Isaac Haynes

An Arctic boat journey in the autumn of 1854

Second Edition

Isaac Haynes

An Arctic boat journey in the autumn of 1854
Second Edition

ISBN/EAN: 9783337128166

Printed in Europe, USA, Canada, Australia, Japan

Cover: Foto ©Andreas Hilbeck / pixelio.de

More available books at **www.hansebooks.com**

AN ARCTIC BOAT JOURNEY.

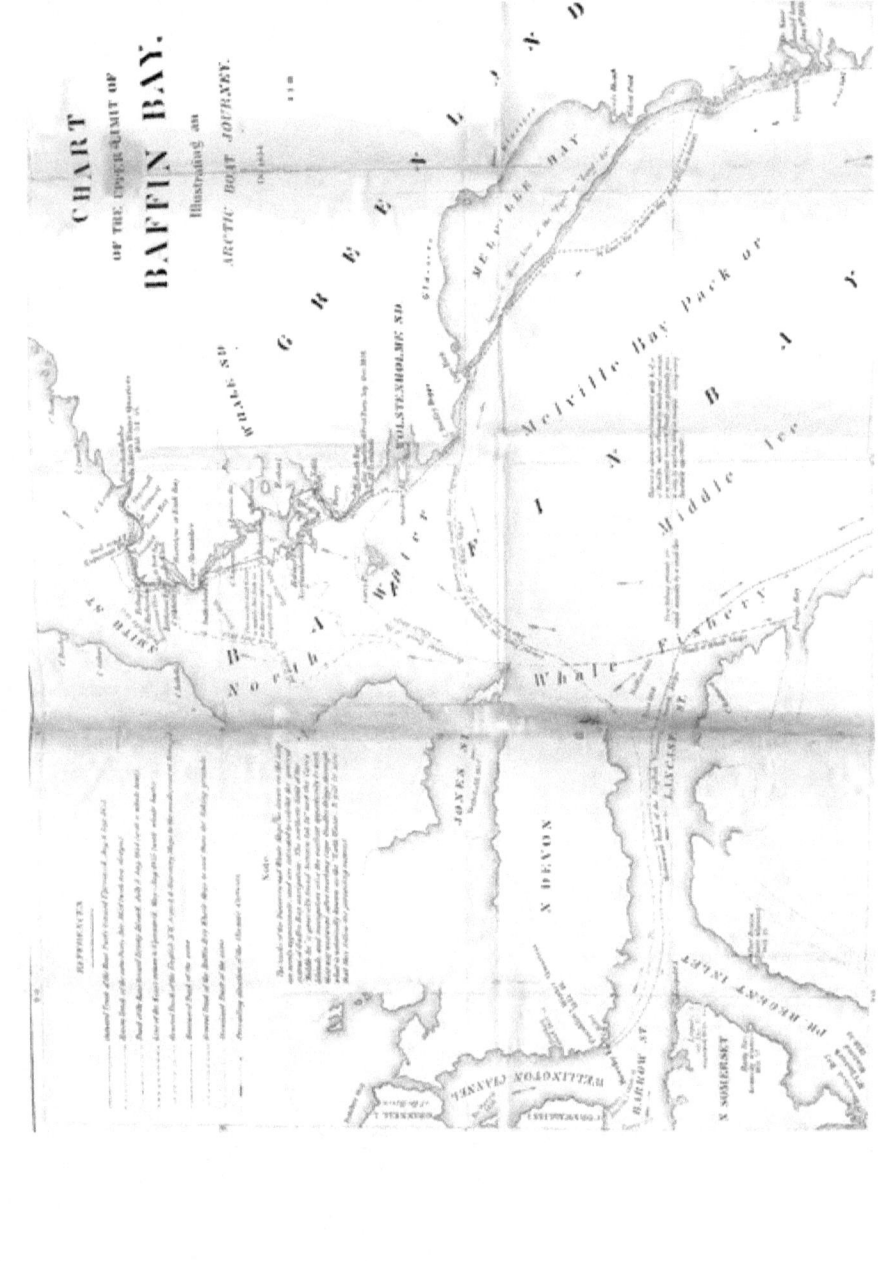

AN

ARCTIC BOAT JOURNEY,

IN THE AUTUMN OF 1854.

BY

ISAAC I. HAYES,

SURGEON OF THE SECOND GRINNELL EXPEDITION.

BOSTON:
BROWN, TAGGARD AND CHASE.
PHILADELPHIA: J. B. LIPPINCOTT & CO.
NEW YORK: SHELDON & CO.
1860.

RIVERSIDE, CAMBRIDGE:
STEREOTYPED AND PRINTED BY
H. O. HOUGHTON AND COMPANY.

I dedicate this Book to the Companions who shared with me the Fortunes which it records.

PREFACE.

The readers of the narrative of Dr. Kane will remember that, in the autumn of 1854, eight persons, being a portion of the officers and crew of the brig Advance, then in Rensselaer Harbor, made an attempt to reach Upernavik, in North Greenland, the nearest outpost of civilization. The party were absent during nearly four months, and they returned to the brig unsuccessful.

It was the wish of Dr. Kane to receive from me a written report of the journey; but as I was disabled at the time of my return, he accepted one from my dictation; and, under the impression that he was thus possessed of all that he required, I gave no further attention to the subject. It subsequently appeared that I was in error; for, when his narrative was going through the press, he informed me that my verbal report was too meagre for his use, and that he had expected a more complete statement of the principal events. Before I could act upon this information, I was prostrated by fever; and, as Dr. Kane's manuscript was put into type as fast as prepared, and was immediately stereotyped, the opportunity was unavoidably lost to me.

After the publication of the main narrative of the expedition, my own memoranda appeared too insignificant to justify the issue of a separate volume. My friends and other persons represented to me, from time to time, that even minute details of life in a region so remote, so peculiar, and so little known as that in which I had passed nearly a third of a year, would not fail to interest the general reader; but it needed a stronger inducement than such persuasions to overcome my reluctance to issue a book.

Having undertaken to conduct another expedition toward the North Pole, as soon as my countrymen will furnish the moderate outfit required for this object, my time and efforts have been exclusively devoted to the necessary preliminary measures. My experienced publishers having encouraged me to believe, not only that a somewhat extended report of the incidents of the journey of 1854 would be acceptable to the public, but also that it would probably contribute towards the expenses of my preparations, I have yielded to the temptation offered by their favorable judgment, and their liberal readiness to assume the risks of the press.

Beside the foregoing explanation of the motives which have led to the issuing of the following pages, the reader is requested to bear in mind that they contain a record chiefly of personal adventure, the interest of which is dependent, for the most part, upon the strangeness of the place and circumstances. I. I. H.

PHILADELPHIA, JANUARY 1, 1860.

CONTENTS.

CHAP.   PAGE

I. INTRODUCTORY 1

    Leaving New York — Entering Smith Strait — Passage up the Coast — Entering Rensselaer Bay — Dr. Kane's Boat Journey to the North — In Winter Quarters — Journey of Mr. Wilson and Dr. Hayes into the Interior — The great *Mer de Glace* — Preparing for the Winter — Fall Work — Journey of Messrs. McGary and Bonsall — Winter Occupations — Preparing for the Spring Work — The Advance Party — Disaster — Rescue — Dr. Kane's Journey — Dr. Hayes' Journey — William Morton's Journey — The Open Sea — The Cruise ended — Dr. Kane's Attempt to reach Beechy Island — Baffled by the Ice-pack — His Return — The Advance not liberated — Dr. Kane makes a final Inspection of the Ice — His Announcement to the Officers and Crew — The Winter closing in — The Question submitted — Dr. Kane's Opinion — Mr. Petersen's Opinions — Conditions — Motives — Fluctuations of Judgment — Division of the Brig's Company into two equal Parties — One of them is to attempt a Boat Journey to Upernavik.

II. PREPARATION 34

    Mr. Petersen chosen Leader and Guide of the Travelling Party — Preliminary Journey — Character of the Travelling — Camp at the Six-mile Ravine — Return on board — Equipment — Meeting in the Cabin — The Pledges — The Parting.

III. THE START 40

    Moving along the Ice-foot — Fairly off — Discouraging Prospect — Ice, Ice, Ice — Relief-Party take leave of us and return to the Brig — A Gale — Its effect upon the Ice — The Boat "Forlorn Hope" — Esquimaux — Hans after them — The "Ice-foot" — An Incident — Difficulty in getting Fresh Water.

IV. ACROSS THE ICE-FIELDS 48

    Taking to the "Floes" — The Sledge breaks through — Cargo

xii   CONTENTS

CHAP.   PAGE

damaged — Spirits damaged — Retreat of Riley and John — John returns — Arrival of a Party from the Brig — The Sledge "Faith" sent back — Shouldering Cargo — Afloat — Breaking a Track — Arrival of another Party from the Brig — The "Faith" returned — Protracted Exertion — The Musk-Ox — The main Open Water reached — Camp at Esquimau Point — A Breeze — Shaking out the Sails.

V. UNDER SAIL... 59

Making Four Knots — Stopped by Ice — Camp on an Ice-raft — Shooting Ducks — A Lead opening — Rapidity of Ice-movements — Hasty Departure — Reaching Life-boat Bay — Hemmed in by Ice — In Jeopardy — Entering a Lead — Landed in Safety.

VI. A GLOOMY NIGHT... 64

After the Life-boat — Transporting the Boat and Cargo over the Ice to Open Water — Crossing the Channel to Littleton Island — Blowing a Gale — Dangerous Landing — A Duck for Supper — Looking for the "Hope" — John on the Pack — The Storm broken — The "Hope" discovered — Re-union.

VII. ROUNDING CAPE ALEXANDER......................... 74

The North Water — Naming the Boats — Under weigh — A stiff Breeze — A fine View — The Boats off the Cape — The Life-boat broached to — Sutherland Island — A Harbor! — Detained by the Storm — A Glacier — View from the Cliffs.

VIII. THE FLEET AT SEA.. 85

Crossing the North Water — Short-lived Felicity — The Ice-pack — Boring the Pack — View from an Iceberg — The "Middle Ice" — Ice-navigation — The Out-side Passage and the In-shore Passage — To Northumberland Island — The Boats nipped — A Fox shot — The Green Hill-side — Cochlearia.

IX. NORTHUMBERLAND ISLAND............................. 94

Repairing the Boats — A Walk to the Cliffs — View to Seaward — Ice all around — No Lead — Reflections — Experience of various Navigators in Baffin Bay — A Fox-chase — The Council — The Resolve.

X. AT SEA IN A SNOW-STORM................................ 103

No Lead yet — An Esquimau Hunter named Amalatok visits the Camp — He lunches on Raw Birds and Oil — Amalatok's Wife and Nephew — Gathering Cochlearia — Change in the

Ice — Hasty Departure — Overtaken by a Snow-storm — Bewildered — The Compass useless — Camp on an Ice-raft — The Adventures of a Night — Landing on Herbert Island — Blowing hard and drifting — The Cook in Trouble.

XI. ACROSS WHALE SOUND............................ 114

The Storm broken — Hunting — Burgomaster Gulls — Breaking through the Ice — Under Sail — Approaching the Main-Land — Esquimaux discovered — Conducted to their Settlement — A merry landing — The Camp — The Village of Netlik.

XII. AMONG THE ESQUIMAUX........................... 121

Kalutunah, the Angekok — Trading for Blubber — A Night Scene — An Esquimau Hut — The Interior — Esquimau Hospitality — An Esquimau Delicacy.

XIII. HOPES CHECKED..................................... 130

Poverty of the Esquimaux — Theft discovered — Leaving Netlik — Cape Parry reached — The everlasting Pack — Beset — The Winter closing in — Progress arrested — Retreat cut off — The Climax — The Prospect.

XIV. BUILDING A HUT..................................... 139

Locality described — Searching for a Site — A Crevice found — Plan arranged — Gathering Stones — Getting Sand — Building the Wall — Roofing — Storm-stayed — Building Fox-traps — Hunting — Moss Food — Roasted Coffee gives out — Comparative merits of Coffee and Tea — Cheerless Times.

XV. HUT-BUILDING CONTINUED.................. 149

Breakfasting under Difficulties — Getting Water from the Lake — A Day of unmitigated Misery — The Canvas Tent — Reading "Ivanhoe" — A clear Morning and a stormy Evening — Gathering Moss — A gloomy Sunday — Stephenson Sick — Housed — Snowing and Blowing — The first Evening in the Hut — Inventory.

XVI. THE HUT DISCOVERED BY ESQUIMAUX........... 160

The Hut imbedded in Snow — Arrival of Kalutunah and another Hunter from Netlik — Description of them — A substantial Meal — Tunnelling the Snow-Drift to get out — Fierceness of Dogs — Bargaining for Supplies — Kalutunah's Cunning — Petersen's Diplomacy — Esquimau Manhood.

CONTENTS.

CHAP.		PAGE
XVII.	A TWO WEEKS' FAMINE..........................	172

Doorway made — **Description of the Hut** — Boat broken up for Fuel — **Building Fox-traps** — Fox-Hunting — Short Allowance — **Eating Stone-Moss** — Reduced condition of the Party — Arrival of Esquimaux — Saved from present Peril.

| XVIII. | SCHEMES FOR MOVING SOUTHWARD............ | 182 |

Supplies obtained — A Cheerful Evening — Two Foxes caught — Visiting the Traps — Thoughts of Home — Schemes discussed — A Young Lover — "David Copperfield" — Doubtful Plans — Communication with the Brig necessary.

| XIX. | PLANS FOR OBTAINING SUPPLIES................ | 192 |

Petersen volunteers to attempt a Journey to the Brig — A Woman and a Baby among our Visitors — Geographical Range of the Esquimaux — Proposals to the Esquimaux — Attempted Bargain — Propositions for going to Cape York — The Widow — Her Meal and her friendly Proffers — Penance — Departure of Mr. Petersen and Godfrey in charge of Kalutunah — Departure of Mr. Sonntag and John for Akbat.

| XX. | PETERSEN.. | 203 |

Hopes of the Party centred in Petersen — His early Life — His Greenland Experience — His Services to the Searching Expeditions.

| XXI. | INTERCOURSE WITH THE ESQUIMAUX............ | 208 |

Low Temperature of the Hut — Occupations — Value of Books — Reading Anatomy — Return of Mr. Sonntag and John, with two Esquimaux, and a small supply of Food — Esquimau Dogs — Esquimau Sledge — Provision for a Journey — Dog-Harness — Watching the Hunters — Happiness!

| XXII. | FAILURE OF OUR PLANS................................ | 222 |

Visiting the Traps — Return of Mr. Petersen and Godfrey — Both broken down — Treachery of the Esquimaux — Keeping Guard.

| XXIII. | PETERSEN'S ADVENTURES AMONG THE ESQUIMAUX.. | 227 |

The first day at Netlik — The Savage Sip-su — Suspicion of Treachery — Dread of Fire-arms — Conspiracy discovered — Flight and Pursuit — Perseverance.

| XXIV. | SUPPLIES OBTAINED WHEN LEAST EXPECTED.. | 236 |

Resources apparently exhausted — Desolation — Arrival of

CHAP.		PAGE
	Kalutunah and other Esquimaux — Reconciliation — Petersen making Knives — Abundant Supplies — The Sentimental Widow again — Kingiktok and his Story — The Witch-Wife— Novel mode of Execution — The Rivals — Hope for the Esquimaux.	
XXV.	GOOD CHEER..	247
	Eleven Visitors — More Supplies — Kalutunah and the Knife — High temperature of the Hut — A savage Feast — Learning to count — Astronomical Fables — Encouragement.	
XXVI.	FURTHER PLANS.......................................	257
	Rations — Animal Food — Health of the Party — Healthfulness of the Climate — Esquimau Beards — Plans for communicating with the Brig — Shunghu — Esquimaux Hunting-grounds — Tattarat and his Family moving away from Cape York — The Sea in that vicinity closed — Purchase of Dogs — Making a Sledge — Provisions all consumed — A Providential Fox — Blubber and Moss-Soup.	
XXVII.	PREPARATIONS FOR ABANDONING THE HUT....	267
	The Alternatives — The Determination — Meagre Clothing — Tailoring — Value of Coffee — Walrus Hide for Food — Mischievous Esquimaux — Purchase of two Dogs — Dog stolen — Equipment for the contemplated Journey to the Brig.	
XXVIII.	DARKNESS AHEAD!..................................	277
	The Hut abandoned — Slow progress of the Party — Stephenson breaks down — Return to the Hut — Stupefied by Cold — Condition of the Hut — Its Temperature — Departure of Petersen and Bonsall — Visiting the Traps — A Fox caught — Thoughts of Home.	
XXIX.	PLOTS AND COUNTER-PLOTS	287
	Kalutunah and two other Hunters arrive at the Hut — They reject our Proposals and reasonable Demands — Plot against them — They are drugged with Opium — The Hut abandoned again.	
XXX.	MOVING NORTHWARD	294
	Difficulty with the Dogs — Cape Parry reached — The Party overtaken by the Esquimaux — Subjection of the Esquimaux — Reaching Netlik — Astonishment of the Natives — The Huts — Abundance of Food.	
XXXI.	OVER THE FROZEN SEA...........	304
	To Northumberland Island — Eating Frozen Birds — News	

| CHAP. | PAGE |

of Petersen and Bonsall — Among the Hummocks — Crossing Whale Sound — Hardness of Snow-Crystals — A cold Lunch — The Main-land reached — Karsooit — Sip-su at home — To the double Hut at Cape Saumarez — An exhilarating Ride.

XXXII. ROUNDING CAPE ALEXANDER AGAIN 313

Up the Coast — Nearing the Cape — Wind from the South — Increases to a moderate Gale — A wild Scene — Meeting a Crack — View from a pile of Hummocks — Broken Ice and Open Water — Mounting the Land-ice — Meeting a Glacier — Another Crack — Crossing it — In the Water — Winding along the Ice-foot — A dangerous Passage — Reaching Etah.

XXXIII. REACHING THE BRIG.... 320

Leaving Etah — A dash after a Bear — Hummocks and Darkness — Myouk — The Hut at Anoatok — Disappointment — Across Bedevilled Reach — The Dogs at full Speed — Sighting the Brig — On board — CONCLUSION — Our Esquimaux Drivers return to their Homes — Experience of Petersen and Bonsall — Scorbutic condition of those who remained at the Brig — The returned Party are one by one stricken down with the Disease — Return of Spring — Partial recovery of the Sick — Final abandonment of the Brig by the entire Company — Journey to Upernavik — The Danish Brig — Passage secured for Copenhagen — To Godhavn — Mr. Olrik — The United States Vessels — Hearty Welcome — Captain Hartstene's vigorous Search — Return to New York.

XXXIV. CONCLUDING REMARKS 331

The popular Idea of the Dangers of Arctic Travelling — Reasons therefor — Dangerous voyages exceptional — Comparison between the difficulties of Arctic exploration and the exploration of other regions — Value of Experience — Illustrations — The experience of the last three centuries shows the Arctic Ocean to be invested by a Belt of Ice — Dr. Kane's Explorations prove that this Belt can be most readily broken, through Smith Strait — By this route the North Pole can be reached — Route of the Discovery, and Whaleships in Baffin Bay — The Current and Ice of Smith Strait — Cause of Dr. Kane's failure to reach a higher latitude — Cape Frazer and the Coasts of Grinnell Land — Scurvy easily avoided — Fresh Food necessary — Health of the Boat-party — Temperature and travelling — The Cold no obstacle to exploration — The Open Sea, and the proofs of its existence — Nature of the Country — Route of Dr. Hayes' proposed Expedition toward the North Pole — Comparison of Distances — Position of Baffin in 1616 — The dangers encountered by Arctic travellers generally less than those encountered by travellers in Africa.

APPENDIX.

PROCEEDINGS OF SCIENTIFIC SOCIETIES, AND LETTERS, RELATIVE TO DR. HAYES' PROPOSED ARCTIC EXPEDITION 355

I. The American Geographical and Statistical Society.
II. The American Association for the Advancement of Science.
III. The American Philosophical Society, Philadelphia.
IV. The Academy of Natural Sciences of Philadelphia.
V. The American Academy of Arts and Sciences, Boston.
VI. The Boston Society of Natural History.
VII. The New York Lyceum of Natural History.
VIII. The Royal Geographical Society, London.
IX. Letter from Professor A. Dallas Bache.
X. Letter from M. de la Roquette.

AN ARCTIC BOAT JOURNEY.

CHAPTER I.

INTRODUCTORY.

It is well known that the Advance, a brigantine of one hundred and forty-four tons, under command of Dr. E. K. Kane of the United States Navy, sailed from New York, May 30th 1853, on her second cruise to the arctic seas, in search of Sir John Franklin.

My connection with the expedition dates from the day prior to that of sailing. Five months before, while yet a student of medicine, I had volunteered to join the party. The offer could not be accepted at that time; and it was not until the 18th of May that I received notice that there was a probability of its acceptance. It was not until the afternoon of the 29th that I obtained my appointment. In a few hours I had purchased and sent aboard my outfit. Next morning the Advance was headed for Greenland.

The historian of the expedition has left nothing new for me to communicate concerning the more important events of the cruise; and I will detain the reader over this introductory chapter, only long enough to recall such facts as are needed to connect the narrative of Dr. Kane with the events which it is the purpose of this book to record.

In consequence of the prevalence of head-winds and calms, the coast of Greenland was not reached until the first of July; but, the season being unusually forward, we made up for lost time by a quick passage through that gauntlet of the Baffin Bay whale fishers, the "middle ice," and were at the seat of our future operations, Smith Strait, by the 7th of August.

Having deposited in a cairn on Lyttleton Island, near the mouth of the strait, a record of our proceedings thus far; and having placed on the main land, about two miles farther to the north and east, our Francis' metallic life-boat, together with a provision depôt upon which to fall back in case of accident, we pushed northward through the strait, on the Greenland side.

Since leaving Cape Dudley Diggs we had encountered no ice, except here and there a vagrant berg; and everything looked bright and promising as we sank the cavernous cliffs of Cape Alexander. With a fair wind and topgallant-sails set we sped over a broad sheet of iceless water, whose white-capped waves, bounding away toward the unknown north, led the imagination on to the *terra incognita* of our dreams; but an ominous "blink" appeared from the top of Lyttleton Island; and, before the close of the next day, our dreams were effectually broken by a heavy pack of massive ice-fields. In this we lay beset, and escaped from it not without some severe shocks, to Refuge Inlet.

During the twelve following days, by hard labor and almost continual battling with the ice, we succeeded in making about forty miles; and then found ourselves at the bottom of a broad, shallow bay, (called then Bedevilled Reach, but named more seriously afterwards in honor of Mr. Peter Force,) and there, hemmed in by grounded bergs, we lay awaiting a change of weather.

On the 20th a violent gale set in from the southeast, and the ice was driven off rapidly from the coast. The Advance was broken loose from her anchorage; and, unable to keep her head against the driving wind, she was swept in the wake of the drifting floes across the bay, and was finally brought up among the loose "trash" which margined a solid field resting on the north face of Cape Ingersoll.

The flight across Force Bay was sufficiently terrific, but worse followed. The dodging among the bergs which dotted the sea, and the plunging over the waves which beat and broke against them; the escape from being crushed between two closing ice-islands; the carrying away of our jib-boom against another in an attempt to wear, after a fruitless effort to go to windward; the losing of our best bower anchor in a struggle to bring up under Cape Grinnell; the general confusion; the clattering of blocks; the jibing of the main boom, from port to starboard, and from starboard to port, as every few minutes we went about; the whistling of the wind through the rigging; the dashing of the spray; the general babel of voices, were, altogether, less startling than the tossing, grinding, surging, of the broken, crushed, and crumbling masses which, riding on the billows, opened to receive us. At first they were few in number and far between, but they thickened as we advanced; and we were soon inclosed in the main body of them, and could no longer hold our course. The bluff of the port bow struck a floe, luckily not large enough to do us damage; the brig veered around and brought up with her waist against a larger mass, which slipped along her side and dropped us around broadside to the wind. Thus we rode, powerless to move but as the elements listed. That we were not ground to pieces seemed a wonder. Thump followed thump in quick succession; bows, quarter, waist, stem, and stern successively received the shocks as the brig rose and fell and plunged with the waves. Soon we had run this gauntlet, and then came the hardest trial of all: we were rushing upon the solid floe, which was firm as a rock. A huge wave lifted us high in the air, and, as it slipped from under the brig, down went her forefoot upon the ice. The shock was terrible; the masts creaked and shivered; every person on board expected to see them fly in splinters, but they held firm. Next moment the stern fell off, and we lay grinding against the floe. Then a large field bore down upon us from the windward, and the brig was squeezed out of the water. The crew, powerless to help her, sprang upon the ice; and there she lay high and dry for several hours. At length the storm abated, the ice relaxed, and the Advance settled down into her proper element. A lead having opened toward the shore, a warp was run out, and we first hauled under the lee of a grounded berg, then to the land. Worn out with constant work, we made fast to the land-ice, the watch was set, and all hands turned in.

The prospect of advancing farther north with the brig was now very unpromising. Dr. Kane had hoped to reach with her at least latitude 80°; and here we were completely beset at 78° 40'. All to the north was one unbroken ice-field, crossed by no crack, and with not a drop of water visible, except here and there a puddle of melted snow.

Along the land, which trended eastward, opened a narrow lead, from twenty to sixty feet in width; which, although clogged with loose, ragged pieces, was, nevertheless, wide enough to admit the vessel. Into this lead she was hauled; and inch by inch, and foot by foot we tracked and warped her along the frozen wall of the land-ice, for the next five days, making thus about six miles. This was along the southern shore of a deep bay, afterwards called Rensselaer. Being close under the land, we grounded at nearly every low tide.

The head of the bay was reached on the 27th. Finding here the ice much more broken, we hauled over to the opposite shore, and then commenced again to track; but the lead was soon found to be completely closed. The winter was now fast approaching; the young ice was forming rapidly; and there was nothing left for us but to retreat and seek a harbor.

Dr. Kane, with a boat's crew of six men, put off up the coast to inspect the ice; the remainder of us meanwhile working to get the Advance to a place of safety. The sailing-master, Mr. Wilson, being sick, and the two mates having accompanied Dr.

Kane, the superintendence of the work devolved upon Mr. Ohlsen, who was ordered to get the vessel clear of the ice, and then to await the return of our chief.

We were four days in making two miles. The "bay ice" was, in places, two inches thick; and, with all the power we could apply with capstan and windlass, we could not force the vessel forward without first breaking a track with poles and handspikes.

The islands at the head of the bay were at length reached; but the ice was there found locked against the outer point of Fern Rock, above which we had passed on our way in; and it was not until the evening of the 6th of September that it became possible to execute further the commander's instructions. Then a gale set in from the southeast, and in a few hours the ice was driven nearly out of sight. Preparations were at once commenced for getting under weigh. The watch was called; the click, click, of the capstan was again heard; the men were sent aloft to shake out the foresail. All was ready, and in a few minutes we should have been off. Then came a cry from the masthead that Dr. Kane and his party were in sight. They were on the ice a mile or so below Cape Leiper. Immediately a boat put off for them, and in a couple of hours they were aboard.

This journey had convinced Dr. Kane that it was practicable to travel over the ice with sledges, and that the search could be thus continued in the spring. Of this there had been not a little doubt at his starting. Mr. Petersen had given it as his decided opinion that, owing to the roughness of the ice, nothing could be done with the dogs; and the prospect certainly looked no more promising for the men.

By his journey up the coast, **Dr. Kane** had decided the question of the propriety of wintering, even in this low latitude. On the following morning, the brig was hauled between the islands, and was moored fast. The temperature fell to 19°. The gale died away, allowing the old floes to drift back about us; the young ice cemented them together; and, by the morning of the 9th of September, we could walk ashore. The Advance was firmly locked up.

Now commenced busy preparations for meeting the four months of the winter which was closing upon us. The hold of the vessel was unstowed, and the stores were carried on sleds over the ice, about thirty yards, to Butler Island, and there deposited in a temporary house. The upper deck was covered in with boards. The between-decks were bulkheaded at about twelve feet abaft the foremast; the cabin and hold were united in one long room, and this was decked and bunked all around. The little stove was retained in the cabin; the cook-stove was placed amidships; the men moved aft from the forecastle; the nautical day was changed to the old-fashioned day which commences at midnight; and, with the Advance thus virtually converted into a *house*, both as concerned herself and her domestic arrangements, we entered upon the winter.

Meanwhile the work of exploration went on. The anchor had scarcely been dropped before Mr. Wilson and myself were sent to the interior, with the view, mainly, of determining how far we might rely upon the land to supply us with game.

We left the vessel on the 8th of September, carrying upon our backs our slender equipment. Our only companion was the Greenlander, Hans Hendrich, a fine little fellow who joined us at Lichtenfels, South Greenland; and who, after serving faithfully the expedition for nearly two years, finally fell in love with a pair of black eyes and a fat face, and left us to live with the wild Esquimaux.

Our route lay, for two days, over an uneven primitive country, from which we emerged upon a table-land of weather-worn greenstone. Over this we travelled for about fifteen miles, when we came again upon the porphyritic and gneissoid rocks; and, on the fourth day, after a laborious travel, we descended into a deep broad valley, which proved to be the bed of a river. This was almost dry, but it bore upon its banks evidences of having recently been a deep and rapid torrent, which, as it rolled and tumbled over the rocks, was fed, through the many gorges which flanked it, by the melting snow from the mountain sides. Here we spread our buffalo skins upon the stones, and rested for the morrow's work.

The morrow found our poor Esquimau unable to travel; and we were in not much better condition. Our route had lain over a very uneven country. The snow of the previous winter having all disappeared, we clambered over the naked rocks; and as each of us carried upon his shoulders a burden of about thirty pounds' weight, this was no slight task.

On the second day there was a light fall of snow, which rendered the rocks slippery and our footing insecure, and added greatly to the difficulties of the journey. No evidences of life were seen, save a solitary rabbit and the footmarks of a fox.

Before us the country was no less rugged than that which we had just traversed, and we resolved to leave behind us, in charge of Hans, all our travelling gear; and each taking in his pocket a lump of pemmican and an ounce or so of coffee, we started, at noon of the fifth day, up the bank of the river, resolved if possible to trace it to its source.

As we proceeded the prospect became more enlivening. The fall of snow had been mainly confined to the coast, and the bare rocks, over which we made our way by springing from one boulder to another, gave us firmer foothold. The hills became more even in their outline; and between them rested picturesque valleys, sloping down to the river banks, which were often broad and clothed with verdure. Patches of andromeda, — arctic type of Scotia's heather, — its purple blossoms not yet nipped by the winter frosts, — gave here and there a carpet to the feet, and furnished us fuel for the cooking of a meal. Beds of green moss and turf, whose roots supplied pabulum to some festucine grasses, on which were browsing little herds of reindeer, gave to the scene an air of enchantment, and brought to recollection the verdure of my native Chester. These meadows often tempted us from our course, sometimes to catch a closer glimpse of the stunted flowers, sometimes to steal a shot at the deer. In the former purpose we were always amply successful, but in the latter we were frustrated by the timidity of the animals, who could not, with all our arts, be surprised, nor approached within rifle shot. The old buck who stood guard over the herd, gave the alarm by a significant snort; and, angry at being disturbed, led away his charge, the whole troop bounding off to the mountains. Thence looking down over the cliffs, they were seen watching us until they were lost among the rocks, from which, in the distance, they could not be distinguished. The vegetation of the marshes and meadow-lands was richer than anything I had seen north of Melville Bay. Dwarf willows, — representatives of the beautiful shade-trees of our lawns and river banks, — with branches which trailed on the ground as thin as one's little finger, and a foot long, (the whole tree being of about the circumference of a large dinner plate,) were, in places, quite abundant.

At length we emerged upon a broad plain or valley, wider than any we had yet seen, in the heart of which reposed a lake about two miles in length by half a mile in width, over the transparent, glassy surface of which we walked. On either side of us rose rugged bluffs, that stretched off into long lines of hills, culminating in series in a broad-topped mountain ridge, which, running away to right and left, was cut by a gap several miles wide that opened directly before us. Immediately in front was a low hill, around the base of which flowed on either side the branches of the stream which we had followed. Leaving the bed of the river just above the lake, we ascended to the top of this hillock; and here a sight burst upon us, grand and imposing beyond any power of mine adequately to describe. From the rocky bed, only a few miles in advance, a sloping wall of pure whiteness rose to a broad level plain of ice, which, apparently boundless, stretched away toward the unknown east. It was the great *mer de glace* of the arctic continent.

At any subsequent period of the cruise this sight would have less impressed me; but I had never, except in the distance, seen a glacier. Here before us was, in reality, the counterpart of the river-systems of other lands. From behind the granite hills the congealed drainings of the interior water-sheds, the atmospheric precipitations of ages, were moving as a solid though plastic mass, down through every gap in the mountains, swallowing up the rocks, filling the valleys, submerging the hills: an onward, irresistible, crystal tide, swelling to the ocean. Cutting the surface were many vertical crevasses, or gutters, some of great depth, which had drained off the melted snow.

It was midnight when we made our approach. The sun was several degrees beneath the horizon, and afforded us a faint twilight. Stars of the second magnitude were dimly visible in the northern heavens. When we were within about half a mile of the icy wall, a brilliant meteor fell before us, and by its reflection upon the glassy surface beneath, greatly heightened the effect of the scene; while loud reports, like distant thunder or the booming of artillery, broke at intervals from the heart of the frozen sea.

Upon closer inspection we found the face of the glacier to ascend at an angle of from $30°$ to $35°$. At its base lay a high snow-bank, up which we clambered about sixty feet; but beyond this the ice was so smooth as to defy our efforts. The mountains, which stood like giant gateposts on either side, were overlapped and partially submerged by the glacier. From the face of this a multitude of little rivulets ran down the gutters already mentioned, or gurgled from beneath the ice; and formed, on the level lands below, a sort of marsh, not twenty yards from the icy wall. Here grew, in strange contrast, beds of green moss; and in these, tufts of dwarf willows were twining their tiny arms and rootlets about the feebler flower growths; and there, clustered together, crouched among the grass, and sheltered by the leaves, and feeding on the bed of lichens, I found a white-blossomed *draba* which would have needed only a lady's thimble for a flower-pot, and a white chickweed. Dotting the few feet of green around me were seen the yellow blossoms of the more hardy poppy, the purple *potentilla*, and the white, purple, and yellow *saxifrages*.

This little *oasis* was literally imbedded in ice. The water which had flowed through it had frozen in the holes, and spread itself out in a crystal sheet upon the rocks and stones around. A few specimens of the tiny blossoms were laid in my notebook, a sprig of heather and a saxifrage were stuck in my button hole, and with these souvenirs we left this garden spot, which the glacier was soon to cover forever from human eyes.

Returning upon our track, we arrived at the camp after an absence of twenty-three hours, having travelled, during that time, between fifty and sixty miles. After halting here until midnight, we set out for the vessel, which was reached in another march.

We found the preparations for winter progressing

rapidly. Before they were completed, and as soon as the ice was sufficiently solid to insure the safety of travel, Messrs. McGary and Bonsall, with five men, were dispatched with a sledge-load of stores, part of which they were to place on the land, as far north as they could reach, the remainder at available points along the Greenland coast. These deposits were to serve as supports of the principal operations, which were to follow in the spring. The party carried upon the sledge, in addition to their own provisions and equipment, about four hundred pounds of pemmican* and bread.

Their route lay up the hitherto unsurveyed coast of Greenland, to the northeastward from Rensselaer Harbor. They soon found, much to their disappointment, that the ice was not completely fast, although the temperature was within a few degrees of zero. The tide, as it rose and fell alternately, opened and closed chasms, or rivers, as Bonsall styled them, sometimes fifty yards wide, across which the party were compelled in several cases to transport themselves and their baggage on a loose cake of ice,—an insecure though cheap substitute for a raft. In this unusual mode of navigation, they were once well drenched, but no more serious results followed; and with a steadfast determination to carry out their instructions, McGary and Bonsall led on their men, until their further progress

---

* *Pemmican* is a preparation of meat. It is made by drying thin strips of the lean portions of beef, or other flesh, either in the sun, or by a slow artificial heat, such as that of a malt-kiln; and then chopping it finely and mixing it with an equal portion of melted tallow. One pound of this preparation is equal in nutritive effect to about three pounds of ordinary meat.

was arrested by a great glassy wall, a huge barricade of ice, from three to five hundred feet in height, which joined the land ninety miles northeast of Rensselaer Bay, and stretched north-by-east as far as the eye could reach.

This cold mass (afterwards named Humboldt Glacier) brought the temperature down below zero; but it changed the course of the party only from northeast-by-east to north-by-east. Parallel with its face, and within two miles of it, they struck out for the land, which loomed up northward. After fifty-two miles of hard toil, they became entangled among bergs and hummocks, through which their heavily laden sledge could not be forced. They were thus compelled to put back, and to deposit their stores upon the land which they had left a few days before. The principal depôts were made at Capes Agassiz and Russell. On the 16th of October, the party reached the brig, after an absence of twenty-six days.

A few days afterward I added a light load to the depôt at Cape Russell; and with this journey closed the preparatory operations for search. We were not yet, however, quite driven within doors. Mr. Sonntag finished the observatory, and began his work in it; and while the light of noonday continued bright enough to enable me to read the markings on the vernier, I was engaged, with Baker for assistant, upon a topographical sextant-survey of Rensselaer Harbor and the region round about. The thermometer being at from ten to twenty degrees below zero, I had of course a fine opportunity to prove the scorching power of frosty metal. Mr. Bonsall and

Mr. Goodfellow, Mr. Petersen and Hans, Morton and Riley, tried successively to reach the Esquimaux, who were supposed to live near the mouth of the strait; and Dr. Kane, in the intervals of his numerous occupations as commander, found time for training and exercising, for future service, the dogs, on which so much must thereafter depend.

The darkness at length cut short these out-door operations, and forced us within the vessel, where we were not idle. Our small force had been reduced by sickness, and the deck officers and effective men had enough of ship's duty to occupy several hours of each day. Mr. Sonntag had still his observatory to look after, and he was assisted there alternately by the commander, Bonsall, and myself; and on board, during "office-hours," he was engaged upon his charts and computations. For myself, I had no room to complain of want of occupation. My duties were multifarious and endless. They included the functions of doctor, hospital steward, naturalist, and captain's clerk. When the winter shut us in, I had a hospital to look after; more than half a hundred birds, hares, and foxes to skin; charts to project, and reports of journeys to draw up; the official records, log-book, and meteorological tables of two months to copy, beside the current days' entries; and withal, now and then, from four to eight hours' watch to keep per diem, as one officer after another was temporarily on the sick-list.

There was no idling on board the Advance during the early part of the winter; and after the "Christmas holidays" were over, new occupation was found in preparing for the spring journeys.

The carpenter was making and mending sleds; the tinkers were manufacturing cooking apparatus; some of the men were sewing tents; others fur-bags to sleep in; others boots, stockings, mittens, and all the et ceteras of personal outfit. Thus, as the winter dragged its slow length along, we found, in constant occupation, the means of rendering the dreariness of our imprisonment more endurable.

The sun came to us again on the first of March, after an absence of one hundred and thirty-five days; and once more we were bathing in an atmosphere of continual sunlight. The season was, however, backward, and this month was the coldest of the year.

Meanwhile the preparations for field-work were completed, and on the 19th of the month the first party started, with the first officer. This, like the fall party of McGary and Bonsall, was to carry out provisions, to be deposited for the use of the main exploring and searching party, which was to follow under the immediate command of Dr. Kane.

The direction given was to pursue a due north course; and upon reaching the opposite side of the channel to deposit there the provisions and return; but unexpected obstacles presented themselves in the shape of heavy hummocks and deep snow-drifts. The ice in the centre of the strait had, during the latter part of the previous summer, been broken up; and drifting masses, crowding upon each other, had been piled in confused ridges, and in this state had been frozen together. Thus the whole surface of the sea was covered; and Brooks and his party for several days, picked a tortuous passage through, or mounted over, heavy piles of crushed ice, varying in height from five to fifty feet. At length the severity of the labor broke down the men; the thermometer fell to 55° below zero, and four of the party, including the leader, were frozen and rendered helpless. Leaving Hickey to look after these, Ohlsen, Petersen, and Sonntag returned to the ship, forty-five miles distant, which they reached in thirteen hours. Immediately a relief party was organized by Dr. Kane, and was guided by Ohlsen into the wilderness of ice in search of his companions, whom he had great reason to fear were lost forever. They were, however, found and brought back upon the sledge. — For a minute history of this heroic rescue I must refer the reader to the narrative of Dr. Kane.

Soon after the return of this party, the brig was visited by a tribe of wild Esquimaux, from whom we obtained four dogs, in exchange for knives, needles, and pieces of wood and iron. These dogs, with the three * already in our possession, made up a full team.

The disastrous effort just made had broken down the efficiency of the ship's company; and it was not until late in April that a sufficient number of men had recovered to make another attempt possible.

On the 26th Mr. McGary started with the leading sledge, and on the next day Dr. Kane followed with Godfrey and the dogs. This was to have been the crowning expedition of the campaign; but the

---

* The four fine teams, obtained by Dr. Kane at Upernavik and Karsuk, had all, except the three dogs above mentioned, died during the winter, chiefly from the effect of salted food.

2 *

same causes again brought defeat. The heavy hummocks and deep drifts made the travelling so laborious, that one by one the men broke down, and symptoms of scurvy added to the complication of troubles. At length the commander, an invalid at starting, was prostrated by the severity of his labors; he fell into frequent fainting fits, and finally became helpless. The party were compelled to put back; and by forced marches they brought him on board. He was carried up the ship's side insensible. The old enemy, scurvy, had again seized upon him, and its attack was aggravated by typhoid symptoms and dropsical effusion. I may truly say that I lost all expectation of seeing him recover, or even rally, from his severe prostration; but, with a wonderful reactive power, he began, in a few hours, to grow better; and he continued to improve rapidly from day to day.

The crew were at this time in a sorry plight. Indeed, both officers and men were all, more or less, broken. Several were down with frostbite, snow-blindness, fatigue, or scurvy; and only six of the whole number were fit for service. The ship was a hospital.

It happened, fortunately, that I had not yet been so exposed as to impair my health. I was consequently able to attend to all the wants of the sick, and to perform other duties.

By the 16th of May Dr. Kane was well enough to move about, and, with the aid of our excellent steward, to administer to the invalid crew. This left me more at liberty, and on the 18th, accompanied by Godfrey, I set out to make another attempt to cross the wilderness of hummocks to the opposite coast. I was directed to follow nearly the track of the first party.

I give our simple equipment. Our sledge weighed twenty-two pounds; on this was loaded eighty pounds of pemmican, and ten pounds of bread, food for ten days, for men and dogs. Eighteen pounds more of weight were added by our lamp and cooking apparatus, with lard and rope-yarn for fuel. On top of these articles were stowed two bags of reindeer skin, each weighing eight pounds, the use of which I will presently describe; and over the whole was spread a light canvas cover, which was lashed down compactly to the sledge, so that sledge, cargo, and all, could be capsized and rolled over and over, as frequently happened, without damage. On my back were slung a Sharpe's rifle, a small pocket-compass, and a sextant. My driver carried only his whip. The dogs were lashed to the sledge, as is the fashion of the Esquimaux, each by a separate line eighteen feet in length, the animals therefore running side by side. They were guided entirely by the voice and the whip. If the driver wished to go to the right, he struck the left-hand dog, or let the whip-lash fall upon the snow at his side, and *vice versa*. The team was thus easily directed; and, but that the dogs were continually jumping over each other's backs, tangling their traces into inextricable knots, they would have been as conveniently managed as a span of horses.

Upon encamping, our first duty was to unlash the sledge and to unharness and feed the dogs; our second, was to light the lamp, for melting snow, and cooking coffee or tea. This lamp consisted of a sheet-iron cylinder closed at one end, a foot high and eight inches in diameter, which was set on the ice. In this was placed a little cup of lard, and some pieces of rope-yarn or canvas, which, being lighted, filled the cylinder with flame; and in this extempore chimney-place, the pot was set to melt snow and to boil the water thus obtained. Supper, of bread and coffee, and cold pemmican, being over, the third duty was to prepare for sleeping. If a wind was blowing, we built a snow-house to shelter us from it; but, if calm, we spread out upon the ice or snow the reindeer bags which have been already described, having previously secured under them the harness, and everything not impenetrable by the tooth of an Esquimau dog. These wolfish fellows will eat anything, from an old shoe up to one of their crippled comrades, or a man; and could they get a chance, would, before morning, effectually prevent themselves from being harnessed. These several occupations over, while my companion smoked his pipe, it was my melancholy task, with cold fingers, to jot down in my journal the doings of the day. Then we went to bed, by crawling feet foremost into the before-mentioned sleeping-bags. In this manner one may rest quite securely, even in the open air, if the temperature be not very far below zero, in which case a snow-hut becomes necessary. Such a hut, if well packed with men, soon becomes quite warm, by the heat radiated from the persons of the occupants. Although with plenty of furs one may generally be warm enough in the open air, at almost any temperature, yet I am compelled to say that a sleeping-bag is no very desirable place in which to spend the night; for, if you expose your head you run great risk of freezing that most sensitive organ, the nose; and if you haul your head within doors, or close up the mouth of the bag, you run equally great risk of smothering. It is a nice operation, and one requiring some practice, to adjust a proper mean between these extremes.

An adequate idea of the rugged track, over which we travelled, can hardly be conveyed by a mere description. One moment we were ascending the slippery, sloping surface of a huge elevated table of ice which had been pressed upward; then we were sliding down another, the sledge on top of the dogs, the dogs tangled in their traces, howling piteously; men, dogs, and sledge in wild confusion, plunging into a snow-drift, or against a cake of ice. Sometimes we were halted by a precipice eight or ten feet high, up which we were obliged to clamber, lifting the sledge, dogs, and cargo, or down which we had to leap, the sledge burying itself head foremost in the deep drift; at other times we picked a tortuous passage among the lesser masses, often being compelled to turn back to seek an opening. Our shelter and rest were invariably obtained in a snow-hut or in our sleeping-bags upon the ice.

One thing the reader must bear in mind in order to get a picture of our condition at this time, namely, that we had constant daylight. The sun was visible, during all the four-and-twenty hours, successively in the north, east, south, and west; and always near the horizon.

This journey was successful; but it would not have been so without the aid of the dogs. In eight days we reached the coast at Cape Frazer, in latitude 79° 42′; but, having only two days' provisions remaining, it was impossible to proceed much further; and, after making a few additional miles of northing, and planting on the top of Cape Frazer a little flag mounted on a whipstock,* we turned down the coast and I connected my survey with the English explorations at the mouth of the channel. This survey embraced about two hundred miles of the eastern coast of the land which now bears the name of the chief patron of the expedition, Mr. Henry Grinnell. It is the most northern known land on the globe. Its eastern and southern limits have been determined, but its western and northern are yet unknown. It probably extends nearer to the pole than any other land.†

I had been attacked on the second day of this

---

* It was at this time that the author observed the harbor at Cape Frazer as a suitable place for the head-quarters of an expedition for polar discovery. It interests him to think that his little flag still floats in the arctic breezes, awaiting the return of the hand which placed it there. No white man but the author and his companion has ever trodden that land.

† It may serve to illustrate to the reader some of the peculiarities of journeys, like that mentioned in the text, to say, that on our ten days' allowance of provision we travelled twelve days, during the last two of which myself and companion were without food of any kind. We fed our team with the lower extremities of our trousers, which we cut for the purpose. These pieces, with an extra pair of boots, were dressed with slush, the remnant of the fuel of our lamp, and were eaten without difficulty by the dogs. On the ninth day, to enable us to push forward to the ship, we were compelled to lighten our load by throwing away our sleeping-bags. This restricted us for shelter to the lee of snow-banks, with the help of such warmth as the sun vouchsafed to us. During the last forty hours we travelled one hundred and twenty miles.

journey with snow-blindness, which did not leave me during my absence; and upon returning to the brig I was so blind as to be unable to get on board without a guide. I volunteered, however, again to take the field; but the commander, with a consideration for my future sight which I appreciate now better than I did then, would not permit me to leave the ship. The next duty, therefore, devolved upon William Morton, the steward, who was the only remaining able-bodied man on board who was sufficiently instructed to conduct even the most rude survey. After having been trained by the astronomer, Mr. Sonntag, in the use of the sextant, Morton left the ship on the 5th of June, with a relief-party, and was followed by Hans, the Esquimau hunter, on the 10th, with the dogs.

In view of the fact that I had, in proceeding directly north from **Rensselaer** Harbor, found the track to be almost impassable, by reason of the heavy hummocks, Morton was directed to keep upon the Greenland side of the strait, and to make a final start from the *cache* established by McGary and Bonsall in October, 1853, near the base of Humboldt Glacier. This spot was reached on the 15th of June; and, separating on the 18th from the relief-party which had accompanied him thus far, Morton proceeded nearly due north. This course took him eastward of the chief line of the drift of the channel; and he found therefore a smoother track than I had previously encountered further westward. On the 21st, he reached the mouth of a new channel, (to which the name of Hon. John P. Kennedy has been given,) extending northward from Smith Strait; and at about ten miles from the eastern shore he came suddenly upon open water. Tracing the margin of this water eastward to the land, he mounted to the land-ice, and travelling thence northward, having open water continually upon his left, he reached, on the 24th, his extreme latitude, about fifty miles up the channel. Finding it impossible to proceed further, he ascended to the top of a bluff, four hundred and eighty feet in height, and thence looked out to the northward upon a boundless, iceless sea. Retracing his steps he reached the brig on the 10th of July.

This journey was the most important one of the expedition, and it was attended with more than the usual share of difficulties and dangers peculiar to ice-travel; all of which were overcome with manly energy and perseverance.

The finding of open water northward of the ice-belt of Smith Strait, is the great discovery of the cruise; and the observations made in connection with it, show the extension of this open water far northward beyond the line of vision; thus indicating the existence of an iceless area at the centre of the Arctic Ocean.

The return of Morton closed the search. Nothing more could be done or attempted at this late period of the summer. The ice was breaking up, was already crossed by numerous cracks, and was covered with sludge. Travelling thus became not only difficult and dangerous, but for any considerable distance over the ice-fields quite impossible.

Our commander, after feelingly thanking his officers and crew for the promptness and energy with which they had seconded his efforts, announced to us that the objects of the cruise had been attained as far as lay within our power. Henceforth our thoughts and labors would be directed homeward; and when the little prayer, with which he opened our simple meal, was changed from " Lord, accept our gratitude, and bless our undertaking," to " Lord, accept our gratitude, and restore us to our homes," every heart manifested the quickening impulses of a new inspiration.

The season, however, showed evident signs of backwardness. The open water to the south was yet more than thirty miles distant. Our situation was critical.

In order the better to insure our escape, Dr. Kane gallantly proposed to lead a party to Beechy Island, to apprise the English, there harbored, of our condition. It was known to us that the squadron of Sir Edward Belcher, or at least a part of it, would return home that fall, as soon as liberated from the ice; and in case our brig should remain locked up, we felt no doubt that he would come two hundred miles out of his way, to render us whatever aid we might require.

The boat "Forlorn-Hope" was once more refitted, and was carried on a sledge down to the open water, which by this time had advanced to Esquimau Point. Here the boat was launched, and, with five as brave fellows as ever pulled an oar, Dr. Kane started.

It was the sixth of August before we saw them again. After an absence of almost three weeks, they brought back only a record of hard labor and sad disappointment. An unexpected obstacle met them in the "North Water." A heavy "pack" stretched from shore to shore, across from Jones' to Whale Sound. After repeated efforts to bore through this barrier, skirting it from coast to coast in the interval, they ran short of provisions, and were forced to put back. They brought their boat through Force Bay, and along the land lead to within six miles of the ship.

This at least was good news. The open water had advanced rapidly, and had thus come up as far as, during the previous season it had reached at a period two weeks later. Every one seemed to feel confident that the brig would be liberated.

With the aid of gunpowder and handspikes, the vessel was loosened in her cradle, and was once more afloat. She was then warped, inside of the islands, down to Fox-trap Point, half a mile from our old quarters. Between this point and the Six-mile Ravine, the ice was fast, and we lay day after day in anxious suspense. Parties were going to and fro continually. All the reports showed that the open water did not advance. It had come up to the Six-mile Ravine as if to permit the entrance of Dr. Kane; and there it had stopped. The commander made a final journey on the 23d.

Soon after his return the ship's company were called together, and the results of his expedition were explained to them. The ice in the centre of the channel had broken up, and had drifted down into Force Bay. Escape for the brig was hopeless. She could not be liberated. Either of two courses was now open to us — to remain by the brig and try in her the chances of a second winter, or to seek safety in our boats to the south.

That everything possible had been done towards the attainment of the objects of the cruise, was not doubted by any officer or man of the brig's company; and certainly the character of the commander might, itself, have been relied upon by them, as a sufficient guaranty of the hopelessness of further efforts, when he had renounced them as fruitless. The question was, simply, when we should set out homeward, — whether we should pass the winter in the vessel, and start for Upernavik in the spring; or make the attempt without further delay. In either case, we must abandon all thought, either of further exploration, or of preserving the brig. The recent observations of Dr. Kane, had been such as to prevent his detaching even an experimental party to the south, so great did the perils of a journey in that direction appear to him. On the other hand, so urgent were our necessities, and so difficult of solution the problems upon which depended the safety of the persons under him, that, although his natural bias as commander inclined him to stay by the vessel at whatever cost, yet he rightly considered it unjust, now that the cruise was in effect ended, to interpose the weight of his official authority to determine the choice of time for our setting out. He called together officers and men, and submitted the whole subject for their reflection, giving them twenty-four hours for deliberation. In case any of them should determine to go, they should have, said he, "the best outfit I can give them, an abundant share of our remaining stores, and my good-bye blessing." *

* Dr. Kane has so clearly explained our circumstances on this trying

In addition to the motives which influenced the resolution of others, there were some which had peculiar relation to myself as medical officer of the brig. To remain in her during the coming winter, and thus keep together so large a number of persons as the entire company, in quarters so straitened, subjected to the worst causes of disease, without the most essential means either of prevention or cure, would, I felt assured, convert the brig into a mere hospital, where the most depressing influences must be engendered. Originally prepared for only a single winter, we had now completely exhausted our fuel, except 750 pounds of coals, after the consumption of which we must break up the ship; and our remaining provisions, although ample in quantity for the entire company through the winter, consisted

---

occasion, that the reader will probably be pleased to have his principal statements repeated in connection with the text.

"'August 18, Friday. — Reduced our allowance of wood to six pounds a meal. This, among eighteen mouths, is one-third of a pound of fuel for each. It allows us coffee twice a day, and soup once. Our fare besides this is cold pork boiled in quantity and eaten as required. This sort of thing works badly; but I must save coal for other emergencies. I see 'darkness ahead.'

"'I inspected the ice again to-day. Bad! bad! — I must look another winter in the face. I do not shrink from the thought; but, while we have a chance ahead, it is my first duty to have all things in readiness to meet it. It is *horrible* — yes, that is the word — to look forward to another year of disease and darkness to be met without fresh food and without fuel. I should meet it with more tempered sadness if I had no comrades to think for and protect.

"'August 20, Sunday. — Rest for all hands. The daily prayer is no longer ' Lord, accept our gratitude and bless our undertaking,' but ' Lord, accept our gratitude and restore us to our homes.' The ice shows no change: after a boat and foot journey around the entire southeastern curve of the bay, no signs!' (p. 343.)

"Everything before us was involved in gloomy doubt. Hopeful as I had been, it was impossible not to feel that we were near the climax of the expedition. (p. 344.)

mainly of salted meat, which, from its effect in producing and aggravating scurvy, as shown by the last winter's sad experience, threatened to be fatal to men in our condition. If one half of the company should leave the vessel to try the southward journey, there would be a sufficient number of men in each party to form a complete organization. Those remaining with the vessel would have the professional skill of Dr. Kane, with augmented means of health and comfort; and the causes of disease would be proportionally diminished. If the travelling party should perish by the way, the deaths would probably not be more numerous than if all should continue together; and whatever the fate of that party, the persons at the brig would be in improved condition in the spring.

"And now came the question of a second winter: how to look our enemy in the face, and how to meet him. Anything was better than inaction; and, in spite of the uncertainty which yet attended our plans, a host of expedients were to be resorted to, and much Robinson Crusoe labor ahead. Moss was to be gathered for eking out our winter fuel, and willow-stems and stonecrops and sorrel, as antiscorbutics, collected and buried in the snow. But while all these were in progress came other and graver questions.

"Some of my party had entertained the idea that an escape to the south was still practicable; and this opinion was supported by Mr. Petersen, our Danish interpreter, who had accompanied the searching expedition of Captain Penny, and had a matured experience in the changes of arctic ice. They even thought that the safety of all would be promoted by a withdrawal from the brig.

"'August 21, Monday. — The question of detaching a party was in my mind some time ago; but the more I thought it over, the more I was convinced that it would be neither right in itself nor practically safe. For myself personally, it is a simple duty of honor to remain by the brig: I could not think of leaving her till I had proved the effect of the later tides; and after that, as I have known all along, it would be too late. — Come what may, I share her fortunes.

"'But it is a different question with my associates. I cannot expect them to adopt my impulses; and I am by no means sure that I ought to

It was remembered by all of us, that to make a southward journey in boats to Upernavik rather than to hazard a second winter in the ice, had previously been repeatedly discussed, as among the alternatives which awaited us; and it was a subject long familiar to all of us. If, after the completion of the spring work, the season should be backward, it had been regarded as one of our recognized means of safety, to transport boats and provisions over the ice to open water, and early in September to push southward. This was one of the considerations which originally influenced Dr. Kane in favor of wintering in Rensselaer Bay.

The failure of his late expedition to Beechy Island, and the prospect of an early winter, (for the young ice was making rapidly,) led him to the conclusion

hold them bound by my conclusions. Have I the *moral right?* for, as to nautical rules, they do not fit the circumstances: among the whalers, when a ship is hopelessly beset, the master's authority gives way, and the crew take counsel for themselves whether to go or stay by her. My party is subordinate and well-disposed; but if the restlessness of suffering makes some of them anxious to brave the chances, they may certainly plead that a second winter in the ice is no part of the cruise they bargained for.

"' But what presses on me is of another character. I cannot disguise it from myself that we are wretchedly prepared for another winter on board. We are a set of scurvy-riddled, broken-down men; our provisions are sorely reduced in quantity, and are altogether unsuited to our condition. My only hope of maintaining and restoring such degree of health among us as is indispensable to our escape in the spring has been and must be in a wholesome elastic tone of feeling among the men: a reluctant, brooding, disheartened spirit would sweep the decks like a pestilence. I fear the bane of depressing example.

"' I know all this as a medical man and an officer; and I feel that I might be wearing away the hearts and energies, if not the lives of all, by forcing those who were reluctant to remain. With half a dozen confiding resolute men, I have no fears of ultimate safety. I will make a thorough inspection of the ice to-morrow, and decide finally the prospect of our liberation.

"' August 23, Wednesday. — The brig cannot escape. I got an eligible

which he announced to his officers, namely, that the "pack" in the North Water, which had baffled him, would still remain, and would interpose an insurmountable barrier to any attempt to escape to the south. This, however, he submitted to our judgments as a question upon which each of us was now called to think for himself.

On the other hand, it was believed by Mr. Petersen, whose long experience of the movements of arctic ice entitled his opinion to great respect, that this North Water "pack" had never previously been observed; that it was merely accidental; and that, such was the rapidity of ice movements, we had every reason to believe that it would entirely disappear within two weeks. Some of the grounds of this judgment will be manifested in subsequent

position with my sledge to review the floes, and returned this morning at two o'clock. There is no possibility of our release, unless by some extreme intervention of the coming tides. I doubt whether a boat could be forced as far as the Southern Water. When I think of the extraordinary way in which the ice was impacted last winter, how very little it has yielded through the summer, and how early another winter is making its onset upon us, I am very doubtful, indeed, whether our brig can get away at all. It would be inexpedient to attempt leaving her now in boats; the water-streams closing, the pack nearly fast again, and the young ice almost impenetrable.

"'I shall call the officers and crew together, and make known to them very fully how things look, and what hazards must attend such an effort as has been proposed among them. They shall have my views unequivocally expressed. I will then give twenty-four hours to deliberate; and at the end of that time all who determine to go shall say so in writing, with a full exposition of the circumstances of the case. They shall have the best outfit I can give, an abundant share of our remaining stores, and my good-bye blessing.

"'August 24, Thursday. — At noon to-day I had all hands called, and explained to them frankly the considerations which have determined me to remain where we are. I endeavored to show them that an escape to open water could not succeed, and that the effort must be exceedingly hazardous: I alluded to our duties to the ship: in a word, I advised them stren-

chapters, as the narrative carries us to the region to which they respectively relate. It is sufficient here to say, that I adopted entirely Mr. Petersen's conclusion, and thought that the escape which we all meditated was practicable at this time.

Again: if a party should succeed in the attempt to reach Upernavik, (the distance to which was not greater than that to Beechy Island,) they would there pass the winter, and being directly in the line of the Baffin Bay whalers, (which go annually within from one hundred to one hundred and fifty miles of Smith Strait,) they could give information of the condition of the Advance, and by means either of one of those whalers or of one of the small sloops known to be at the Danish settlements, communication could be reopened with Rensselaer Harbor in the spring.

Perhaps no one, who has never been placed in

---

uously to forego the project. I then told them that I should freely give my permission to such as were desirous of making the attempt, but that I should require them to place themselves under the command of officers selected by them before setting out, and to renounce in writing all claims upon myself and the rest who were resolved to stay by the vessel. Having done this, I directed the roll to be called, and each man to answer for himself.'

"In the result, eight out of the seventeen survivors of my party resolved to stand by the brig. It is just that I should record their names. They were Henry Brooks, James McGary, J. W. Wilson, Henry Goodfellow, William Morton, Christian Ohlsen, Thomas Hickey, Hans Christian.

"I divided to the others their portion of our resources justly and even liberally; and they left us on Monday, the 28th, with every appliance our narrow circumstances could furnish to speed and guard them. One of them, George Riley, returned a few days afterward; but weary months went by before we saw the rest again. They carried with them a written assurance of a brother's welcome should they be driven back; and this assurance was redeemed when hard trials had prepared them to share again our fortunes." (pp. 348 to 351.) *Arctic Explorations: the Second Grinnell Expedition in Search of Sir John Franklin, by Elisha Kent Kane, M. D., U. S. N.*

similar circumstances, can appreciate the conflict of motives which affected the persons interested in the pending question. Yet a decision must be promptly made; and suffice it to say that, after some fluctuations of judgment, the company was divided into two equal parties. One of these was to remain with the vessel during the winter. The other, which was to venture the journey over the thousand miles of ice-girt water which lay between the brig and the nearest outpost of christian men, consisted of J. Carl Petersen, August Sonntag, Amos Bonsall, George Stephenson, George Whipple, John Blake, William Godfrey, and George Riley. That party I accompanied. These pages are a record of its fortunes.

CHAPTER II.

PREPARATION.

As the enterprise upon which we were about to start was of our own choosing, and rested upon our own individual responsibility, the commander very properly required as a condition of his consent to it, that we should formally detach ourselves from the organization of the brig's company, and that we should effect a separate organization under officers elected by ourselves. We had no hesitation in the choice of a leader; for, beside Mr. Petersen there was no one in the company who had sufficient acquaintance with the region through which we were to journey, to guide us toward Upernavik. He had the experience of twenty years in all the phases of arctic life and travel, and he was accordingly unanimously elected to conduct our party. A future chapter shall be enlivened by some biographical notices of him.

Our preparations for departure were immediately commenced. They were simple and soon completed. We could carry with us very little, either in weight or bulk, since everything had to be transported over the ice to the open water. Of the character of the ice down to Esquimau Point we had had already a foretaste when Dr. Kane started for Beechy Island. It was now incomparably worse.

All hands turned to with a will to help us off, and the 25th was a busy day on board the Advance. Dr. Kane directed the boiling of a barrel of pork and some beans, and the coppers were filled early in the morning. I was chiefly occupied, during the day, in getting together my collections of natural history, the gatherings of two summers; and in stowing them away in the hold, and in my little room down by the forecastle. The floral specimens, altogether about two thousand individual plants, were wrapped in brown paper packages, labelled with date and locality, and delivered to the commander. The same was done with the small entomological collection, which was in a cigar-box. The bird skins, in all nearly two hundred, were secured in a rat-proof chest. The geological and mineralogical specimens; the musk-ox, human and other skulls and bones; the bear and seal skins; the fishes and other wet preparations, were in barrels or in the Smithsonian copper-tanks. This work seemed, at the time, very useless; but we knew not what might come, nor how many of these things might in the end be saved. I parted with deep regret from these old friends of my wanderings and dredgings — pets mostly collected by myself, which had slowly accumulated about me.

We commenced passing our equipment over the ship's side about noon of the 26th; and whilst some of us were thus engaged, others were sledging it to the land-ice, and with a rope hauling it up the vertical wall. The carpenter had made us a sledge of inch-plank, shod with hoop-iron, on which and on the "Faith," the companion of many a weary day's work, was stowed what we would carry; and at half-past five o'clock in the afternoon, accompanied by Mr. Wilson, Ohlsen, and Hickey of the remaining party, we moved southward, with the first load.

The travelling was bad. The snow-drifts were half frozen, half melted; and the ice-foot was covered in places with the overflow of the flood-tide, now skimmed over with thin ice, too thin to bear, thick enough to retard the sledge. In half an hour we reached the first ravine, and found that the torrent formed by the melted snow from the mountains, had worn the land-ice completely away. The sledges were unloaded, and the cargo was carried over upon our shoulders. The same operation was again performed about a mile further on.

At five o'clock next morning we reached the Six-mile Ravine. The rocky slope was here found to be exposed for a space of about forty yards. Being too much fatigued to carry over more than our sleeping fixtures, and preferring a berth where we were, to quarters in the brig at the expense of a walk back, we spread out our buffalo skins and blankets upon the rocks.

Our sleep was such as tired men get everywhere; and it lasted until three o'clock in the afternoon. By seven o'clock we had shouldered the remainder of our cargo over the ravine, and turning back toward the brig, we reached it in three hours. Stephenson and Godfrey, being broken down, were left at the encampment.

Our now dismantled bunks offered a sorry temptation, and we made only a short stay in them. By eleven o'clock A. M. of the 28th, all was ready for a final start. Our full cargo and equipment may be summed up as follows.

We were to take the life-boat from Life-boat Cove, near Lyttleton Island, and the whale-boat Forlorn Hope, left **by Dr. Kane** at the Six-mile Ravine; and for transporting our cargo over the ice, the little sledge made for us **by Ohlsen**, and the sledge Faith which was loaned to us for a few **days.**

For provisions, we had one barrel of parboiled pork, a half barrel of raw ditto, fifty pounds of boiled beans, five barrels of bread, fifty pounds of coffee, and about five of tea; all sewed up in canvas bags.

For fuel, we had a large keg of lard (slush, **rather)** and a coil of rope-yarn; our cooking apparatus being a rough portable sheet-tin furnace, a foot in diameter, and fourteen inches high. Our other culinary articles, tossed into a bag of India-rubber cloth, were an old copper teakettle, and a well-worn tin pot; six one-pint, and three half-pint tin cups, and ten spoons. Our luxuries were a bag of flour, (about twenty pounds,) **a two-gallon keg of** molasses, a case of Borden's meat-biscuit, a half dozen bottles of lime-juice, and two **ditto of vinegar.**

These articles were estimated to last us from four to five weeks.* **For** the rest, we were to rely upon our guns.

---

* This was **the** time in which we were expected to reach Upernavik, if at all. The amount of our provision **was** liberally left **by the** commander to our own **option**; and it was the more readily taken **by the party** as the men who **continued with** the brig had all that remained of the stores, which would have sufficed, **in** quantity, **for** eight months for the entire company of eighteen, officers and men.

Our personal equipment was on a par with the state of the larder. Every man who had a complete change of clothing, carried it with him; and most of us were thus furnished. We had worn out nearly all of our furs. Our outer garments were, therefore, either pilot cloth, seal-skin, or canvas. Each took his private stock of blankets, averaging about one and a half pairs per man. From the ship's stores we had half the buffalo robes, (two India-rubber lined skins,) relics of the spring journeys. We were supplied by the commander with a sextant, spy-glass, chronometer, boat-compass, barometer, one shot gun, and a reasonable quantity of ammunition. Bonsall and Petersen had each his own rifle. Dr. Kane, Mr. Wilson, Mr. McGary, and Morton, who were best provided, generously shared with us their clothing. From Wilson I received an under-shirt, and two pairs of good woollen socks, and I left him, in exchange, a coat. Sonntag added to his bag something from Wilson, and received a blanket from the captain. Petersen's rifle was a present from Dr. Kane to Petersen junior, at Upernavik.

During the morning, while some were packing up their "traps," others were carrying our remaining stores to the land-ice. Before noon the sledges were packed, and all was ready. Dr. Kane then called us to the cabin. In some nook or corner of the after-port-locker the careful steward had stowed a couple of bottles of champagne, the existence of which was known only to the commander and himself. One of these was drawn from its hiding-place, and in broken-handled teacups we exchanged mutual pledges. The "God speed you" of those who remained was answered with a reciprocal good wish from those who were about to leave. Next moment we had shaken hands and said good-bye all around, and, mounting the companion-ladder, were off.

As we slowly moved down the ice-foot, we endeavored to make up in firmness of tread what we lacked in lightness of heart. Although our judgments could not waver, after the serious discussions which had led to our choice of alternatives, yet the contingencies which awaited each party were sufficiently impressive to weigh heavily upon us. Our messmates at the brig waved us a silent adieu from the deck.

CHAPTER III.

THE START.

Mr. McGary, Hickey, and Hans were detailed by Dr. Kane to assist us in transporting our cargo to the open water, a lead of which we expected to meet at ten miles from the brig. The Six-mile Ravine was reached late in the afternoon, and here we again camped.

We were now fairly off; but it was not until next day that we fully realized the amount of labor which was before us. I was awake at four o'clock in the morning; and, calling one of the men, started the lamp to boil some coffee. Leaving him to look after the breakfast, I walked a short distance down the ice-foot in company with Petersen. The prospect was rather disheartening. There was scarcely a foot of water to be seen. The land lead was closed with lumps of wasted ice, cemented together by the last few days' freezing. All to the northward appeared as one unbroken field; while down the coast to the south and west we could see only an impacted mass of broken floes, the chasms separating which were bridged over with thin ice. Returning to the encampment we found our companions busy with preparations for starting. The first load was packed on the Faith; and with all hands on the track-ropes, except Mr. Sonntag and Stephenson who were both unwell, we moved slowly southward; and in three hours reached the Ten-mile Ravine, four miles further on our course.

As we approached the outer extremity of the cape, our people felt keenly disappointed; for they had confidently expected here to take the water. Ice, ice, and nothing but ice was anywhere to be seen. There was certainly little that was tempting in the prospect. The succor for which they perilled their lives seemed a long way off, when they looked out over this boundless waste of frozen water. Ten miles behind them was the ship, which they had left the day before. Between her oaken walls was to be found the only shelter within more than a thousand miles. Before them, at that distance, was Upernavik, with safety, if it could be reached; but what a wilderness intervened! A less important object, and a less desperate motive to persevere, would have been insufficient to sustain us.

There was certainly some excuse for melancholy faces, and questionings as to whether it were not wiser to turn back. However, the men all stood firm through fourteen hours of continual labor, in the teeth of a southerly wind, accompanied with occasional gusts of snow. During this time we brought up all our cargo in three separate loads, leaving behind only the boat Forlorn Hope; and we were glad enough, after a supper of cold pork, bread, and coffee, to find, in the tent, shelter from the wind, which was fast increasing to a gale. The relief-party, which had accompanied us thus far, having exhausted its allotted time, left us at noon to return on board.

The barometer went down in the night to 28.7, and the temperature rose from 26° to 33°. The gale broke upon us directly after we had camped. It soon started the ice. First a few open leads appeared at the head of the bay, and toward Godsend Island. At length the floes to the northwest gave way, and the loose drift down toward Esquimau Point drove rapidly up the channel; but the shore-ice near us did not move. A chain of heavy bergs lay grounded off Cape Ingersoll, and they held the ice firmly. Our hope was that the gale would set these bergs in motion; but this hope forsook us when we discovered the barometer to be rising and the thermometer falling.

The force of the gale was broken in the afternoon, and it died away toward evening, leaving the sea open to the southwest. From this water we were most provokingly shut out by a narrow belt of hummocks and trash which were all joined together by thin ice, not sufficiently strong to bear. We had a good night's rest in our tent, notwithstanding the wind, and turned out at eight o'clock.

Godfrey fixed the lamp in the lee of a large rock, and cooked us a comfortable breakfast of scouse and coffee. The gale was then at its height, and we waited from hour to hour in readiness to take the water when the ice should move off; but five o'clock came, and brought no change. There was no alternative but to resume our work. Our tent was pitched at the mouth of a deep ravine, and before us the land-ice* was entirely gone for at least fifty yards. Beyond this it was much wasted away. By noon we had brought up the boat, and then we carried the greater part of our stores a mile further on. While this was being done, Petersen was repairing the boat. The fact had been disclosed to us the day before, that the **Forlorn** Hope was a forlorn affair indeed. As she lay under the cliffs where she had been left by Dr. Kane, she had become seriously damaged. A stone, about the size of one's fist, had fallen upon her from the cliff, and, striking her sternpost, had started it; then, glancing off, it had gone completely through her half-inch cedar planking; while another had rolled down under the bilge, and, pushing a plank out of its place, had broken it in two. We had the good fortune to possess a hatchet, some nails, a few pieces of board, and a little pot of white lead; and with these Petersen patched up the holes, and made all right again.

The boat was then launched; that is, run down over the stones upon her keel toward the water. She stuck fast, and we found much trouble in doing anything with her. The ice would not support her, and yet it was so thick that we could not cut through it. We therefore hauled her out again, and resolved to await the flood-tide.

We crawled back into the tent and slept soundly until three o'clock next morning, when we were

---

* This "land-ice," or "ice-foot," as it is indifferently called, is a belt which, being glued to the rocks, does not rise and fall with the tide. Its outer face is vertical, and its upper surface is mainly smooth and level, until toward the close of summer, when the melted snow poured upon it from the hills and cliffs on the one side, and the sea on the other, wear it rapidly away.

aroused by voices outside. Three Esquimaux, a boy of about eighteen years, and two women, stood at the door of the tent, chattering away as unintelligibly, and many times as fast as a poll-parrot. The boy we had seen before, but the women were new to us. They were a miserable looking set. Their faces were mottled with soot and oil, through which only here and there could be seen the natural coppery tint of the complexion. They were dressed in skins, or rather were scarcely dressed at all, for their clothing was in rags and tatters, and seemed just ready to drop off. Their hands and faces looked as if they had never been washed; and the boy, with his long black matted hair cut square across his eyebrows, and the women with theirs drawn together on the top of the head, where it was tied with a piece of leather, presented a most unattractive appearance. One of the women carried a baby not more than six months old. It was stuck, stark naked and feet foremost, into the after-part of her coat or jumper, being supported by a rope, on which it seemed to sit, and which came around under the mother's arms and was tied about her neck; its innocent baby-face, peering out over the woman's left shoulder from beneath her hood, was the very image of stupid unconsciousness.

They were shivering with cold, and asked for means to light a fire. We gave them some matches, a bit of wood, and two or three needles; and after sharing with us our breakfast, which, salt though it was, they were hungry enough to relish, they started off down the coast. A few hours after, we learned that they knew more than they chose to communicate. Hans came running down the ice-foot, out of breath and in a great rage. It was sometime before we could get out of him what was the matter. When he recovered his breath, he told his story in his own language to Petersen; but in the mean time it was nothing but "Smit-Soun Eskemo, no koot! no koot! All same mickey!—all same dog! steal me bag!—steal Nalegak buffalo!"

The truth was, they had been to the ship and carried off, among other valuables, a small buffalo-skin, and a wolf-skin bag which Dr. Kane had presented to Hans. Hence the lad's indignation. The cunning thieves had taken good care to secrete these articles from us. They had probably travelled over the land, and approaching the sea, a mile or two below, had seen us from the hill-tops, and come to beg a trifle. Certainly all they could get by fair means or foul was not more than they needed, and could we have spared any important articles, I am sure no one would have objected to giving them what they most required. We were about as badly off as they. Hans stopped with us long enough to refresh himself with something to eat and a cup of coffee, and then continued after the thieves.

When the full tide had come in we found that the ice had relaxed a little, and that there was a narrow lead close alongside the ice-foot. The boat was again run down and launched. For about a hundred yards we got on well enough, but the lead was then closed up by pieces of heavy ice, some of which had been carried there by the spring-tides and were grounded. These obliged us to haul outside where the young ice lay in one continuous sheet.

It was found to be of the same character as that which we had before encountered. It would not break before the bows of the boat, nor would it bear. We tried all sorts of expedients. First we cleared the thwarts, and four men were put to the oars. The points of the blades were driven into the ice, the bow having been previously lightened, and everything stowed in the sternsheets; but no force that we could exert in this manner would drive the boat forward. Then two men were stationed in the bow and broke the way with the boat-hooks; but this was so slow an operation, and fatigued us so much, that it was abandoned. We therefore drew back once more, and after unshipping the cargo, we dragged the boat upon the ice-foot, and hauled her on her keel, down to the place to which we had carried the remaining stores the day before.

These stores were then taken forward upon the sledge, at two separate loads, one and a half miles further on; and the boat was afterward carried to the same place. Here we again found that a portion of the ice-foot was washed away; and beyond this break the foot was impassable by reason of the frequent fissures which occurred, some of them wide and deep. Beside, the icy ledge was in many places so narrow or sloping as to be impracticable to a sledge.

The labors of the day had much fatigued us. In addition to the fruitless exertion which we had made on account of the boat, we were five times obliged to unship our cargo from the sledges; and, making pack-horses of ourselves, to transport it piece by piece across the broken places in the land-ice, or over the narrow fissures on a bridge which we made with the sledges. We were, beside, greatly vexed by a little accident, which seemed likely to deprive us of one of our few luxuries. Bonsall had taken the keg of molasses upon the back of his neck, grasping either end of it with one hand, and, while trudging along near the edge of the ice-foot, tripped and fell upon his face. The keg went rolling over his head and down into the sea. Then more than two hours elapsed before we could find any water for our coffee. The streams seemed to be all dried up; and we were obliged to await the return of a party from our last encampment before we could start the fire. It was seven o'clock when we pitched the tent, and we got to bed after ten; not, however, before we had the satisfaction of learning that, the tide having fallen, Mr. Bonsall and Godfrey had, by means of boat-hooks, fished up the molasses out of four feet of water!

CHAPTER IV.

ACROSS THE ICE-FIELDS.

For reasons which appear in the last chapter, no course remained to us but to leave the land-ice and try once more the "floes." A sudden fall of the temperature, during the night and the latter part of the previous day, to ten degrees below the freezing point of sea-water, had come to our aid. The young ice was found to be, in places, three inches in thickness, and would securely bear us.

Accordingly, after breakfast, everything was made ready; and the tide being at its ebb, the boat was run down the sloping beach and upon the ice; and although this bent under the weight, yet we reached in safety an old floe at about a hundred yards from shore. The large sledge was then loaded with our clothes-bags and buffalo robes, and started; but, as bad luck would have it, the slope was steep, and the two men at the after-guy found it impossible to maintain their hold. Their heels flew up, and away went the "Faith" down to the right where the ice was thin. First, this bent; then one runner broke through; over went the cargo, and into the water went everything.

Fortunately there was nothing on the sledge that

would not float; but our clothes-bags were thoroughly soaked before we could get our boat-hooks and save them. The buffalo robes were wrapped in India-rubber cloth, and were scarcely touched by the water. Nothing of importance to us was seriously damaged except the spirits of our men. Petersen was the principal loser. He had brought with him from Upernavik a fine bed of eider-down, under which he was accustomed to stow himself out of sight every night when on board of the Advance. This bed he had compressed into a bundle not larger than his head, and had put it in his bag. It was thoroughly soaked, and was of course worthless. I pitied the man as he unwrapped the flabby thing; yet I could not repress a smile at the workings of his rueful face, while he wrung the water from his treasure. Smarting under my mirthfulness, and his great disappointment, he hastily rolled the whole up into a wad, and with an expression, too Danish for me to detect of its meaning, more than "Doctor!" and "Sa-tan!" he hurled it among the rocks. — Forty Danish dollars gone forever!

During the last four-and-twenty hours the courage of some of the party had been steadily on the wane. They could see no possibility of our getting at this rate to Upernavik. This accident was the straw which broke the camel's back; and while we were yet busy with the wet cargo, Riley and John, concluding, no doubt, that prudence was the better part of valor, beat a hasty retreat toward the brig. John rejoined us soon afterward, but Riley remained on board. The number of our party was thus reduced to eight persons.

The work nevertheless went on. A half hour was sufficient for wringing the water out of our baggage and spreading the articles upon the rocks. With more caution than before, we ran another load over to the boat. At six o'clock in the afternoon, we had collected together all of our cargo, and were ready once more to move onward. In the mean time Godfrey had been moping on the rocks. I gave to him peremptorily the option, to go back to the ship at once, or to go to work. He chose the latter.

Hans joined us again at noon. He had overtaken the Esquimaux, but had not found the stolen articles upon them. It was his wish to go with us, and now that our party was reduced to seven, (John had not yet returned,) and the party on board increased to eleven, he thought it unfair that we refused him. I desired Petersen to tell him that we could not take him without the permission of Dr. Kane. He worked with us during the remainder of the day, no doubt hoping that by this act of devotion we would be induced to relent; but it was clearly our duty to send him back.

The old floe, to which we had brought our boat and cargo, was rough and rotten. On the further side of it was a belt of new ice. Beyond this we could see open water, which Hans informed us continued nearly to Godsend Island, to the south of which, with the exception of a narrow belt, all was free. We worked hard, hoping to reach this open water, but eleven o'clock found us only at the margin of the old field. Already we had been in the traces fourteen hours; and at least six more would be required to make the remaining distance. The people were exhausted and must have rest, come what might. We therefore pitched our tent, and, by midnight, were all fast asleep.

An hour after, we were aroused by McGary and Goodfellow, who had come down after the Faith. I explained to them that they must have mistaken their orders, since we were to have the sledge until we reached the water; that they had two good sledges at the ship, and the one which we had was not needed in addition; but they showed a letter from Dr. Kane containing an order to bring the Faith to the ship. Although satisfied that a misapprehension existed (as subsequently was ascertained to be the fact), we sent back the sledge. The party left us in half an hour. They made in one continuous march the journey to and fro, altogether little less than thirty miles, without rest or food, over a bad road, with the thermometer at 17°. We afterward learned that they had worked all the day before at the ship, had started after supper, and were at home to breakfast.

We were out of our blankets at six o'clock next morning. The temperature had fallen to 15°. The air was perfectly calm. The open water, which looked so hopeful yesterday, was now covered with a thin crust of ice. The day began rather discouragingly.

The sledge made for us by the carpenter had been found to be utterly worthless; and, after the first day, it had been carried, not under, but on top of the cargo. It was so frail that it would not hold together; and the thin hoop-iron sole was cracked. Bad, however, as it was, it was all that we had, and we must make the most of it. Petersen, whose ingenuity we had reason to commend on many subsequent occasions, did the best that he could under the circumstances. The broken iron was patched, and the lashings were re-arranged. By nine o'clock, all was ready to start.

Meanwhile, some of the party had been carrying forward such articles as they could transport upon their backs; and some of the heavier ones were swung upon oars and carried, upon two men's shoulders, to the place where open water had been seen the previous evening. Such articles as could not be thus transported were left for the sledge, which brought them up in three loads. Then the boat was dragged to the same spot upon her keel. The water was now found to be covered with ice about an inch in thickness.

The stores being placed in the boat, we ran her out upon the thin ice; and as the bows sank down, we sprang over the gunwale, and found ourselves afloat in a puddle of water which fitted us exactly. How to get on was the next question. Three men took oars, the others took poles and boat-hooks. The blades of the oars were planted in the ice, and the boat-hooks astern. The result of the operation was to split an oar, to break a thole-pin, and to precipitate the surgeon of the expedition into the water. He was stationed in the sternsheets, and was pushing with much energy with a boat-hook, planted in the ice, when the hold broke, and the area of the open water was increased by the size of his body.

The ice was too strong to be cut by the boat's

stem; and, but for Stephenson, we should have been obliged once more to haul back upon the floe, and try again the sledging. Stephenson wore a pair of thick cowhide boots, professedly water-proof, which came up a foot above his knees; and with these he proposed to tramp a track. He stationed himself astride of the bow, seized the top of the stem-post with both hands, and, treading to right and left, he broke up a passage from two to three feet in width, through which the boat was squeezed. The ice became thinner as we advanced, and we made better progress.

Thus we gained about four miles, which brought us to the land at the head of Force Bay. Mounting to the ice-foot, which was here very narrow and almost impassable, we tracked the boat, in true canal style, a mile or two further, when we again brought up against ice which would bear us. Again the cargo was unshipped, and was carried over to an old floe, about a hundred yards from shore. Here we pitched our tent.

This kind of work was rapidly reducing the strength of our people. Constant labor during sixteen hours is not child's play anywhere; but, with wet feet and often wet bodies, in a temperature varying from 12° to 20°, it was more than any one could prolong. Several of us had fallen through the ice during the day; and Stephenson, who was a scorbutic invalid at starting, felt seriously the effects of having his feet so long in the water. Petersen, who had suffered during the whole summer from scurvy and rheumatism, felt his pains coming back; and Mr. Sonntag was threatened with his old heart trouble.

I believe there was scarcely one of us who did not take his sick man's growl as he rolled into his blankets.

While the supper was cooking, I went with Petersen and Sonntag to the shore, and from a bluff about one hundred feet in height we had a fine view to the westward. About six miles away, the sea was perfectly open, and a light wind which blew in from that direction was eating into the young ice which margined it, and, by keeping its surface agitated, prevented its freezing. With a good sledge, another day's pull would finish this soul and body killing work; but, with the rickety affair with which we had occupied eight hours in making half a mile, we had a hopeless task before us. Indeed, it looked very much like folly to attempt it. We could not hope to make the six miles in less than three days. Already the temperature was down to 12°. Three days would carry us to the 6th of September, and then the prospect of getting out of the bay would be slight indeed.

We had just got fairly into the midst of our nap when we were aroused by Morton. He had come down to bring back the Faith, and he carried a letter from Dr. Kane, explaining the cause of its withdrawal. From what he had learned, he had feared that adverse counsels existed in the party, that it had been divided, and that the sledge no longer remained in the possession of the officers.

Hickey and Riley accompanied Morton. Riley was to remain with us until we got to open water, and then take back the sledge. Morton and Hickey were to go in pursuit of the Esquimaux thieves.

A bed was fitted up for them in the boat, and there they slept soundly until ten o'clock next morning. By eleven, everything was packed up, and the sledge loaded; and, as the men ran away with it, the despondency which settled over them the previous evening took hasty flight. There would be now no difficulty in reaching the water.

Hickey was sick, and stayed at the camp, while Riley took his place and went on with Morton. In half an hour Riley came back dripping wet; he had fallen through the ice. Morton had gone on alone. He returned late in the afternoon, having the Esquimaux with him. He had overtaken them near Refuge Inlet, where they had halted to divide their booty. The skins were all nicely made by them into coats and pantaloons, which had usurped the place of their old ragged, filthy seal-skins. They looked much improved in their borrowed plumes, and strutted about, seeming not to be aware of the fact that they were prisoners; and very proud were they, supposing that they had obtained the skin of an umingmak, (musk-ox,) an animal of which they had heard, but which they had never seen. The tribe have, however, traditional knowledge of the existence of the musk-ox to the far north. They were once inhabitants of that part of Greenland visited by us above Cape Alexander. My collections of natural history, left at the Advance, contained at least a dozen skulls, picked up at different points along the coast; and, eighty miles eastward of Rensselaer Harbor, nearly at the base of the *mer de glace*, specimens of them were found by Mr. Wilson and myself in the autumn of 1853. It seems, therefore, that they were numerous in that region in former times; though, from the fact that no living specimens were observed by us, nor any seen by the natives, we may infer that the animal has long since become extinct in Greenland. I do not doubt the truthfulness of the Esquimau tradition of their existence to the far north, on an island in an iceless sea.

To return to the narrative: Morton and Hickey soon left us with their newly-clad prisoners, and the work of transportation went on in much the same manner as during the two previous days; but we progressed more slowly than we had anticipated. Once we reached a wide crack that had been opened by the tide, which obliged us to ship our cargo into the boat, and unship it again on the other side, thus occasioning the loss of much time. Another crack we attempted to cross on its bridge of thin ice. It held up very well, bending slightly, but not breaking, under our several loads, until the boat broke its back, and let all of us down into the water except those who had hold of the track-ropes.

The main open water was not reached until midnight. Everything was embarked in the boat, and, leaving Petersen with four men to bring it over to Esquimau Point, which was about two miles distant, I walked with the remainder of my comrades around upon the ice to the land. After taking a look-out from a neighboring bluff, we joined the others where they were hauled up at a short distance from the shore, being unable to approach nearer on account of the heavy ice which had set in, and which lay grounded and hemmed in by the rocks. We found that they had preceded us by an hour and a half, as was shown by the steaming pot of coffee with which we were welcomed.

On our way down to the beach from the hill-side, we stopped at the old dilapidated hut which gives the name to the locality. Here we had the good fortune to find a piece of walrus meat, which we supposed had been left by Morton's prisoners; and which, as we had tasted no fresh food since leaving the ship, we thought it no sin to appropriate to our own use. We left in its place a wooden staff, which, in the eyes of the Esquimaux, would be ample compensation. With the addition of a few pieces of pork, the meat thus provided made us a fine supper.

The view which we obtained from the hill showed the coast to be mainly free from ice as far down as the eye could reach, and out to sea for three or four miles. Beyond this distance there lay a heavy pack, which was held off from the shore by a long chain of dangerous looking bergs. The lead was tempting, but there was no wind, and we could only go on under oars. Our people were incapable of such exertion. They had had another day of sixteen hours' continued work, and must have rest. Hoping for the best, — that the lead would remain open, — we pitched our tent upon the level surface of a piece of old ice which lay grounded near the shore; and at three o'clock in the morning we turned in, weary and cold, as men with wet clothes would naturally be after so protracted exertion, with the temperature at 11°, but happy as temporary success could make us. We were so far overcome that we retired to rest without setting a watch.

When we awoke next morning, a smart breeze was blowing from north-northeast. Petersen went on shore to reconnoitre, and soon returned, reporting the ice closing in with the land. Our baggage was shipped into the boat as quickly as possible. Giving the Faith into the charge of Riley, and bidding him a hasty adieu, we pulled up to windward to clear the Point; and then, shaking out our sails, we stood away exultingly on our course, west-southwest.

CHAPTER V.

UNDER SAIL.

The Forlorn Hope was an ordinary New London whale-boat, twenty-four feet in length, two and a half in depth, and with five and a half feet beam. She had been rigged by Mr. McGary for Dr. Kane's southern journey in July, with a foresail and a mainsail, — the first with twelve, and the last with fourteen feet, lift; and a jib. Eight men, with their baggage, brought her gunwale down within four inches of the water. Notwithstanding this, we made nearly four knots; and for a while everything looked promising; but below Anoatok, which is five miles southwest of Esquimau Point, we found that the icebergs came in close to the land, and no longer held off the pack. Our lead was closed.

After beating about for a while in search of an opening, we drew up, much disappointed, alongside of a lump of old ice, which was about twenty yards square and thirty feet in thickness. Its surface lay about four feet out of the water; and, being quite level, afforded a good camping-ground. Upon this table we unshipped our cargo; and Petersen taking the boat, with two men, pulled up to a little berg near which we had observed a flock of unfledged ducks. He returned in an hour with eleven birds, eight of which made us a good supper.

We waited here until late in the evening, hoping that a change of tide would open a passage; but the pack only closed tighter and tighter, finally compelling us to haul our boat up on the ice, to save it from being crushed. The wind still blew from the north-northeast, bitterly cold; temperature 15°. At ten o'clock we pitched the tent and turned in.

Petersen had the morning watch, and went on shore to observe the ice. At first everything remained as it was the evening before; an apparently endless collection of immensely heavy floes were locked against the capes of Refuge Harbor. Suddenly something appeared to give way. First a few pools of water were visible; then lead after lead opened in every direction through the pack. In a little while the ice had spread itself out over the sea, and was moving off to the west and south. Petersen watched the shifting scene until he became satisfied that the change was permanent. Then running quickly down the hill, he cried to us from the shore, "Haste! haste! the lead opens." He was just in time to spring aboard the frozen raft on which we had taken refuge, as it moved away.

We were out of our blankets and buffaloes in a twinkling. The Hope was quickly launched and stowed. While this was being done, the cook had prepared a hasty breakfast, which being more hastily swallowed, we dropped down into the boat, and, with all sails set, ran off before the wind for the capes of Refuge Harbor.

The movements of these ice-fields are as strange

as they are rapid. We started from Esquimau Point with every prospect of an unobstructed passage, and before we had gone six miles the lead was closed. So it remained during the day. In a few hours the wind hauled around two points to the east, and the whole aspect of things was changed. The ice began to move; the floes separated; the cracks widened; until finally there was no barrier at all; and in an open sea, dotted only here and there by a floe, we were spinning down the coast at the rate of four knots an hour.

In three hours we left behind us the brown knobby bluffs which form the horns of Refuge Harbor; and in another hour we were close under the granite wall of Cape Hatherton. Then opened the low lands of Life-boat Bay, and behind these the dark stratified cliffs supporting an extensive table-land which, elevated a thousand feet above the ocean, stretches away far into the interior.

Life-boat Bay is a broad shallow arm of the sea. It is studded on its northern side with little islands; while its eastern shore is cut into numerous coves or bights, by low rocky points. On the main land, two miles northeast from Lyttleton Island, and six miles south of Cape Hatherton, at the head of the most southern of these coves, lay the Francis' metallic life-boat, left by Dr. Kane in August 1853, which was to form the second vessel of our fleet. Of this boat we were now in search.

We made good progress for nearly an hour after rounding Cape Hatherton, having, during that time, passed about three miles of the coast, and we were congratulating ourselves that all was free, when the look-out cried, "ice ahead!" There it was, sure enough, about a mile before us, — a long white line, against which the surf was breaking.

We ran down within a quarter of a mile of it, hoping all the time that we should find a lead; but no opening could anywhere be seen. The pack was jammed tight together, and against the southern shore of the bay; and stretching off to the southwest, it seemed to block up the channel between Lyttleton Island and the main land.

The course of the boat was changed to the west, and, although the wind was increasing, we determined to run outside the island and endeavor to reach the cove from the south; but here, again, we were headed off; a tongue of the pack stretched up to the north as far as we could see. To haul close on the wind and run up the edge of the ice was out of the question. With a less heavily laden boat this could easily have been accomplished; but already we were shipping much water, with the wind on the quarter. Two points more around must swamp us. A sea breaking over the gunwale convinced us of the danger of the attempt, and again the boat was headed south.

It became now evident that we were in great jeopardy. We had run down into a bight, with a lee-shore to the east, and ice to the south and west. We were in the bend of a great horseshoe.

There was no time to get out the oars and pull up to windward; the boat could not have lived long enough to get her head around to the waves. The cargo was piled upon the thwarts, and a quarter of an hour would scarcely have sufficed to clear them.

Something must be done, and that quickly. The wind increased in violence, the waves rolled higher and higher. We could only run down upon the ice and trust to luck. Choosing a point to the southwest, where the pack looked weakest, we brailed up the mainsail, took a hasty reef in the foresail, hauled in the jib, and ran for it. John took the steering oar, Petersen conned the boat from the forecastle, Stephenson held the sheet, Bonsall stood by the brail of the foresail, and the rest of us took whatever of boat-hooks and poles we could lay hands on, to "fend off."

The boat bounded away. "See any opening, Petersen?" "No, sir!" An anxious five minutes followed. "I see what looks like a lead; we must try for it." "Give the word, Petersen." On flew the boat. "Let her fall off a little — off! — Ease off the sheet — so — steady! — A little more off — so! — Steady there — steady, as she goes!" Our skilful pilot was running us through a narrow lead which terminated in a little bight, where the water was, fortunately, smooth. We were beginning to hope that it would carry us through the pack, when he cried out, "It's a blind lead!" "Tight everywhere?" "I see no opening!" "There's a crack to windward." "Can't make it! — Let go the sheet — brail up — fend off!" Thump, crash, push. The stem struck fair, and the force of the blow was broken by the poles. In an instant all hands sprang out upon the floe. The boat did not appear to have been seriously damaged.

Our harbor was only temporary. The ice was in rapid motion, and in a moment the whole face of things about us was changed. A large floe, which had kept off the waves, commenced to revolve. In few minutes there was only a tongue, a few feet wide, to protect us from the surf. The ice pressed close upon the boat; the spray dashed over our heads. The cargo was unshipped as quickly as possible, and the Hope was hauled up in time to save her. The stores were next tumbled into a heap, out of the reach of the spray. This had scarcely been done, when the floe broke in two. The crack opening rapidly, separated the Hope from her cargo. Here was a dilemma, and it promised to be a serious one; but, luckily, the piece upon which the boat stood was caught by another drifting mass, which slewed it around and tongued it upon a corner of the field from which it had been detached. The boat was quickly run over; and, with thankful hearts, we now saw, what we had no reason to expect at any time during the last fifteen minutes, all of our valuables together in, at least, temporary safety. The whole pack was moving, grinding, squeezing, and closing. Presently, a large floe revolved to the eastward and settled down against the field upon which we had taken refuge. In half an hour there was no open water within a hundred yards of us.

CHAPTER VI.

A GLOOMY NIGHT.

Everything now appearing to be secure, Bonsall and myself, accompanied by two of the men, set off over the ice to try to reach the life-boat on foot. The head of the cove where it lay was distant two miles; we were at about the same distance from Lyttleton Island. The floes were tightly packed, and we found no difficulty in accomplishing our purpose. The depôt was reached in an hour.

It remained undisturbed; evidently not having been discovered by the natives. The boat was turned bottom up, and under it lay the articles deposited there by Dr. Kane. These were, besides the oars and sail, two barrels of bread, one of pork, and another of beef; about thirty pounds of rice, the same quantity of sugar, a saucepan, an empty keg, a gallon can of alcohol, a bale of blankets, an ice anchor, an ice chisel, a gun, a hatchet, a few small poles, and some pieces of wood.

We could not take much of this provision, since we were compelled to carry everything upon our backs. We, however, selected such articles as were most needed, and as could be most readily transported in this manner. These were, one barrel of bread, the saucepan filled with sugar, ten pounds of rice, the empty keg, the hatchet, the gun, and the boat's equipment, including the ice anchor and chisel, two poles, and a small bundle of wood. We needed badly some of the pork for fuel, since our slush keg was getting low; but we could not take it.

Ascending the hill-side a little way, we observed that the eastern shore of Lyttleton Island was mainly free from ice, while the pack was locked upon its northern cape, and stretched up the west and north as far as we could see. From the beach where we stood, to the open water of this island, was about a mile. It was fully double that distance to where our companions lay with the Hope.

Since we must drag the boat and carry the cargo, we chose the shortest distance, intending to reach Lyttleton Island, and there await the breaking of the storm, the loosening of the pack, and the arrival of the Hope. The boat was run down over the ice-foot and dragged out upon the floes. The barrel of bread was swung upon an oar and carried by John and Godfrey. The smaller articles, oars, sail, &c., were brought on as we could manage them.

The boat was light, and had the track been smooth we should have progressed well enough; but after leaving the land-ice our route lay over a closely jammed pack of pieces of ice, of almost every shape and size; some of them being a foot out of water, others ten feet. One moment we were hauling the boat up a precipice, the next letting her down over another. Added to this difficulty was the feeling of constant insecurity, for it would have been perfectly in character for the whole raft suddenly to take flight to seaward. We were consequently compelled to keep our different articles as near together as possible. First we carried forward the boat about a hundred yards, then piece by piece the cargo and equipment. The same operation being repeated about a dozen times, we reached finally, in six hours, the open water.

By this time it was blowing a regular gale, still from the northeast. The pack had partially broken, and some loose pieces were drifting rapidly down through the channel. To work between these driving masses was an operation attended with no little difficulty. Once we came near being crushed.

Lyttleton Island, which was at length reached, is the largest of the granite knobs which lie in a cluster at the south side of Life-boat Bay. It is about three quarters of a mile in diameter, and is separated from the main land by a channel about half a mile in width. We pulled down this channel to the southwest, and sought a lee on the southern side; but no lee could we anywhere find. Reaching the extreme point we were met by a gust of wind which came howling through the narrow strait separating Lyttleton Island from McGary's Rock, driving us back to face a similar blast which came from the other side.

Everything gave promise of a dirty night. The sky was overcast. Light clouds went flitting wildly across the sky, breaking now and then and disclosing a twinkling star of the first or second magnitude. It was not dark, for the sun was not yet far beneath the horizon; but a dull, gloomy twilight. Already we were wet to the skin with the dashing spray. The mercury stood at 22°, and the water was freezing upon our clothes. We must either land on the island, or run before the wind down under Cape Ohlsen, five miles south. This last would carry us too far from our comrades of the Hope, and we determined to land on the island if possible. Our metallic boat would stand a good deal of thumping. There were no breakers; but the swell, which came in from the west, made the sea anything but smooth. With a wooden boat it would have been dangerous to approach the rocks.

The shore was steep, almost perpendicular; and it was some time before we found a place which offered the least chance for executing our intention. At length we discovered a little cove, or rather a cleft in the rock, about twenty feet in width and twice as deep. The rocks to the right and behind were vertical; but the cleft ran off to the left, and there the rock sloped gradually upward. If we could strike this inclined plane, by a fortunate turn of the boat after entering, we should be landed in safety. The boat was headed square for the opening, the men gave way on their oars, and we rode in on the top of a swell which, as it retreated, left us high and dry. Next moment all hands sprang out, and, seizing the boat by the gunwale, hauled her out of danger.

As we came across the ice, John had discovered a wounded duck sitting behind a hummock, and secured her with an oar. A fire was kindled in a crevice in the rock; the saucepan was half filled with sea-water, and the four quarters of the unfortunate eider were soon boiling in it. The head was knocked out of the bread-barrel, and eight biscuits were added to the contents of the pot.

We were too cold and too nearly famished to wait with much patience, and the stew was speedily pronounced *done*. Plates and spoons we had none, so each one handled his share of the duck, and then we took turns with the lid for the soup.

This hot meal warmed us up a little, but with it vanished our stock of comforts. With a cup of coffee, or even tea, we should have made out very well.

There was a gloomy prospect for the night. Nowhere could we find protection against the wind, which not only swept in from the sea, but came furiously down upon us through the rocky gorges. We had not as much as a blanket to cover us, and the cold gusts blew most cruelly through our water-soaked cloth coats and canvas pantaloons. We clambered about in the darkness along the rocky ledge, under a great black wall, hunting in vain for a lea; but no sooner had we found a place which seemed to offer us protection, than the wind shifted. Indeed, it seemed to blow, in one and the same minute, from every quarter of the heavens, north, south, east, and west; and when it could not get at us from either of these directions, it rolled down over the cliffs and fell upon us like an avalanche. We returned to the place where we had landed, and erected an extempore tent. One end of an oar was thrust into a crack in the rock, the other end was supported upon the barrel. Over this was spread the sail. After securing the corners with heavy stones we crawled in, but we thus obtained only a sorry protection. The wind came in on every side. Bonsall and Godfrey finally gave way under the pressure of fatigue and long exposure, and shivered themselves to sleep. I would have given much to be able to forget, in like manner, all care and trouble; but it was out of the question. Unable longer to bear the cold, I drew myself out from the sail, determined to thaw my frozen blood by a run about the island. John followed, muttering something like, " I believe they could sleep with their heads in a tub of water."

I was nearly blown off as I clambered up the steep rocks, but I reached at length the level table above, and ran to and fro from east to west, and from west to east, for about an hour, until I had got pretty well warmed; I then faced about and ran in the teeth of the gale to the north cape of the island. To the north, west, and south, the sea was dotted with bergs, loose hummocks, or streams of pack-ice, against which the waves were lashing themselves into frosty foam. To the northeast I could trace the outline of the solid pack in one long line of dashing spray. There I had left four comrades. There they must have remained, but the mist and darkness were too great to permit me to detect them. It was now about midnight.

I took another turn about the island and came back to the same spot. The wind was blowing less fiercely; the clouds opened, and moved sullenly away; and the stars shone out in unobstructed beauty. The pack had separated, and great streams of ice were pouring down through the channel to the eastward, as through a sluice-gate. I went down to a point where I could command a full view of the channel and watched every piece of ice, expecting to see the Hope and her crew adrift. I had not looked long before I discovered something dark upon one of the floating fields. It was a man, and I soon made out that it was John. I called to him, but he either did not hear, or did not heed me. The tumult might well have drowned my voice. What he was doing there, or how he had got there, I could not imagine. He was standing in the middle of the crystal raft, with nothing around him but the raging waters which were breaking over it. Directly the floe floated into the midst of a long stream of broken masses. The moment the collision came he sprang forward, and then away he went bounding from floe to floe, springing crack after crack with the fleetness of a deer. Once again I saw him adrift upon an isolated field, and thus he must have floated several minutes, before the pack closed up. I watched him until he was lost to sight in the mist and spray and darkness.

I had for some time entertained serious apprehensions for the safety of our comrades with the Hope, and these apprehensions were sharpened by this incident. With these fears were now mingled anxiety for the safety of John. It was evident that he was not upon the ice by any accident, but designedly; and I could imagine nothing that would induce him to run such a dare-devil's race, but to render assistance to Petersen and his party. He was making directly for the point where we had left them, as nearly as the elements would allow; and I could give no other explanation of his conduct than that he had detected the party, had seen them in distress, and had run this risk to help them.

Bonsall and Godfrey were at length frozen out of

the tent and joined me on the hill. I communicated to them my fears respecting the party. I sent Godfrey to watch to seaward. Bonsall went to the north cape, and I remained in my old position. The night wore on; daylight came slowly back; the wind died away to a fresh breeze; the sea was going down; the spray leapt less wildly; yet nothing could we see of the boat.

At length a change of tide brought a change of scene; the ice was set in motion; the pack, which had so closely hugged the land, was loosened; and it stretched its long arms out over the water to the westward. Broad leads ran through the body of it. Bonsall's quick eye first detected something dark moving upon the water. "I see the boat," he shouted to me, — "Where away?" — "Coming down through the in-shore lead." There she was, with all sail set, bearing directly for the island. By eight o'clock her party brought up on the south side of our encampment. I counted them as they floated by: one, two, three, four, *five* — John was there.

The swell was still too high to permit them to touch the rocks with their frail boat; we therefore launched the metallic boat, and following them under oars, pulled around behind Cape Ohlsen. Here was found a snug little harbor with a low shingly beach. The cargo was unshipped, and the boats were hauled up at half-past eleven o'clock. The sun's slanting rays shone directly in upon us from the south; the mercury went up to 28°. Not a breath of air rippled the water. No surf beat upon the shore. What a contrast to the tumultuous scenes of yesterday! From a little stream of melted snow which trickled down the mountain side, we filled our kettles; the lamp was fired; and in an hour and a half the cook had ready for us a good pot of coffee, and a stew of the young eiders which were left from the day before; to which were added some pieces of pork, and a young burgomaster gull, which had been shot on the way from Lyttleton Island. While this substantial breakfast was being eaten, we interchanged our stories of the night's adventures.

Our friends had had a fearful night. Bad as had been our fortune theirs was incomparably worse. Soon after we left them, the protecting floes to the north shifted their position; and from that time until the storm subsided, they were frightfully exposed. The waves rolled in upon them, frequently breaking over the floe on which they were, while the spray flew over them continually. They wrapped the bread-bags in a piece of India-rubber cloth, and thus kept them tolerably dry; but everything else became thoroughly soaked, — clothes, buffaloes, and blankets, especially. They pitched their tent and tried to get some rest, but the water very soon drowned them out. They tried to cook some coffee, but the spray extinguished their lamp. They were thirty hours without water to drink, and during all that time they tasted nothing warm, their sole provision being cold pork and bread. Their suffering was great, and our tale sounded tamely enough after theirs.

I questioned John why he had so recklessly exposed his life; he "wanted to see what had become of them." He did not see them when he started; had no certain knowledge as to where they were; he only wanted to "look them up."

CHAPTER VII.

ROUNDING CAPE ALEXANDER.

It was now the 6th of September. Eleven days had been occupied in making about seventy-five miles. We were out of the strait, and seemed to be free of the ice. Before us opened Baffin Bay, disclosing no ice except here and there a straggling berg.

In these arctic waters, channels like Smith Strait are the first to become locked upon the closing in of the winter, and the last to break up in the summer; while the larger bodies, as Baffin Bay, remain mainly open until late in the fall, and indeed may be said never to close completely. The centre of the upper limit of Baffin Bay, the "North-Water" of the whalers, continues open throughout the winter. About Upernavik the sea is chiefly free from ice until late in October; while the Melville Bay pack, to the northward of Upernavik, is in motion throughout the year. These facts were well known to us; and, although the winter was rapidly setting in, we confidently hoped for at least a month of navigable season. This hope was greatly heightened as we looked out upon the iceless sea, which stretched away to the south as far as the eye could reach.

We congratulated ourselves that the hardest part of the journey was over, and we seemed to have some ground for anticipating that henceforth all would be plain sailing. How far these anticipations were realized will be seen by what follows.

With more spirit than had been shown on any previous occasion, our people prepared for what seemed a final embarkation. We were thus occupied until six o'clock in the afternoon. The Hope needed repairs; the repeated straining to which she had been subjected, by hauling her out of the water, and by dragging her over the ice, had opened her seams, and she leaked badly. For the life-boat we had no mast; and it was necessary to transfer to her the mainmast of the Hope. John made for her a snug little jib. Petersen, whose trade had been that of a cooper, and who was an excellent mechanic, acted as carpenter. The step of the foremast of the Hope was shifted two feet further aft, her seams were re-caulked, and the holes in her sides were repatched. Those who could not assist the carpenter and sail-maker in these operations, were at first engaged in spreading out to dry our water-soaked clothing; which being done, they threw themselves upon the rocks to rest and to sleep. We were all worn out with the last thirty hours' constant labor and exposure; but since there was a light breeze blowing outside, we could not afford to lose time by camping.

Everything being ready, the boats were launched and stowed. The crews were distributed evenly between them. Petersen took the whale-boat, with Mr. Sonntag, George Stephenson, and George Whipple; and I the life-boat, with Mr. Bonsall, John Blake, and William Godfrey. It remained only to name the vessels. It was, I think, Mr. Bonsall who suggested "Ironsides" for our craft; and at the instance of Mr. Petersen, "Forlorn Hope" was changed to "Good Hope."

We pulled out from under the land, to catch the wind which still blew lightly from the northeast; and spreading our canvas we gave three lusty cheers for Upernavik, and stood away for Cape Alexander, which was fourteen miles distant. A watch was set in each boat. Petersen took the steering oar of the Hope, John that of the Ironsides, and the rest of the crews crawled under their blankets and buffalo robes.

Soon after our starting, an ominous cloud was observed creeping up the northern sky. As it spread itself overhead, the wind freshened, and after fluttering through a squall, settled into a heavy blow. The white-caps multiplied behind us, and everything looked suspicious; but whatever might be our misgivings as to the fortune in store for us, out at sea in a storm, with our frail heavily laden boats, we could do nothing but hold our course, and take the risks. To run back under the land which we had just left, did not at all accord with our tastes, nor with the nature of our undertaking. Off the larboard bow lay a long line of iron-bound coast, which offered no sign of a harbor. Come what might, we must keep on, and sink or swim off Cape Alexander.

To be at sea in a snug ship with a deck under your feet, the wind roaring and the waves breaking about you, is a pleasure, and as the vessel bounds forward one scarcely feels that he is not in the most secure place in the world; but it is quite a different affair in an open boat twenty feet long.

As we ran out from the land, we obtained a fine view of Hartstene Bay. The coast which bounds it to the north is high and precipitous, trending a little to the north of east, and terminating in a large glacier, about twelve miles east of Cape Ohlsen. The face of this glacier, dimly traceable in the distance, appeared to be about three miles in extent, sloping backward into an extensive *mer de glace*. To the south of the glacier the land trends nearly parallel with the north shore for three or four miles, when it falls off to the south, terminating in another glacier larger than the first, which, like it, sweeps back around the base of the mountains into the same glassy sea. From the southern extremity of this glacier the coast runs southwest, presenting an almost straight line of high, vertical, jagged rocks, which end in the noble headland for which we were steering.

Although closely watching the sheet, while John steered and Bonsall and Godfrey slept, I was yet at leisure to enjoy the magnificent scene which spread itself before me as we approached the cape. A parhelion stood in the sky on my right hand, presenting a perfect image of the sun above, and a faint point of light on either side. On my left lay the before-mentioned line of coast, its dark front contrasting grandly with the white sheet of ice a few miles further back, which seemed to be in the act of pouring down into the sea from some great inland reservoir. The sandstone rocks, at the base of the cliffs, were worn and wasted by the frost and breakers, and looked like the ruins of some ancient castle or dismantled fortress. The waves which tossed the boat about seemed to be at play; and, after licking their frothy tongues across her poop, they chased each other swiftly to the shore, where, breaking through the breaches in the wall, they threw their snow-white caps about as if in triumph over the ruins that their revelries had made, and then came roaring down again into the sea.

The wind continued to increase, and the waves to roll higher, yet we reached within a half mile of the northern extremity of the cape without accident, and shipping little water. Here the current, setting rapidly around the point, had produced an irregular and chopping sea. It became necessary to shorten sail; we could not hold on at our present speed through such uncertain swells. Mr. Petersen took a reef without difficulty, and the Hope, admirably constructed for a heavy sea-way, doubled the cape in gallant style. The Ironsides was shorter, and much less manageable. Although laden with the heaviest articles of our cargo, she rode, in consequence of her large air-chambers, high out of the water; and the stern-chamber embarrassed the steersman. The watch was called up to lend a hand. The halyards were lowered away; but the sprit was found to be a foot too long, and in the effort to shorten it by hitching it up, the point dropped from its thimble, the stick fell across the boat, and the sail flapped loosely in the wind. Bonsall attempted to gather up the flying canvas, Godfrey grasped after the sprit, and John, instead of attending to his own business, watched them both. His oar flew out of the water, and the boat, no longer under its control, broached to. The next wave broke amidships and filled us. The air-chambers, which had hitherto made the boat so crank, now saved us from sinking. The steersman was knocked down from his seat, and before he could regain his oar, and bring the boat into the wind, sea after sea had broken over us.

Finding that they were not absolutely drowned, and that nothing worse could happen than a good ducking, the men returned to their posts, and in a few minutes the sail was reefed and set, and the boat righted. The increased load which she now carried sank her lower in the water, and in spite of all our efforts, there remained an unwelcome cargo; for, as fast as we bailed out one portion, another poured in. Discouraged at length by our fruitless efforts to get her free, we gave up the attempt; and being now satisfied that the life-boat would not go down, we held on to the mast and gunwale to prevent the seas from washing us overboard, and in this manner drifted around the cape. Here we were met by our consort. Her crew, fearful that we had swamped, were gallantly beating up in smoother water to our assistance.

It was dead calm under the cape. After bailing out some of the water, we took in the sails, unshipped the mast, and pulled over to Sutherland Island in search of a harbor. This little rock lies about three miles to the southeast of Cape Alexander. It was found to be precipitous on its northern and eastern sides, and unprotected to the south and west from the winds and waves which eddied around the cape. Finding no safe anchorage, we were compelled to pull back. By this time our people had become almost disheartened. We had been exposed to cutting blasts during the two hours which were occupied in circumnavigating the island; the sun had sunk beneath the horizon, and it had grown quite dark. To make the annoyance worse, a cold sleety rain began to fall. The thermometer stood at 21°. Our clothing was stiffening on us like pasteboard. Our cramped limbs were almost rigid; and the long continued exertion, under circumstances so depressing, had nearly exhausted our strength. It was as much as we could do to stem the wind and waves, as we rounded the north side of the island and struck out for the main land. The gale, broken by the cape, fell upon us in fitful gusts, which often drove us to leeward. Then came a lull; the men "gave way" with all the force which their paralyzed muscles could command; and we recovered our lost ground, and gained a few boat-lengths before the next squall struck us.

Thus we continued to oscillate, gaining a little with every lull, until at last we were once more in smooth water; and soon after, we lay under the high wall of the protecting headland. Then we crawled slowly down the coast, more for the purpose of keeping ourselves from freezing, than with the hope of finding a landing; for the shore appeared to be everywhere precipitous. Better fortune, however, awaited us than we anticipated. We had not gone more than two miles when we came suddenly upon a low point of granite rock, behind which lay the snuggest of little harbors. A faint cheer broke involuntarily from the boat's crew when I announced to them the discovery.— "Here we are, Petersen; a harbor! A harbor, boys; a harbor! Give way! give way!"

We were soon ashore; and as we looked out from the rocks on the foaming sea, and listened to the moaning wind as it fell over the cliffs above us, and to the breakers thundering against the coast, we had reason to be thankful that we were once again on *terra firma*. The Ironsides was hauled upon the beach and capsized, to free her of her load of water. Petersen anchored the Hope with a couple of heavy stones. Having no dry clothing to put on, we ran about until we were a little warmed and dried; and then, pitching the tent, we spread over us our water-soaked buffalo, and slept away fatigue and disappointment.

Everything in the Ironsides was thoroughly wet. Among the articles of food were a two-barrel bag of bread and our large bag of coffee. The cargo of the Hope was as dry as when put on board at Cape Ohlsen. She had behaved admirably, and had weathered the gale quite comfortably. She shipped more water through her leaky sides than over her gunwale.

The wind lulled a little in the night, but rose in the morning, and increased again to a gale. The storm was too heavy to allow us to put to sea. The wind had hauled around to the north, and the swell came into our harbor. The anchorage of the Hope being thus rendered insecure, she also was dragged upon the beach. Our wet cargo was spread out upon the stones to dry; and we awaited with much anxiety the breaking of the gale, which continued with unabated force through the day. The clouds had, however, cleared away, the sun shone brightly, and the thermometer went up to 30°. We seized the opportunity afforded by our detention to obtain the rest which we so much needed. A little blue fox, doubtless attracted by curiosity, came near the mouth of the tent, and, perching himself upon a rock, set up his wild but cheery cry. Petersen, with an eye to the pot, fired at him, and sent him, badly wounded, up the hill to die under a pile of stones to which he escaped.

Toward evening the wind abated a little, yet the waves rolled too high to make it safe for the boats; and we reluctantly found ourselves compelled to spend another night where we lay. The discovery of the fox gave us hope that others might be found, and the hunters were busy, during the afternoon and evening, in clambering over the rocky hills; but they all returned unsuccessful. There were no signs of life about us.

While some of the party were thus occupied, others were rambling about, seeking adventure, or gratifying their curiosity. The coast here trends nearly due east, and, at about two miles from our encampment, terminates in a glacier. This stream of ice was visited by me in the afternoon, and by Bonsall and Sonntag later in the day. It was the first glacier protruding into the ocean which I had had opportunity to inspect closely; and although small compared with other similar formations, it had nevertheless all their principal characteristics. It presented to the sea a convex mural face seventy feet in height and about two miles in length, its centre projecting into the water beyond the general line of the coast to the east and west of it. Its surface rose by an abrupt angle to the height of about two hundred feet, and, sloping thence backward at a less inclination, seemed to be connected with an extensive *mer de glace* above. From where I stood, I observed several fissures or crevasses, apparently of great depth, running vertically through the body of it, and extending far up into its interior; and others more shallow which seemed to have been formed by the streams of melted snow which poured in cataracts down into the sea. I was struck with its viscous appearance, as I had been before with that of the inland glacier visited by me in the autumn of 1853, to which allusion has been made in a former chapter.

Parallel with its convex face ran a succession of indistinctly marked lines, which gave it the aspect of a semifluid mass, moving downward upon an inclined surface; and this idea was more forcibly impressed upon me by its appearance about the rocks on either side. Over these it seemed to have flowed; and, fitting accurately into all their inequalities, it gave the effect of a huge moving mass of partially solidified matter suddenly congealed.

Returning from the glacier, I mounted on my way through a ravine to the top of the cliffs, where a fine view was had to the south and west. Below me was the ruddy rock of Sutherland Island, with a chimney-like peak at its eastern end, and a heavy belt of ice hanging on its northern side. To the south-south-east stood, as distinctive landmarks, the snow-crowned headlands of Saumarez and Robertson. The tops of Northumberland and Herbert Islands, exhibiting alternate streaks of brown and white, lay in dim outline to the south. The sea was covered with foaming white-caps. No ice was visible. The sun's glaring disk, like a wheel of fire, rolled slowly northward, dipping so gently as to create the impression that it was revolving on the plane of the horizon. Its rays fell upon the hoary heads of the mountains behind me, and bathed in purple the long streaks of stratus clouds which hung over the dark waters.

CHAPTER VIII.

THE FLEET AT SEA.

It was not until noon of the 8th of September that we broke up our encampment, and set out for Northumberland Island. The wind blew fresh from the northeast, having now held from that quarter during four days. The sea was still rough.

I took the first watch, and was relieved at four o'clock. When I came again on duty, four hours afterwards, Cape Alexander lay whole leagues behind us, and the capes and glaciers of the coast to our left were blended into one long, straight, streaked, white-capped wall, abruptly terminating in Cape Robertson. The boats were cutting through the water in glorious style. The Hope lay right abeam, and was climbing over the waves, and knocking the spray to right and left, in a manner which it did our hearts good to see. There were no troublesome ice-fields in sight; water — a great wide waste of swelling water — was all around us. The men were in high glee. The boats approached near enough to exchange salutations. "Isn't this glorious?" cried Whipple — "we have it watch and watch about!" —"And so have we!" answered Godfrey. — "We're shipping a galley, and mean to have some supper!"

said Stephenson.—"And we've got it done.—Look there!" said John, flourishing in the air a pot of steaming coffee. Our tars were in their element, and alive again.

Our felicity was short-lived. A few bergs soon showed their heads above the horizon; and, as we approached nearer, we found among them loose streams of ice, which compelled us frequently to change our course, but occasioned for a time no other embarrassment. At length, these streams became more dense, and in places were found cemented together with young ice. The night closed around us whilst we were dodging among these fields; yet we managed to hold on, and, in spite of the darkness, to pick a tortuous passage; and we brought up, at six o'clock on the morning of the 9th, in a little cove on the north side of Hakluyt Island, having been eighteen hours on the way. After halting upon the rocks, long enough to cook and eat our breakfast, we again put to sea. A narrow stream, which lay against the western cape of the island, arrested our progress for an hour; but it opened as the tide changed.

We then made for the southwestern cape of Northumberland Island. Passing the south side of Hakluyt, we discovered the narrow channel, which separates it from Northumberland, to be closed with a heavy pack, which, joining the land, headed us off. Changing our course first to south, then to south-south-west, then to south-west, as the margin of the pack varied its direction, we held on until one o'clock in the afternoon, when we found ourselves about eight miles from Northumberland. Here the ice became more dense to the westward, but appeared to be open to the southeast. Entering a narrow lead which ran in that direction, we continued for about half a mile. The lead was in places covered with a thin crust of ice, the wind had died away to a light breeze, and we therefore made slow progress. The young ice was cutting the whaleboat badly.

Reaching the end of this lead, and uncertain which way to turn, we hauled the boats alongside of a little berg, to the top of which I clambered in company with my brother-officers. This gave us an elevation of about fifty feet. The pack extended throughout the entire circuit, though in no place was it tightly closed.

The selection of our course became now an important question. Either of two was open to us: to stick to the land, running thereby the risk of meeting the heavy ice, which always hugs the shore; or to try the more immediately hazardous experiment of an outside passage. A short description of some of the physical features of this sea will better enable the reader to appreciate the critical nature of our position.

Baffin Bay, or more properly Baffin Sea, is the great estuary through which the Polar ice of the American division of the Arctic Ocean is drifted into the Atlantic. This ice is poured into it through Lancaster, Jones, and Smith Sounds on the west and north. It receives, also, accessions from Whale and Wolstenholme Sounds on the east, and by berg-discharge from the numerous glaciers of both coasts. Added to these sources of supply is the immense sheet which, during the winter, forms upon the surface of the bay itself. Its central portion, lying between Capes York and Bathurst on the north, and the Island of Disco and Cape Walsingham on the south, forms the grand receptacle into which are poured the rafts which float down through the different channels. These accumulated masses constitute the "middle-ice," or "Melville Bay pack;" the whole body of which is undergoing constant movement southward, discharging continually from its southern margin through Davis Strait into the Atlantic, and receiving proportionate accessions from the north. The great highway through which these accessions come, and into which they are first discharged from the above-mentioned channels, is styled by the whalers the "North-Water;" and in consequence of the rapid flow of the current southward, this, the north part of Baffin Bay, is, throughout the greater part of the year, mainly free from ice; and, as stated in a former paragraph, it is never closed completely.

We were now about midway between the usual northern margin of the Melville Bay pack and Smith Strait, on the Greenland side of the North-Water, and directly in the mouth of Whale Sound. The pack which lay around us on every side, was doubtless made up of the discharges from this sound, and from those of Jones and Smith, which, owing to some cause to me inexplicable, had not yet joined the middle-ice. This pack lay separate and distinct from that of Melville Bay, leaving, in all probability to the south of the Carey Islands, a belt of open water, and thus dividing the North-Water into two parts.

It will be seen that the navigation of this ice-encumbered sea is necessarily peculiar; yet, so long and carefully have the movements of the ice been studied, that this navigation has been reduced to almost as great precision and certainty as the navigation of the high seas. The whalers, who have for almost two centuries frequented these waters, have always, at certain seasons of the year, adhered to the land, holding on to what is technically known as the "fast ice." I allude now chiefly to Melville Bay; in which deep indentation there is to be found, always early in the summer, and sometimes throughout the entire season, an unbroken belt of ice, commencing at the Devil's Thumb, widening gradually as it approximates the centre of the bay, and narrowing again toward Cape York; presenting an irregular, though, in its general trend, an almost straight, line from one to the other of these extremes. This belt it is, which is properly designated as above mentioned; and in holding on to this, vessels are secure against the risks and embarrassments attendant upon the ever-shifting pack which lies to the westward, and which is, throughout the year, as already observed, undergoing a generally southward movement. To the north of Melville Bay, this "fast ice" does not exist with the same regularity, nor does it possess, at any season of the year, the same characteristics as the "fast ice" previously described.

The chief seat of the Baffin Bay whale-fishery is at Pond Bay, a little to the south of Lancaster Sound. To get to this once profitable fishing-ground, the whale-ships always take the Greenland side, in the manner above described, and after reaching Cape York, or Cape Dudley Diggs, run over to the westward; but later in the season the "fast ice" becomes broken and insecure, and therefore, following the current southward, they return home down the American coast in September. Although at this late season of the year, the whalers do not hesitate to throw themselves into the pack, yet they most scrupulously avoid it in the northward passage during the months of June and July.

It was a question of the utmost importance to us to decide, whether we would follow the spring or the summer plan of the whalers. With a ship under us, our course would have been plain enough, but with only our boats, the case was different. The winter was closing in rapidly. The young ice was forming whenever the wind fell to calm, and we were liable to be frozen up at almost any moment. The ice being in more constant motion in the centre of the bay, this danger was there less imminent; but there was no absolute safety anywhere. If we should attempt to make our way along the coast, and should be there caught by the winter, we would have at least, a temporary lease of life. If, on the other hand, we should haul to the westward, and attempt to run down the centre of the strait, outside of the Carey Islands, while it was certain that we should have open water longer, and run less risk of being frozen up, yet, if frozen up, there would be no possible escape for us — we must speedily perish. We were, however, bound on a desperate adventure, and must use desperate means.

Petersen was our ice-man, and the party had confidence in his caution and judgment. Beside him, none of us had, at that time, much knowledge of ice-movements or ice-navigation. Twenty years' constant experience had certainly given him some claim to the dignity of an oracle. He recommended the in-shore passage. It was decided that we should hold our course to the eastward, and reach, if possible, Northumberland Island, trusting to find a lead over to Cape Parry, and thence down the coast. In the neighborhood of the island the ice appeared to be quite open; but beyond this we could not determine anything with certainty.

By the time that our conclusion was reached, there had fallen a dead calm; the masts were therefore unshipped, and we again took to our oars. The attempt was attended with much difficulty. The tide ran swiftly, and the ice was in rapid motion. The boats were fearfully exposed. We could find no regular lead, and had therefore to trust to the changes of the fields to give us a passage. The suddenness with which they sometimes closed together, subjected us to frequent nippings, to escape which we were obliged, repeatedly, to toss our cargo upon the ice and drag up the boats. The back of the Hope was nearly broken by these operations; her timbers were severely strained, and her seams were so much opened that one man was constantly employed in bailing. The Ironsides was dented in a dozen places, and her bilge was pressed in below the thwarts fully four inches, by a nip which she received while attempting to run the gauntlet of two closing fields.

As we approached the island, the ice was found to be even more closely packed than outside, and in more rapid motion. There was no lead along the shore: the tide was against us. It was with the utmost difficulty that we could hold our place. Our efforts to advance were only sufficient to prevent our being drifted back. It was clearly of no use to continue at this work, wearing ourselves out, endangering our boats, and, withal, making no headway. It was therefore determined to strike more directly for the land, reach it if possible, and there camp, and reconnoitre from the mountains. Running now across the direction of the drift, the boats were in greater peril than before. We made our way by edging up diagonally against the current, boring through when we found an opening.

We reached the land at seven o'clock in the evening, but could find no harbor. Discovering a point of rock projecting about twenty yards into the water, we drew in behind it, and were thus protected against the drifting ice while the boats were unloading. This done, they were again hauled upon the beach, beyond the tide-line. The tent was pitched upon a terrace, about thirty feet above the water, and about fifty yards from the beach. This terrace was covered with a thick sod of grass; and the hill-side above, which sloped upward at an angle of forty degrees, to a red sandstone cliff, whose base stood three hundred feet above the level of the sea, was equally rich in vegetation. We had lighted upon a weary man's paradise. For more than two hundred yards, on either side, this green sward continued; and we all agreed that nothing like it had been seen since we had left South Greenland, fourteen months before. A blue fox was shot by one of the hunters, immediately after our landing; and while the cooks were preparing him for supper, the rest of the party, forgetting their fatigue, rambled over the green hill-side, and, like colts in spring pasture, rolled themselves in the thick grass.

If the sight of this green spot gave joy to our spirits, it held, too, treasures for our scurvy-riddled men. Knowing what was to be expected, in such a locality, I took Mr. Bonsall with me; and we had not searched long before we were rewarded by the discovery of some patches of cochlearia and sorrel, in sufficient quantity to satisfy the wants of a hundred men. The plants were only slightly wilted by the frost; and their juicy stalks, which grew in some places three or four inches in length, were plucked and eaten by our people with a ravenous zeal that told how badly we stood in need of something fresh and green. Stephenson and Whipple carried their caps full of it to the cook, who boiled it with his fox, and made us such a supper as we had not had since we left New York. Although disappointed of getting on in our course, the spirits of our people were better, after this hearty feast, than they had been at any time since leaving the brig. They declared that they felt the cochlearia in their very bones.

It was midnight when we retired to our tent, having previously set a watch, to be relieved every two hours, with directions to keep a close look-out upon the ice, and to give the alarm in case it showed any signs of opening. The moon shone out brightly, the air was calm, and the thermometer stood at 30°.

CHAPTER IX.

NORTHUMBERLAND ISLAND.

When we awoke, the sun was shining brightly upon us; the air was warm. So long had we been accustomed to this arctic climate, that we had almost forgotten that there was such a thing as summer. This noonday heat brought it to our recollection, and it felt quite sultry, with the thermometer in the shade standing at 36°, and in the sun at 73°.

The ice remained nearly the same as on the previous evening. There being clearly no chance, for the present, of getting on, we embraced the opportunity to dry our wet cargo. The boat-sails were spread upon the grass, and on them were poured the contents of our water-soaked bread and coffee bags. The buffalo skins, and blankets, and clothing, were treated in a similar manner. We also overhauled the boats. The Hope was much damaged, and it was found necessary to recaulk her. Her tin sheathing had been, in places, loosened, or torn off, and required to be tacked on again. The metallic boat was not materially injured: her sides needed only to be beaten out straight. Those to whom was assigned the duty of superintending the drying of our cargo, having finished their work, returned to the hill to feast again on the cochlearia.

In the afternoon Mr. Bonsall and myself set out to climb the mountain for a view. Bonsall carried his gun with the hope of getting a shot at one of the foxes, which were heard barking in the cliffs above us.

We started up the shore, and, the tide being at its ebb, we walked along the beach, sometimes picking a passage among the cakes of ice which lay stranded by the retiring waters, sometimes clambering over the rough knobs of porphyritic rock, which here and there cropped out, or edging along the face of a low slate-stone cliff, which, deeply worn and wasted, bore evidence of the destructive powers of the frost and sea. A heavy ground-swell was rolling up at our feet, tossing the ice about in tumultuous confusion.

We had gone nearly a mile before we found a break in the cliffs; then, climbing up the stony slope, we emerged at length upon a broad plateau, five hundred feet above the level of the ocean. To the left lay a glacier which ran down into the sea; to the right stretched the long line of cliffs, under which we had travelled; and before us rose a low, round-topped mountain. We walked parallel with the cliffs until we came back opposite to our encampment. Advancing then to the edge of the precipice, a charming sight broke upon our gaze. Far beneath our feet lay the green hill-side, appearing, as we looked down upon it, almost like a level plain, the slope increasing the perspective distance and in effect doubling the dimensions of the field. The tent lay at its farther edge; strewn around were our travelling accoutrements. One of our companions was manœuvring along the base of the cliffs to get a shot at a ger-falcon, which constantly eluded his stealthy vigilance. Flitting from rock to rock, screaming wildly all the while, the noble bird of prey managed to hold a middle course between two fires — from above and from beneath — without abandoning his favorite haunt. Others of the party were basking in the sun, asleep upon the lawn; while one individual was stretched out at full length, feasting in the "garden," as we called the patch of cochlearia. It was a gypsy-like camp, and, viewed separately from its surroundings, was altogether a most un-arctic scene.

We were as much disheartened by what lay beyond as delighted by what lay beneath. Before us, to our right, and to our left was ice, ice, ice. We could see full forty miles; and, although not able to determine positively the condition of the water for more than twenty, yet what we saw assured us that a probably impenetrable pack lay in our way. To the southwest, toward the Carey Islands, whose tops were dimly visible, the sky indicated open water, which seemed to run in toward Saunders Island, whose long, flat, white roof, supported by a dark vertical wall, appeared above the horizon to the south. Under Cape Parry was a large open area, from which diverged several narrow leads, like the fingers of an outspread hand, toward Northumberland. One of these leads came up within four or five miles of our camp; but inside of it all was tightly closed. Below Cape Parry several small leads appeared, and much open water seemed to lie along the land.

Although this pack was in fact the same that had baffled Dr. Kane in July and August, yet its existence here surprised me as it had him. It had never been noted before. Our track had been traversed by Baffin and Bylot in August, 1616; by Sir John Ross, between August 7th and 30th, 1818; by Capt. Inglefield, August 28th, 1852; and by Dr. Kane, in the Advance, August 7th, 1853; and by none of them had any considerable quantity of ice been seen north of Melville Bay. I was not prepared for such a rebuff at this part of our voyage.

Could we pass it? would it open? was there any hope for **us**? I confess that, as these questions came in succession to my mind, I could only meet them by gloomy doubting. The ice was more firm and secure than we had anticipated finding, even in **Melville Bay**. All of our bright dreams of **succor and safety** seemed to be ending.

I was still not wholly without hope. There were yet twenty days of September; and, although signs of winter had been about us ever since we left the brig, yet it was now much warmer here than at Rensselaer Harbor a month earlier. Altogether, September promised more of summer than of winter.

It was with mingled feelings of hope and discouragement that I started to return. These feelings were shared by my companion, who, like myself, could not, without a shudder, think of the prospect of undertaking to bore the pack at this late season; and yet to put back for the brig was a thought equally unwelcome. Apart from any feeling of pride, it was evident that to turn back not only would involve the certain loss of that relief which we sought, but, by nearly doubling the vessel's crew, would induce that very condition of ill health to prevent which was one of the reasons for our leaving the vessel. However, we had yet some days before us to watch and wait; and if, in the end, we were forced to retreat, we should then have at least the satisfaction of knowing that we had done our duty. We had had nineteen days of as constant hard striving against the elements as could be reasonably asked of us.

If there was not at least some chance (and at present none appeared) of getting through the pack, it would be madness to enter it farther. We determined, therefore, to have the matter discussed in a formal council, of the men as well as the officers; and, after Petersen should have demonstrated what he knew of the laws of ice-movements, and the nature of the seas to the south of us, then to call for a vote, and let the party thus decide the choice of risks: namely, to wait and take the consequences, or to put back while it remained possible so to do. All had a right to be consulted on such an occasion, however the impulses of a few might prompt to a continuance of our journey.

To undertake to winter where we were, or anywhere upon the coast, which we must do in case we should not be successful and our retreat should be cut off, seemed like folly. We had barely food to last us eighteen days, and fuel for less than half that time. That the Esquimaux lived somewhere, and somehow, we knew; but where, or how, we did not know, nor could we imagine. Thus far our guns had brought us nothing of consequence. We had seen several seals, and had got within thirty yards of one of them, but the rifle missed its aim. We had passed a school of walrus but we had no harpoon, and our bullets would not pierce their hide. The birds, which swarm upon the shores and waters during the summer, had brought forth their young, and had flown away. We had seen only a few foxes, and not a single bear. Petersen, whose experience as a Greenland hunter entitled him to judge of the resources which would probably be opened, desponded at the thought of wintering, when I talked with him about the contingencies against which we must provide, as far as we were able.

We sought along the cliff a place where we might descend, and came at length upon a gorge which sloped down between two precipitous walls to the lawn, a little to the east of our encampment. As we were commencing the descent, a fox was seen scampering away over the plain. Bonsall gave chase, but could not get within shooting distance. Another was heard barking overhead at us when we reached about half-way down. I took the gun, and, climbing back over the huge boulders which filled the bottom of the gorge, tried, by crawling behind a rock, to approach him; but he seemed to be aware of my intentions, and scampering away, led me a wild chase across the plain over which Bonsall had before run. The cunning animal first made off, so that I could not corner him upon the cliff; and, when out of danger, perched himself upon a stone and barked at me until I came within long range, when, as I was about to bring my gun to my shoulder, he dropped behind the stone and fled to another, where he set up the same wild chatter,— a shrill "huk! huk! huk!"— which sounded like a mixture of anger and defiance. I tried again to approach him, but with no better success: he ran round and round me until at length, becoming weary with following him, I fired. Some shot must have touched him, for he screamed as if half murdered, and flew away as fast as his little legs would carry him.

We reached the camp at six o'clock in the evening, tired and foot-sore. We found some of our companions seated on the grass-plot, near the tent, smoking their pipes and playing "forty-fives," as unconcernedly as if they were already at home. Danger, and the hard prospect before them, seemed furthest from their thoughts. Sonntag was busy writing a geological description of the island. Petersen was out hunting.

They had not, however, been idle at the camp during our absence, as was shown by a pile of cochlearia, which lay near by. They were only waiting for us to bring them in something more substantial for supper, to start the fire. They had found along the shore, half a mile below, a little glacier, over which poured a stream of crystal water, from which they had filled the kettles. This discovery came most opportunely; for we had hitherto, since landing on the island, been obliged to melt ice, thus consuming rapidly our fuel. Petersen came in soon after, like us, empty-handed. He had seen several foxes but could not get near them. We were compelled, therefore, to fall back again upon our rapidly vanishing stock of pork and bread, of which, with the addition of some cochlearia, John made us an excellent scouse. To this he added our never-failing source of comfort — a pot of coffee.

While the plates were passing around, the subject of advancing further was introduced. Petersen's observations coincided with Bonsall's and my own. The party received the intelligence with a coolness quite characteristic; and, when the possible contingency of being compelled to turn back was put before them, the response was most gratifying. I knew, beforehand, that the views of Messrs. Sonntag and Petersen accorded with those of Bonsall and myself. Whipple made quite a neat little speech, which I wish that I could record literally. I give it as nearly as I can remember it: " The ice can't remain long, — I'll bet it opens to-morrow. The winter is a long way off yet. If we have such luck as we have had since leaving Cape Alexander, we'll be in Upernavik in a couple of weeks. You say it is not more than six hundred miles there in a straight line. We have food for that time, and fuel for a week. Before that's gone we'll shoot a seal." It was a right gallant and hopeful little speech, and " Long George " (as his messmates always called him) looked quite the hero. It reflected the spirit of the party; and it is one of the pleasantest recollections of my life that, notwithstanding nineteen days of danger and suffering, during which they had been wet, cold, and often half famished, the men who were my companions did not quail at this crisis.

In order that the nature of our situation might be more fully understood, Mr. Sonntag brought out his charts; and after we had carefully discussed together the difficulties and dangers on every hand; the possible chances of our success, and the probable chances of our being caught in the ice; and having all arrived at a full comprehension of the uncertainties which were before us, and our facilities for availing ourselves of the temporary security which was behind us, a formal vote was then taken upon the question, " Whether we should go back, or wait and go on with the slightest opening."

There was but one voice in the company. — " Upernavik or nothing, then it is!" "That's what I mean!" — " and so do I!" were the prompt responses. — The thing was settled.

CHAPTER X.

AT SEA IN A SNOW STORM.

I FEAR that I am prolonging this history beyond the limit which my readers will consider reasonable, even for a merely personal narrative; but I find the temptation to detail almost irresistible, as the recollections of the past crowd upon my memory. I will be more brief with the next few days.

September 11*th*. The ice drifts rapidly out of the sound, opening wider the leads toward Cape Parry and the southwest; but it is closing up more tightly against the southeast corner of the island. The floes have left the shore opposite our camp, and we could put to sea and make some headway toward the Carey Islands; but this is not the course we have determined upon pursuing. We could not advance more than half a mile in the direction of the main land. Godfrey has shot a fox, and he reports having seen several others among the mountains. Petersen brought down a young raven; it is not good, but we must eat it and save our pork. The sky is overcast, and the temperature has gone down to 25°. The air remains calm.

September 12*th*. The ice remains close to the land below us, but is still loose off the camp. It continues to drift out of the channel, and moves toward the southwest. The clouds and mist have cleared away; the sun shines out brightly; and the thermometer comes back at noonday to 35° in the shade, and to 72° in the sun.

We were surprised about noon by the appearance of an Esquimau. He came up the beach, and was as much astonished as ourselves. We recognized him as one of those who were at the ship last winter. His name was Amalatok. After exchanging salutations, he seated himself upon a rock with a cool dignity quite characteristic of his people, and began to talk in a rapid and animated manner. He was dressed in a coat made of bird-skins, feathers turned inward; bear-skin pantaloons, hair outward; tanned seal-skin boots, and dog-skin stockings. He told us that he lived on the eastern side of the island; that he had a wife, but no children; that his brother, who had a wife and children, lived with him; and that they had been visited by white men (*kablunet*) not long since. They were evidently the same people whom Dr. Kane had met on his southern journey in August. Judging from our visitor's description, his house was distant from our camp about three miles. It could be reached, he said, only by climbing over the mountain, which was a difficult undertaking; or by walking along the beach at low tide. He carried in his hand two little auks, a bladder filled with oil, a coil of seal thong, and two or three pieces of half-putrid walrus flesh. He was on an excursion round the island to set fox-traps; and the flesh was intended for bait. While talking with us, he took up one of his auks, twisted off the head, and, inserting the index finger of his right hand under the integuments of the neck, drew it down the back, — and in an instant the bird was skinned. He then ran his long thumb-nail along the breastbone, and as quickly produced two fine fat lumps of flesh, which he generously offered to anybody who would take them. He evidently intended a great courtesy; but the raw meat coming from such hands and treated in this manner was not to our liking. Petersen explained to him that we had just breakfasted, and begged, most politely, that he would not rob himself. It did not please him that we declined his hospitality; which was evidently kindly meant, and was bestowed in a manner which showed plainly that he felt the importance of proprietorship. He did not wait for further invitation, and took his lunch with a gusto quite refreshing to see, washing it down with a drink of oil which, in turn, he offered to us; but again we were compelled to commit the discourtesy of declining the proffered attention. The remainder of his oil, which furnished us fuel for cooking two meals, the other bird, and the coil of thong, we purchased of him for three needles. He had, he said, no stock for his whip, and he begged for a piece of wood. We gave him a splinter from a piece of board, which we carried to patch the boat in case of accident. Notwithstanding his greasy face, matted hair, ragged dress, and disgusting propensity to drink oil, he was the most decent looking native I had yet seen.

Ceremonies over, Petersen questioned him respecting the resources of the island, and the condition of the ice to the eastward. He told us that to the eastward there was much open water; and that his brother had captured a walrus, and would probably trade some of it for a knife. Petersen, accompanied by Godfrey, set out immediately in search of the settlement; but the Esquimau, being intent upon examining the multitude of curious things of which he found us possessed, could not be induced to accompany him. Knowing from experience the light-fingered propensities of his race, we watched him closely.

Petersen came back in a couple of hours, accompanied by a woman and a boy. The woman was the wife of Amalatok, who still remained with us. She appeared to be twice his age, and was ugly beyond description. The boy was quite a good-looking, sprightly, thieving rascal, and her nephew. They had been met on the way, and upon being told what was wanted, the woman replied that her husband's brother, with his wife and entire family, was setting fox-traps on the north side of the island, and that she could not supply him with anything before seeing her husband. Petersen coaxed and persuaded, but to no purpose; and he was reluctantly compelled to return to the camp.

Our newly found friends left us in the evening, in time to get home before the tide came in. Petersen would have gone with them, but it was not thought prudent, as the ice showed signs of loosening. The sun went down through a calm, cloudless atmosphere. As it sank below the horizon, the moon brightened; and first one star, and then another, and another, twinkled in the gray sky. A heavy, ice-incumbered swell rolled up the beach, and its long, deep pulsations broke the stillness of the night.

September 13*th*. No change in the ice. This state of inactivity greatly affects our spirits. Every hour is precious, and it is hard to be kept thus closely imprisoned.

It is wonderful how the fine weather holds; nothing like it was ever experienced at Rensselaer Harbor, even in midsummer. The people amuse themselves in wandering about the green, in plucking and eating cochlearia, or in lounging about the camp, smoking their pipes; sometimes relieving the monotony with a game of whist, or in sewing up the rents in their dilapidated clothing; casting now and then wistful glances on the sea, and wondering impatiently "when the ice will open?" Petersen shot a fox and a young burgomaster-gull; the former was secured, but the latter fell into the sea and floated away with the tide. Although the men suffer morally, they improve physically. The cochlearia has driven from their systems every trace of scurvy; and the few good meals of fresh animal food which we have eaten have built up all of us and filled out our cadaverous cheeks.

September 14*th*. This is our fifth day upon the island. Everything has been put in complete order. Our coffee and bread are thoroughly dried.

The ice showed some signs of opening in the morning, and I went with Mr. Sonntag to the top of the cliffs, for a better view. Our hearts bounded with delight. To the south and west the pack was loose; below and about Cape Parry the coast appeared to be mainly clear; very little ice was to be seen up the channel; the floes which had so long hugged the island were giving way. We returned hastily to the camp with the joyful intelligence, and commenced packing up. Bonsall and Petersen were absent, hunting. They came in as we were beginning to stow the boats, having also seen the sudden change. Each of them had captured a fox. At four o'clock, P. M. we pushed off from the shore, and pulled straight for Cape Parry.

The fine summer weather, which had blessed us during our stay on the island, was now gone. The sky was clear, and the air soft and balmy early in the day; but one of the mists peculiar to these cold waters settled over us while we were preparing to embark; and as we stepped into the boats it began to snow. The cape for which we had steered was, in less than half an hour, invisible; and even the loom of the land we had just left was lost. A great white curtain shut out from view everything but the dark water under us. The temperature was at 24°. The snow was making, upon the surface of the sea, a thick, heavy sludge, which greatly retarded the boats, and made the labor of rowing excessively severe.

Having now no landmarks by which to steer, Mr. Sonntag brought out the compass, which hitherto we had had no occasion to use; but, to our keen disappointment, it was found to be so sluggish as to be utterly unreliable. The needle stood wherever placed, within a range of eight points. Striking a mean between the extremes, we applied the necessary connection for variation, and held on. At length we struck some ice-fields, and in working through them became completely bewildered. The compass was condemned by general consent. Petersen declared that it was leading us into "the pack," of which no whaler had ever greater horror than himself; Bonsall thought that we were steering in the opposite direction, up the channel; Stephenson declared that we were going in a circle; and nobody thought that we were going right. In this state of opinion, it was deemed most prudent to halt and wait for better weather. Discovering a piece of old ice, whose surface floated about two feet above the water, we pulled alongside, and moored the boats. The tent was pitched upon one corner; and, after shaking the snow from their backs, all, except Godfrey and myself who remained without, crawled inside. Our floating ice island was about twelve feet square.

By this time it had grown quite dark. A more gloomy prospect for a night's adventure can scarcely be imagined, drifting as we were on a crystal raft, we knew not whither. We were cold, wet to the skin, covered with ice, and cruelly disappointed. Our boats were literally filled by the snow, which continued to fall faster and faster. We could not unwrap our bedding without getting it wet; and we were, therefore, compelled to huddle together in the tent, and to keep one another warm as best we could. We collected some of the newly fallen snow; and, although everything was so damp that we could scarcely ignite the lamp and keep it burning, yet the cook managed, in about one hour, to melt a kettle of water, and in another to produce a pot of coffee. This warmed us, and dispelled the melancholy which had settled over the party.

The night wore slowly away. Of course we could

not sleep. The watch tramped up and down the few feet of space which lay between the tent and the water, and was relieved every hour. The tent was tightly closed, and the smoke of the pipes brought up the temperature a few degrees. At one time it reached 30°.

That we should feel despondent under the circumstances was, perhaps, quite natural; but now, as on other occasions, there was exhibited in the party a courage which triumphed over the distressing fortunes of the day. Stories, such as sailors alone can tell, followed the coffee, and interrupted the monotonous chattering of teeth; and Godfrey, who had a penchant for negro melodies, broke out from time to time with scraps from " Uncle Ned," in all its variations, " Susannah," and " I'm off to Charlestown, a little while to stay." Petersen recited some chapters from his boy-life in Copenhagen and Iceland; John gave us some insight into a " runner's " life in San Francisco and Macao; Whipple told some horrors of the forecastle of a Liverpool packet; but Bonsall drew the chief applause, by " Who wouldn't sell a farm and go to sea?"

A strange mixture of men crowded the tent on that little frozen raft, in that dark stormy night of the Arctic Sea! There were a German astronomer, a Baltimore seaman, a Pennsylvania farmer, a Greenland cooper, a Hull sailor, an East River boatman, an Irish patriot, and a Philadelphia student of medicine; and it was a singular jumble of human experience and adventure which they related.

We were near being precipitated into the water

during the night. An angle of the raft on which rested one of the tent poles, split off; two of the men who lay in that corner were carried down, and their weight was almost sufficient to drag the others overboard. Fortunately the bottom and sides of the tent were fast together, or two of us at least would have gone into the sea.

September 15th. The air cleared a little as the morning dawned; and, although it continued to snow violently, we were conscious of being near some large object, which loomed high through the thick atmosphere. Whether it was land or an iceberg we could not make out. We were soon in the boats, and pulling towards it through the thin ice and sludge. Before its character became clear, we were within a hundred yards of a low sandy beach, covered with boulders. Two burgomaster-gulls flew overhead while we were breaking through the young ice along the shore; and they were brought down by the unerring gun of Petersen. These supplied us with food, of which we stood greatly in need.

The boats were drawn up above the tide; and we piled the cargo together on the rocks, and covered it with one of the sails. The tent was pitched near by; and with another sail an awning was spread in front, to shelter the cook and to protect the lamp. This precaution was well timed, for it soon began to blow hard from the southwest, the wind being accompanied with hail. We brought our clothes-bags under the awning, and changed our wet garments before retiring to the tent.

We had reason to congratulate ourselves upon having borne the sufferings of the previous night rather than expose the buffalo-robes, which were now found to be quite dry; and never did hungry, cold, and tired men enjoy anything more than we enjoyed the luxury of such means of warmth. We were soon fast asleep.

Meanwhile, John was braving the cold, and the eddies of snow which came whirling into his extempore kitchen. He must have been exposed during several hours; six, according to his own account. He certainly suffered enough to make the number seem to him twelve. Poor fellow! he was almost frozen; his face and hands were blackened with soot, and from his eyes were running great tears, which were forced out by the blinding smoke that he was compelled to confine within the galley, by closing up the sail in order to protect the lamp against the wind. Notwithstanding his care, the flame was blown out no less than five times; and the reader will appreciate how great was the annoyance, if he has ever tried to strike a spark in a little box of light tinder, which he held between his legs, and endeavored to protect with his body,— every moment expecting that a drifting snow would pour down upon and spoil it, or a whiff of wind come and carry it away. Once he was about half an hour relighting his lamp, which had been blown out when the pot over it was nearly boiling. The tinder was damp, and he could not, for a long time, make it take fire; and when he succeeded, and was getting ready a brimstone match, the wind scattered the contents of his box over the ground. He had then to hunt to the bottom of his bag for a little roll of charred rags, which he was fortunate enough to find not wetted. By the time he had succeeded in relighting the fire, the contents of the kettle were covered over with a crust of ice.

Fortunately John, whatever might be his faults, was not easily conquered by difficulties, or we should have been deprived of our meal; for Godfrey, who alone of the party equalled the other as cook, lacked his dogged perseverance. Everything, therefore, depended upon John. At length, at three o'clock in the afternoon, he aroused us, and served to us a plentiful stew of fox and burgomaster. We had not tasted food for more than four and twenty hours. While we were engaged with our meal, our tent was almost blown over. Some time elapsed before everything could be made safe. An additional guy was placed on the windward side, and those at the ends were fastened to heavier stones. The awning was also tightened; and everything being thus rendered apparently secure, we once more drew our heads under cover. We could do nothing for our brave cook but give him some dry clothing, the best place in the tent, and our thanks.

It was still snowing hard; the wind had increased to a gale, and as it went moaning above the plain, it carried up into the air great white clouds, and pelted mercilessly the side of our tent with sleet and hail. I put my head out of the door; I could not see fifty yards. The boats were nearly covered by a great drift, and our cargo was almost buried out of sight. It was not due to ourselves that we were not at sea in that fearful storm. We knew not even where we were. We came by no will of our own. There was a Providence in it.

CHAPTER XI.

ACROSS WHALE SOUND.

THE storm broke at about midnight, but the sky remained overcast during the following day. We turned out early in the morning, and looked around us to ascertain our position. Everything was wintry. Deep snow-drifts lay along the shore and under the hill. Our tent was nearly buried. Above us rose a dark cliff, on the south of which was a steep declivity, from which the snow had all been blown into the deep valley on the margin of which we were encamped. The ice had been driven in by the gale, and was pressed tightly against the shore. The coast of the mainland, terminating in Cape Parry, lay on the left, and Northumberland Island on the right. We had drifted far up Whale Sound, and now occupied Herbert Island, — at least such was our conjecture.

There appearing no prospect of our being able to put to sea, I took a gun and, accompanied by Godfrey, set off up the valley in search of game. After a toilsome journey through the deep snow, we reached the table-land which forms the culminating ridge of the island. There our views respecting our position were confirmed. The ice-pack filled up the channel and extended far to the southwest.

We reached the camp late in the afternoon; having seen, but not captured, a fox, and having discovered the footmarks of a hare. Petersen had had better fortune. He was sleeping soundly in the tent, after dinner, when he was aroused by one of the men calling to him that a flock of "burgomasters" were floating in a pool a little way up the beach. Running hastily out, without stopping to dress, he killed and secured nine out of eleven. The materials for two good meals were thus added to our commissariat. What we most needed, was fuel. . There remained only a few pounds of the fat which had been brought from the ship for such use. This we were saving for an emergency; and during the last few days we had been burning pork, confidently expecting to capture a seal or a walrus, and thus to secure a good stock of blubber; but hitherto we had been uniformly disappointed. Several of these animals had been observed, but they were so shy that we could not approach them. The foxes had exhibited the same timidity. Many of these, as already stated, had been discovered on Northumberland Island, and I was puzzled to explain the cause of their shyness. Petersen declared that a little fellow whom he wounded soon after landing, had told his comrades of the murderous character of our guns, and that thus forewarned, they kept clear of us! At all events, be the cause what it might, they sustained the reputation of their race for cunning. The readiness of the seals to take alarm I could more easily understand, for a relentless war is waged against them by the natives. They are often wounded, and escape from their pursuers; while the foxes, taken only in traps, never live to tell tales. The product of our guns, thus far, had been eighteen burgomaster-gulls, twelve eider ducks, seven foxes, and one raven,— in all, about forty-eight pounds. We had obtained, besides, from the hut at Anoatok, eight pounds of walrus meat, half of which remained to us; but the great question now was, how should we procure material for fire? If necessary, we could eat, uncooked, such food as we might have; but how, without fire, should we obtain water? for, henceforth, we must mainly depend upon melting the snow or ice. In the afternoon Mr. Sonntag was fortunate enough to find a little rivulet, from which the kettle was filled. This enabled us in the evening to obtain a cup of coffee, which luxury the scarcity of our fuel would otherwise have compelled us to deny ourselves. The day was calm, for the most part; but as the sun went down, the wind blew again from the southwest. Temperature, $26\frac{1}{2}°$.

I was too much fatigued to make the circuit of the island; and I am, therefore, not able to add anything to the chart of Captain Inglefield, who, in the little steamer Isabella, ran up the channel in August 1852. The cliffs above us were composed of sandstone and slate, resting on primitive rock, which was visible near our camp. About a quarter of a mile above us were discovered two well built Esquimau huts, which appeared to have been recently occupied.

Hoping that fortune would continue to favor our effort, we retired again to our tent, and awoke on the following morning to find that the wind had hauled around to the northeast, and that the clouds were breaking away. By one o'clock, P. M., it was quite clear. The thermometer went up to two degrees above the freezing point; the ice was giving way, and long leads were opening through it, in every direction. A narrow belt of heavy floes joined together by young ice, unfortunately lay close along the shore; otherwise we could have launched our boats at two o'clock. To break through this belt would have occupied us until night; and deeming it imprudent again to trust ourselves in the darkness to an uncertain channel we concluded to remain where we were, and to start fresh with the early morn.

The morn broke upon us bright, clear, calm, and summer-like. The young ice, neither strong enough to bear nor frail enough to yield easily, seemed for a time likely to baffle us; but by breaking it up with our boat-hooks and poles, we finally succeeded in effecting our escape; not, however, until an hour after the sun had passed the meridian. The way appeared to be free toward the mainland, for which we pulled. After we had been under oars a couple of hours, a light breeze sprang up from east-northeast; once more our canvas was spread, and our ears were again gladdened by the music of gurgling waters as the boats rushed onward through the rippled sea.

We struck the coast at about twenty miles above Cape Parry. Passing under the north cape of Burden Bay, we were surprised to hear human voices on the shore. That they were Esquimaux we knew from the peculiar " Huk! Huk! Huk!"— their hailing cry. Upon approaching the land, a man and a boy were discovered running down the hill toward the beach; and when we came near they were standing close to the water's edge. Petersen held a conversation with the man, while the boy ran off over the rocks and was soon out of sight.

The man was "Kalutunah," the Angekok* of his tribe, and one of our friends of last winter. He informed us that he lived at a short distance up the bay, where there was a colony of his people, to which he invited us to accompany him; promising that we should have some blubber and meat, and that he would pilot us into the harbor if we would take him into our "Oomeak." The boy had gone to spread the alarm; and, while we were parleying with Kalutunah, a crowd of men, women, and children, with a great number of howling dogs, were seen streaming toward us along the shore, all running at full speed, flinging their arms about, and mingling their voices together in unintelligible gleefulness. The chief burden of their exclamations seemed to be "Kabulenet! Kabulenet! Oomeak! Oomeak!"—"White men and ships! white men and ships!" To avoid the impetuous avalanche, we drew hastily alongside of a rock, and, taking the Angekok on board, pushed off and pulled toward the settlement, the crowd following us along the beach. The prospect of getting some blubber justified us in losing a little time.

Our pilot had never been in a boat before; and he seemed to experience all the enjoyment of a child at the possession of a new toy. "Tek-kona! tek-kona!"—"Look at me! look at me!" was his

---

* The Angekok of the Esquimaux corresponds, very nearly, to the Medicine-Man of the North American Indians.

oft-repeated salutation to his envious, yet admiring friends, who were unceasing in their importunities to be treated in like manner. The Oomeak and the pale faces were probably the greatest wonders they had ever seen.

The bay was covered with pancake-ice,* which greatly retarded our progress; and it was nightfall when we reached the settlement, a mile and a half up the bay. The whole colony eagerly assisted us in landing the boats and in carrying up the cargo. About twenty of them, as if it were fine sport, seized the painter and the gunwale, and endeavored to imitate us in every motion; breaking out into loud peals of laughter whenever they made a mistake. The subject which caused them most merriment was the "Heave-oh!" of the sailors. This they attempted to imitate; and it was very amusing to observe their efforts to chime in and keep time. They could not approach nearer than "I-e-u!" They afterward i-e-u-d everything, and "I-e-u! i-e-u!" rang through the settlement the livelong night.

We were landed in a little cove. To the right and left, about thirty yards apart, stood two masses of rock twenty feet high, which nicely protected our harbor. The summits of these little capes were level; and on the table to the right we pitched our camp and stowed our cargo. From the head of the cove the land rose by a gentle slope, which, at the distance of a hundred and thirty yards, terminated

---

* This term is applied to young ice mixed with snow, which has been broken up by the waves, and which, being tough, has been rounded into little cakes by the water agitated by the wind.

abruptly against a long line of cliffs similar in appearance and formation to those of Northumberland Island, already described. Directly in front, on the slope, and at fifty yards from the beach, in the midst of rocks and boulders, stood the settlement, — two stone huts, twenty yards apart! It seemed more fitted for the dwelling-place of wild animals than for the home of human beings. Around it was a wilderness of rocks and snow and ice.

CHAPTER XII.

AMONG THE ESQUIMAUX.

Our savage friends were kind and generous. They anticipated our every wish. One of the young women, true to the instincts of her sex, ran off to the valley, with a dozen boys and girls at her heels, and filled our kettles with water. Kalutunah's koona (wife) brought us a steak of seal, and a dainty piece of liver. All smiled at the slowly-burning canvas wick of our lamp, and at the sputtering salt fat; and the chief sent his daughter for some dried moss and blubber. We gave them a share of our meal, offered them a taste of coffee, and passed around some pieces of ship-biscuit. The biscuit proved too hard for their teeth, and, until they saw us eat, they could not divine its use. They laughed and nibbled at it alternately, and then stuck it into their boots, — their general temporary receptacle for all curiosities. They made wry faces over the coffee, and a general laugh arose against the Angekok, who persisted in taking a drink of the hot liquid. We had, altogether, an amusing time with them. The evening being warm, we sat upon the rocks for several hours; and after supper, our men lighted their pipes. This capped the climax of our strange customs. The Esquimaux seemed amazed, and looked first at us, then at each other, then at us again. They evidently thought it a religious ceremony, seeing how solemn were our faces. At length I could not abstain from a smile; the signal thus given was followed by shouting, clapping of hands, and general confusion among the troop. They ran about, puffing out their cheeks, and imitating, as nearly as they could, the motions of the smokers. Kalutunah, who was determined to try everything, begged to be allowed to smoke a pipe. One being handed to him, he was directed to take a long and deep inhalation; this accomplished, he desired no more, and his rueful face brought the mirth of the party again upon him.

Having thus established the most kindly relations, we presented a needle to each of the women, which greatly delighted them; and having nothing else to offer us in return, they started off in a body and brought us a few pieces of blubber. This was what we most wanted, and they were asked to barter more of it for a knife. The question must have been misunderstood; for, an old woman who was called Eglavfit, (meaning intestines,) and who seemed to be one in authority, told a long story representing how poor they were, how unsuccessful they had been in the hunt, how they would soon have no fire and nothing to eat, and how the winter would soon be upon them; in short, if we could believe her, they were just on the eve of dying. I had heard such stories before, nearer the equator, when substantial favors were likely to be required; and I began to suspect that we had commenced at the wrong end with our negotiations. Accordingly, I suggested to Petersen the propriety of saying that we came for the purpose of bestowing numerous blessings upon them; that we abounded in knives, needles, wood, and iron, and that we expected, in return for our bountiful gifts, such of their paltry goods as we might require during our journey among their people. Petersen acted upon the suggestion, and interpreted my speech to them in a very solemn manner. Whether because of the speech, the sudden exhibition which followed of the coveted knives, or the disposition to do a good thing, I cannot say, but certain it is, that the voice of the old woman gave place to that of the dark-skinned Nalegak (chief) who replied, quite laconically, " The white men shall have blubber!"

They were in fact badly provided. The hunt had latterly been unproductive, and they had not, in the whole settlement, food for three days. They were to hunt on the morrow, and, if successful, they would give us the required supplies, in case we would wait. This was all very fine, but the game was still in the sea.

There was clearly manifested a disposition to furnish us with what they could command. They all went away in a body, and returned in a few minutes, each with a piece of fat, — some of the pieces being not larger than one's hand. Every one expected, of course, his or her reward; but it was quite impossible to pay them in this manner, and we therefore divided them into families, giving to each of these something. Thus were distributed a few small pieces of wood, a dozen needles, and a couple of knives. Altogether, the supply of blubber was sufficient to fill our keg.

We obtained, also, a small bagfull of dry moss, which served us much better for lamp-wick than canvas or rope-yarn, which we had previously used. We could not obtain any food; for the poor creatures had none either to give or to barter.

It was nearly midnight before these negotiations were completed. Being told that we wished to sleep, the Esquimaux left us with numerous friendly professions; and the camp was soon quiet. They could not, however, wholly resist the temptation to be with us; and, arming themselves with a little piece of blubber or moss, they would steal quietly down to the camp, one or more at a time; and, offering their present to the watch, would cautiously open the tent door and look in upon the sleepers, and then scamper away like children caught in some forbidden act.

With Stephenson, who was on the first watch, I marched up and down the short plain in front of the tent, talking of home and of our future prospects. It was a glorious night. Twilight hung upon the mountains; the stars twinkled through the clear atmosphere; and there were no sounds to break the stillness save the heavy breathing of the sleepers, the cawing of a solitary raven, and the occasional bursts of merriment which broke from the huts upon the hill-side.

Leaving Stephenson at his guard, I embraced the opportunity to pay a visit to these huts. I have already indicated their locality; and I will, as nearly as possible, describe their form and *interieur*. I found them to be in shape much like an old-fashioned country clay oven, square in front, and sloping back into the hill. They were now covered with snow, and until after entering one of them, I could not discover of what material they were made. To get inside I was obliged to crawl on my hands and knees through a covered passage about twelve feet long. Kalutunah, upon hearing my footsteps, came out to welcome me, which he did by patting me on the back and grinning in my face. Preceding me with a smoking torch, which was a piece of burning moss saturated with fat, he advanced through the low narrow passage, tramping over several snarling dogs and half-grown puppies. After making two or three turns, I observed at last a bright light streaming down through a hole, into which my guide elevated his body; and then, moving to one side, he made room for his guest. I found myself in a den in which I could not stand upright, but which was crowded with human beings of both sexes, and of all ages and sizes. I was received with a hilarious shout which assured me of welcome. Like a flock of sheep crowding into a pen, they packed themselves in the corners to make room for me on the only seat which I could discover. I had come to gratify my own curiosity, but theirs was even more rapacious than mine, and must be first satisfied. Everything I had on and about me underwent the closest examination. My long beard greatly excited their interest and admiration. Being themselves without this hirsute appendage, or at most having only a few stiff hairs upon the upper lip and the point of the chin, I could readily appreciate their curiosity. They touched it and stroked it, patting me all the while on the back, and hanging on to my arms, legs, and shoulders. I was a very Peter Parley among a crowd of overgrown children. They were greatly puzzled over my woollen clothing, and could not comprehend of what kind of skins it was made. The nearest that I could approach to a description was that it grew on an animal looking like an "Ukalek" (hare). That it was not skin I could not make them understand. Hans, being once importuned at the ship on the same subject, told some of them, rather pettishly, that it was "man skin;" and this I found seemed to be the general impression. My pockets did not escape them; and my pipe, which one of the boys drew out, occasioned much amusement, as it passed around from hand to hand, and from mouth to mouth. Kalutunah drew my knife from its sheath, pressed it to his heart, and then with a roguish leer stuck it in his boot. I shook my head, and, with a laugh, he returned it to its place. It was a prize which he greatly coveted. He had not yet heard of the Ten Commandments, and he could not resist the desire to possess it. He drew it out half a dozen times, exclaiming beseechingly, as he hugged it, "Me? give me?" There was an air of innocent simplicity about the fellow which pleased me; and I had nearly paid for my admiration with my knife. Fortunately, however, I did not wholly forget that charity begins at home. My pistol they handled with great solemnity; with the marvellous effect of our firearms they had already been familiarized; for, as we entered the harbor, Bonsall had, with his gun, dropped a burgomaster-gull among them.

During the incidents just detailed, I found leisure

to examine the hut. The whole interior was about ten feet in diameter, and five and a half feet high. The walls were made of stones, moss, and the bones of whale, narwhal, and other animals. They were not arched, but drawn in gradually from the foundation, and capped by long slabs of slate-stone, stretching from side to side. The floor was covered with thin flat stones. Half of this floor at the back part of the hut was elevated a foot. This elevation was called "breck;" and it served both as bed and seat, being covered with dry grass, over which were spread bear and dog-skins. At the corners in front were similar elevations; under one of which lay a litter of pups, with their mother, and under the other was stowed a joint of meat. The front of the hut was square, and through it, above the passage-way, opened a window; a square sheet of strips of dried intestine, sewed together, admitted the light. The hole of entrance in the floor was close to the front wall, and was covered with a piece of seal-skin. The walls were lined with seal or fox-skins, stretched to dry. In the cracks between the stones were thrust whipstocks, and bone pegs on which hung coils of harpoon-lines. On one side of me, at the edge of the "breck," sat an old woman, and on the other side a young one, each busily engaged in attending to a smoky, greasy lamp. A third woman sat in a corner, similarly occupied. The lamps were made of soapstone, and in shape much resembled a clam-shell, being about eight inches in diameter. The cavity was filled with oil, and on the straight edge a flame was burning quite brilliantly. The wick which supplied fuel to the flame, was of moss. The only business of the women seemed to be, to prevent the lamps from smoking, and to keep them supplied with blubber, large pieces of which were placed in them, the heat of the flame trying out the oil. About three inches above this flame, hung, suspended from the ceiling, an oblong square pot of the same material as the lamp, in which something was slowly simmering. Over this was suspended a rack, made of bear ribbones lashed together crosswise, on which were placed to dry, stockings, mittens, pantaloons, and other articles of clothing. The inmates had no other fire than was supplied by the lamps, nor did they need any. The hut was absolutely hot. So many persons crowded into so small a space would, of themselves, keep the place warm. I counted eighteen, and may, very probably, have missed two or three small ones. Centering each around its own particular lamp and pot were three families, one of which was represented by three generations. These three families numbered, in all, thirteen individuals; but beside these there were some visitors from the other hut. The air of the place was insufferable, except for a short time. The half decomposed scraps of fur, fat, and flesh, which lay on the floor and breck, or were heaped in the corners; the poisonous multiplicity of breathing lungs; the steam which rose from the heated bodies of the inmates; and the smoke of the lamps,— altogether created an atmosphere which was almost stifling. There may have been a vent-hole, but I did not see any. I perspired as if in the tropics. Perceiving this, the company invited me to imitate them, and instantly half a dozen boys and girls seized my coat and boots, preparatory to stripping me. But I had brought from home certain conventional notions, and I declined the intended courtesy, telling them that I must go back to my people. First, however, I must have something to eat. This was an invitation which I feared; and now that it had come. I knew that it would be unwise to decline it. The expression of thanks (koyenak), was one of the few in their language that I knew, and of this I made the most. They laughed heartily when I said " Koyenak," in reply to their invitation to eat; and immediately a not very beautiful young damsel poured some of the contents of one of the before-mentioned pots into a skin dish, and after sipping it to make sure, as I supposed, that it was not too hot, she passed it to me over a group of heads. At first, my courage forsook me; but all eyes were fixed upon me, and it would have been highly impolitic to shrink. I therefore shut my eyes, held my nose, swallowed the dose, and retired. I was afterwards told that it was their great delicacy, which had been proffered to me, — a soup made by boiling together blood, oil, and seal-intestines. It was well that I was ignorant of this fact.

I felt a great relief when again in the cool fresh air. The Angekok and his daughter escorted me to the tent, each with a torch. Dismissing them at the door, I sought my narrow place, among my sleeping comrades, and was soon wandering far away from the Esquimaux and their filthy huts.

CHAPTER XIII.

HOPES CHECKED.

We were stirring with the dawn; and, aided by the people of Netlik, prepared to continue our journey. The valuable addition which we had made to our cargo, greatly encouraged us. It came most opportunely, when we had begun to despair of procuring anything important with our guns.

Our short intercourse with these simple people seemed to have created a mutual attachment; and very decided manifestations of sadness were exhibited by our savage helpers as we parted from them. We had to regret that it was not in our power to leave with them more substantial proofs of our regard. They were poor beyond description. Nature seemed to have supplied them with nothing but life, and they appeared to have wrested from the animal world everything which they possessed. They were clothed wholly in skins; their weapons of the chase were fashioned of bone; they had neither wood nor iron; and they subsisted exclusively on animal food. The few pieces of iron which we had, our knives, or even the hoops upon our kegs, would have been a mine of riches to them; and our oars and poles would, for many years to come, have placed them beyond want for harpoons and lances. We gave them what we could spare of our slender stores, and received, in return, a few presents valuable to us. These were, an addition to our stock of blubber, and two or three pairs of boots and mittens.

Not recognizing, "Thou shalt not steal," or any equivalent precept, as more than a suggestion of public convenience among themselves, it was very natural that they should embrace every opportunity to rob us. Although a close watch was kept upon them, yet, when we had passed our equipment into the boats, piece by piece, the hatchet was found to be missing. Nobody, of course, had seen it. Petersen openly charged them with having stolen it. They boldly scouted the charge, — the good old gray-haired, honest chief declaring, that "his people did not steal." One fellow, in particular, was loud in protesting against the imputation, and on this account he was suspected. He was actually standing upon the hatchet, trying to conceal it with his huge bear-skin moccasins. Petersen alone could talk to them; and, therefore, the rest of us kept quiet. I soon perceived that his Danish blood was up, and the thief was not slow to make the same observation. With a laugh he stooped and picked up the hatchet, offering, with the other hand, as an olive-branch of peace, a pair of mittens. Had it not been for the detention, I should have felt more disposed to laugh than to be vexed at the incident. The Esquimaux followed us along the beach, and as we pulled across the bay we could hear their shouts long after they were lost to sight.

The air being quite calm, and the temperature not

above the freezing point, the young ice which had formed during the night was not broken up; so that our progress was necessarily slow, and our labor severe. It was after sunset when we reached Cape Parry; and here, again, was the everlasting pack. How far it extended out to sea we could not tell; but it came in close to the land, and being in motion, in consequence of a heavy swell from the southwest, we thought it unsafe to attempt to penetrate it in the darkness; and accordingly we sought a harbor behind a low point of land, and camped.

We were not prepared for this rebuff, and we felt keenly disappointed. Cape Parry was the point at which had centered all our hopes. To reach this cape, had been our constant aim for ten long days. Failing to reach it, we must fail in our enterprise: reaching it, there was, at least, a fair prospect of success. From Northumberland Island, as has been previously stated, we could see long leads running down the mainland; and as we looked out from that island none of us entertained a doubt of the general openness of the sea to the south. The reader will, I am sure, appreciate our disappointment.

A good view was obtained, in the morning, from a neighboring elevation. The sea appeared to be everywhere mainly free from ice, except directly along the shore, the very place where it had been previously most open. The heavy swell which came in from the southwest, proved conclusively that most of the great pack which lay spread out over the North Water when we landed at Northumberland Island, had drifted away. The belt which now lay in our path, had clearly been brought in by the recent gale. What should we do? The way was open back to the east side of Northumberland. In that direction there was very little ice in sight. We could still retreat, if we should so choose.

Our case was apparently not yet hopeless. It was conjectured, that if we could succeed in penetrating this narrow belt, the sea would be found free beyond; yet, an attempt to bore the pack at this late period, with the temperature at 22°, and falling, would be an undertaking fraught with serious danger. There was but one expression of sentiment in the party, and that was, "try!" and try we did, long and laboriously. Time after time were the boats thrust into the leads, — into the very jaws of the grinding ice, and as often were they forced back. Tired and defeated, our boats badly battered, the Ironsides deeply-dented along her water-line, the Hope nearly crushed, and leaking badly, we could only avail ourselves of the change of tide, and work slowly down the shore through the lead which it opened. Darkness overtook us near Hoppner Point, about seven miles below Cape Parry. During the day, we saw several small flocks of eider and king-ducks flying southward, but they did not come within shot. Petersen, however, brought down a Kittiwake gull, and Godfrey killed a diver.

The following morning disclosed to us a broad lead starting from the land, about twelve miles below us, and stretching southwest toward Saunders Island. We gave up the idea of boring the pack, and made for this water, if we could reach which, we anticipated that there would be little difficulty in crossing Wolstenholme Sound. The swell kept the bay-ice broken up, — but opposite Blackwood Point, a low ledge of rocks checked its force; and the water inside being smooth, was covered with a crust too thick to break through, which, at two o'clock, obliged us to haul in to the land and await a change of tide.

The tide not having accomplished for us what was expected of it, we were compelled to camp at ten o'clock, P. M. During the day two seals were seen; one of them, a large male, came up near the boat and within close rifle shot. Petersen took a long and true aim at him, but the rifle missed fire. One of the men shot a king-duck from a flock which flew overhead; and Petersen a ptarmigan, on shore. I give the incidents of the next few days in the more concise log-book form.

September 22d. Sky clear. A strong breeze from the southwest packs the ice closer, and keeps us prisoners. We avail ourselves of the opportunity to dry our bedding, spreading it upon the rocks. We also clear the ice out of the boats.

September 23d. The wind died away during the night, but it had brought in more floes, and the calm favored the formation of bay-ice. The tide opened along the shore a narrow lead, which we entered, and advanced in it about a mile. It was there found closed, and during the remainder of the day we progressed by breaking through the young ice. By this operation, everything in the boats became covered with spray, which was beaten up by the poles, and which soon formed an icy coating. Our clothing was as stiff as pasteboard. We passed the mouth of Booth Sound, and were finally arrested within about two miles of the open water for which we had been steering. This water still remained mostly free from either young or old ice. At three o'clock in the afternoon, it blew heavily from the northward. This looked unpromising; but, having only two miles more of this hard work, we kept up our courage.

September 24th. The wind continued through the night to hold from the northward, and it set the ice slowly in motion down the coast. It encroached a little on the water below us. In the morning, the wind hauled to the westward, and finally, about noon, settled in the south-southwest, and blew a gale. It sent in a heavy swell, and again we were close prisoners. Sky overcast. The day was spent in wandering along the coast in search of game. Five ptarmigans were shot by Petersen; some burgomaster-gulls flew over the camp, and were fired at by Bonsall, but they were out of reach. A school of walrus were observed blowing in a little pool, near a berg, but they could not be approached. Temperature 20°.

September 25th. It fell calm during the night. The ice tightly hugs the shore, and is grinding tumultuously with the heavy swell, which abates slowly as the day advances. There are no signs of a lead opening off our camp, and many floes have drifted into the open water below us. Our boats could not live among the ice, and we remain ashore. The hunters have been out scouring the plain, but they saw nothing.

September 26th. No change except for the worse. The swell has subsided; the air is calm; the temperature sinks rapidly, and it is freezing hard. A great quantity of trash-ice, broken up into small fragments by the late swell, hugs the shore. — Every attempt to bore through it is fruitless, and the new ice will not bear. — We are forced to retire again to our camping-ground of yesterday, as the night comes on, and trust to a shore-breeze, or a change of tide, to loosen the pack. The night is dark.

September 27th. Worse and worse! The old ice is all cemented together. The open water which lay below our camp yesterday, is clogged with drift, and is covered with a glassy sheet. The temperature is still falling. At eight o'clock, 15°. Calm and clear.

We hauled the boats upon the land, and cleared them of ice which had accumulated under the lining. At least a barrelfull was dug out of the Hope.

By this brief record the reader will perceive what were the struggles, hopes, and fears of our little party during this critical period of the expedition. To be thus checked, so near to the spot where a broad expanse of water had been seen; and which, when discovered, promised to give us a passage southward, was felt to be a hard fortune. A strong wind from the east might open the ice and release us, but otherwise our fate was sealed, — or at least so it seemed. To retreat was quite as impossible as to advance. We could neither travel over the ice nor cut through it. To live long where we were, seemed equally impossible. The shore upon which we were cast was more bleak and barren than any other that we had seen in this inhospitable region. The summer was gone, and the winter was pressing close upon its heels. The hills were covered with snow; the valleys were filled with drift; the streams were all dried up; the sea was shrouded in its gloomy mantle. Night — the long arctic night — was setting in; already the sun was beneath the horizon during the greater part of each twenty-four hours, and in a short time he would sink to rise no more until February.

To meet this period of winter darkness we were literally without any preparation. Our remaining provisions were scarcely sufficient for two weeks; our fuel was still more scanty; and this fuel was merely of a nature to cook our food and melt water, but not to give warmth to ourselves.

We were not, however, morally unprepared for such a fortune. It was one to which, when leaving Rensselaer Harbor, we well knew ourselves to be liable; and for several days we had made up our minds that the chances were at least ten to one in favor of such a termination to our undertaking; yet the open water, toward which we had so determinedly bent our course since the 21st, offered so tempting a bait, that we had steadfastly pursued it until we fell into this trap.

Our great sorrow was, that we had failed in our purpose. Yet, although the object for which we had striven was not attained, we knew that it was not through our fault, but our misfortune; and, since it had been our duty to persevere as long as there was the least possibility of succeeding, it was now no less our duty than our instinct to endeavor to preserve our lives.

Accordingly, as soon as it became evident that the sudden closing in of the winter had hopelessly beset us, we began to look about us, and to devise means for meeting future emergencies. We must first preserve what was left of our stores; secondly, construct a place to shelter us; and, thirdly, add to our means of subsistence. We could draw no inspiration from the desolation around us. Our trust was in God and our own efforts.

CHAPTER XIV.

BUILDING A HUT.

I AVAIL myself of the opportunity offered by the beginning of a new chapter, to describe our locality. We were about sixteen miles below Cape Parry, nearly midway between this cape and Saunders Island, — or, more accurately, midway between Whale and Wolstenholme Sounds. The coast trends southeast by south. It is low, and of course rocky; the rocks are primitive. The shore is marked by numerous small indentations, and several low points run out into the sea. The largest of these indentations is Booth Sound. This sound, or rather the bay inside of it, is about four miles in diameter; and appearing at a little distance to be surrounded by land, looks much like a lake. The entrance to it is very narrow; its low capes overlap each other, and as you look in from seaward, they appear to be connected. In the centre of this bay stands a very remarkable island, called Fitzclarence Rock, which is about two hundred and fifty feet high; a truncated cone surmounted by a square-faced cap. At the head of the bay rises a vertical cliff from four to five hundred feet in height, which stretches northward, and is continuous with the abrupt wall of Cape

Parry. At a little distance from the shore, the low land in front, which is a belt varying from one to four miles in width, would be overlooked; and the long range of cliffs would seem to be the coast line.

The cape which bounds Booth Sound on the south, is thirteen miles below Cape Parry; and beyond it to the south are two other capes, at the distances respectively of five miles and six miles. Between the last two opens another bay or inlet running, like Booth Bay, back to the base of the cliffs,— or rather, to the foot of their sloping *debris*. Into this bay descends a small glacier; another glacier rests in a valley opening into Booth Bay. These are about four miles apart, and they seem to join, or rather to originate, in the same *mer de glace* above.

It will thus be seen that between the ocean on the one side, and the cliffs on the other; and between Booth Bay on the north, and the other bay on the south, we have a low rocky plain, four miles in diameter, rudely estimated. Its surface is undulating, its highest point being about thirty feet above tide; and it is covered with boulders of large and small sizes. We occupied this plain; and our tent was pitched on the flat surface of a rock about thirty yards from the sea, and midway between the bays which bound the plain on the north and south. A more bleak and barren spot I thought could not be found in the whole world. Here we were to struggle for existence.

It was not until the morning of the 28th of September, that we fully made up our minds that escape was hopeless. Without wasting time in useless lamentation, we at once proceeded to secure our equipment; which we did by carrying it, piece by piece, to a ledge on a rock near at hand, carefully keeping tally to see that no small articles were missing. Everything being thus made safe, we spread over the whole our sails, and fastened them down with heavy stones, that the wind might not carry them away. The boats were then capsized to prevent their being filled with snow; and the oars were stowed under them.

This being done, we began to look about us for a place to build a hut; as we could not live in our tent. It was first suggested that we should construct a house after the manner of the Esquimaux; but it was soon concluded that we could not in a fortnight collect together a sufficient quantity of stones for such purpose, if indeed we could do it at all. Accordingly this plan was abandoned as, under the circumstances, quite impracticable. While we were anxiously considering what we should do, wandering about without discovering any feasible mode of overcoming our difficulty, one of the party accidentally found a crevice in the rock, not far from the camp, — indeed directly opposite to the landing, and about forty yards from the shore. This crevice which ran parallel with the coast, was about eight feet in width and quite level at the bottom. On the east side the rock was six feet high, smooth, and vertical, except that it was broken in two places, forming at each a shelf. The other side was lower, being not more than from three to four feet high, and was round and sloping. As if to make up for this defect it was, however, cut by a lateral cleft.

We at once determined upon this place for the hut. The rocks would save us the labor of much carrying of stones and building, and the little break on the western side would answer for a doorway.

Having now fixed upon a site, the next thing was to obtain materials for building. Thus far we had seen none whatever, everything being covered with snow. We now found, however, that there were some stones scattered about; but unfortunately they were all frozen tight, so that we could not lift them; and here the ice-chisel, which we had brought from the Life-boat depôt, and for which we had not hitherto found use, was of great service. Indeed, without it we should not have been able to effect anything.

An ice-chisel is a bar of iron an inch in diameter and four feet long, which is bent at one end in the form of a ring, to be grasped by the hand; and is sharpened and tempered at the other end like a stone-quarrier's drill. With this instrument Mr. Bonsall loosened the stones, while the rest of us brought them together. Some were carried two hundred yards, and all of them of course upon our shoulders.

Having accumulated a considerable pile, the masons began to construct walls; but here another difficulty arose. We had nothing with which to fill up the cracks. This set us again to searching, and at length a bed of sand was discovered near the beach. The ice-chisel was now called in requisition as a pick; and load after load of the sand was shovelled with one of our tin dinner-plates into a discarded bread-bag, and thus carried up to the builders.

During two days we thus worked, and had then the satisfaction of seeing the area of the hut enclosed. The walls were fourteen feet apart, four feet high, and three feet thick. We had labored hard and almost continuously during our working-hours, reserving only a short time for our scanty meals.

On the following day we built upon the rock, on the west side, a gable, of which the apex was six feet from the ground, and which sloped down on each side to the walls. Through this western side opened the lateral cleft, which was spanned by the gable, which rested at this place on the rudder of the Hope; leaving an orifice three feet high and two feet wide. Next day Petersen made for this opening a door, which was hung at an angle, so as to close by its own weight, when it had been pushed open from the outside. Not having a piece of board wide enough for the purpose, he constructed a frame-work of narrow strips, and covered it with canvas. The cracks around the doorposts were filled with moss. Above the doorway was left another opening for a window. Across this was stretched a strip of an old muslin shirt, greased with blubber for the better transmission of light.

Now came the more difficult operation of roofing. One of the boat's masts served for a ridgepole; and on this and the walls were laid the oars, for rafters. Over these were spread the boats' sails, which were stretched taut, and secured by heavy stones. Then we collected moss to thatch the canvas. This was even a more laborious task than carrying the stones; for we were compelled to scour the country in all directions, and as the snow was almost everywhere a foot deep, to dig for each piece of moss that we obtained. Indeed, four times out of five, we were unsuccessful in finding a single lump, after clearing away cart-loads of snow. This labor would not have been so severe, but that we had no shovel, and were obliged to use our tin dinner-plates. Our carpenter endeavored to supply this defect by making a shovel out of the staves of our now useless molasses keg, tacking them together, and fastening to them a tent-pole for a handle; but as this contrivance soon came to pieces, it failed to answer our purpose.

The moss was frozen hard, and was found rarely in larger quantities than a patch two or three feet in diameter, but more frequently in lumps the size of one's hand. It was dug up with the ice-chisel, and carried on our backs in our clothes-bags, the contents of which we had previously emptied into the tent.

We made excellent progress with our work; and on the fifth day, although feeling uncertain as to what fortune awaited us, yet we had at least the comfortable reflection that, on the next day, we should have a house to shelter us, and should thus be protected against some of the terrors of our position. On that day, however, just before nightfall, when we were distant three miles from the camp, the clouds, which had been gathering since morning, suddenly began to discharge their frozen vapor, and the whole heavens soon became thick with falling snow. Everything that was not very near to us, was hidden from our view; and, fearful that we should lose our way, we crowded into our bags what moss we had dug, and trudged back toward the tent.

Our outward footmarks were almost obliterated, even before we set out to return; and, misled by a casual track, we held too far to the north, and came upon the sea almost two miles above the camp. By this time a light southerly wind was blowing, and, being compelled to face it, we reached the tent much chilled and exhausted. We held on to our moss-bags, however; and, after spreading their contents upon the hut, we found that, with what had been previously collected, there was sufficient to cover the south side with a layer a foot thick.

The wind continued to increase with the darkness, and, by the time supper was over, blew strong from the south-southeast. The drift was whirling in eddies through the air, and a gloomy night was coming on, as we drew under our canvas shelter.

Thus closed Monday, the 2d of October, the ninth day of our stay at this desolate place, and, as previously stated, the fifth of our hut-building. Of our labors I have only recorded a part, for the building was performed chiefly by one half of the company, — the other half being necessarily occupied in roaming about in search of game. Petersen was our general mechanic and tinker, and when anything was required of him in either capacity, he stayed at home, and Bonsall or myself took the gun or the rifle. He was not often absolutely needed, and was therefore usually out hunting during the day; yet he always came home empty-handed, except on one occasion, when he brought in five ptarmigans, all of which he shot within a hundred yards of the camp on his return. There were several cracks in the ice not far from the shore, which were kept open by the changing tide; and in these cracks were frequently seen walrus and seal, but they were too timid to be approached. Petersen fired at them several times, but they were always beyond his range. Along the shore, to the south of our position, he built several fox-traps, which he visited daily; but hitherto no foxes had been caught.

All this was discouraging. It seemed ominous of starvation at a very early day. Our provisions were running very low; we had only a few pounds of pork left, and of bread only a small quantity beside that in the barrel brought from the Lifeboat depôt, of which a small portion had been consumed. There remained a little of the meat-biscuit and a few pounds of rice and flour. Altogether we had not enough to furnish us with full rations during a single week, and we were trying to make our stock suffice for a longer period. Already we were upon the shortest daily allowance which our labors permitted. Men working during twelve or fourteen hours of the twenty-four, in a temperature not much above zero, require a large amount of food to sustain them. We were becoming thin and weak, and were constantly hungry.

To appease the gnawing pains of hunger by at least filling up the stomach, we resorted to an expedient which I remembered of Sir John Franklin's, in his memorable expedition to the Copper-mine, in 1819. This was, to eat the rock-lichen, (*tripe de roche*,) which our party called "stone moss." When at its maximum growth, it is about an inch in diameter, and of the thickness of a **wafer**. It is black externally, but when broken the interior appears white. When boiled it makes a glutinous fluid, which is slightly nutritious. Although in some places it grows very abundantly, yet in our locality it, like the game, was scarce. Most of the rocks had none upon them; and there were very few from which we could collect as much as a quart. The difficulty of gathering it was much augmented by its crispness, and the firmness of its attachment.

For this plant, poor though it was, we were compelled to dig. The rocks in every case were to be cleared from snow, and often our pains went unrewarded. The first time this food was tried it seemed to answer well; it at least filled the stomach, and thus kept off the horrid sensation of hunger until we got to sleep; but it was found to produce afterward a painful diarrhœa. Beside this unpleasant effect, fragments of gravel, which were mixed with the moss, tried our teeth. We picked the plants from the rock with our knives, or a piece of hoop-iron; and we could not avoid breaking off some particles of the stone.

I must not neglect to mention a most important discovery made about this time. I allude to a little **fresh-water** (melted **snow**) lake, which was found by one of the party in a hollow, three quarters of a mile east from the camp. This lake was about fifty by thirty yards in diameter, and about five feet deep in the centre. When it was first discovered, the ice upon it was only a foot and a half thick. By breaking through this crust with the ice-chisel, we obtained an excellent supply of pure water. This enabled us greatly to economize our fuel.

Neither should I neglect to mention a circumstance which, perhaps, will not strike the reader as of great importance, but which occasioned us for several days not a little suffering, since it deprived us of almost our only comfort. This was the failure of the stock of roasted coffee which we had brought with us from the ship. There still remained to us a good supply of the berries, but we had no means of roasting them. We were, therefore, compelled to use tea; and having of this only a small quantity, we were reduced to a meagre allowance at each meal. The luxury of hot, strong coffee, to a cold, hungry, tired, and dispirited man, will, I am sure, be appreciated. Tea was less grateful to us. I do not know how we could have dispensed with a hot drink in the morning and evening, when everything else was so chill and cheerless.

CHAPTER XV.

HUT BUILDING CONTINUED.

Tuesday, October 3d. The storm which set in last evening, continued through the night and during the next day; the snow fell thick and fast; the wind blew fearfully, and the air was filled with drift. We could scarcely stir out of the tent or do anything else except cook the necessary food. This service was performed by Godfrey and myself, it being our turn to-day at the galley.

We crawled out in the morning at eight o'clock, amid cries of "Shut the door! Shut the door!" from our half-slumbering comrades, as the snow came whirling in upon their faces; and after digging the cooking apparatus out of a deep snowbank, which was piled up alongside of and against the tent, we faced the storm, and carried the different articles over to the hut, with the view of there obtaining shelter. The hut was found to be almost covered; on the south side the drift was level with the comb of the roof. All access to the doorway was obstructed, and we could gain entrance only by tearing up the canvas on the northwest corner. Through the orifice, thus made, the blubber-keg, lamp, and kettle were lowered.

To our sorrow the hut was half filled with snow, feathery streams of which came pouring in through the cracks around the roof. These fine particles filled the air, and made everything so damp that it was with much difficulty that the fire was kindled. Leaving Godfrey engaged in this delicate operation, I took the kettle, determined to get if possible some water from the lake. The fuel which must otherwise be used for melting snow, might thus be saved for roasting coffee, the want of which was greatly felt by all of us.

Clambering up through the hole in the roof, I turned to the right around the base of a pile of rocks, and then beat up diagonally against the gale. The drift was almost blinding, and my face grew so cold that I was frequently forced to turn my back to the wind to recover breath and warmth. It was with great difficulty that I picked a passage among the boulders and drifts; but, growing warmer as the exercise heated my blood, I at length came directly upon the lake. This was an unexpected piece of good fortune; for, as I had guessed my way, I could not have even hoped to come exactly to the right spot.

Pieces of ice which lay scattered around the well, had formed a centre for the accumulation of a large drift; and I was therefore compelled to dig another hole. Selecting a spot which the wind had swept clear, I set diligently to work at cutting the crystal sheet with the dull chisel. This, luckily, had been placed upright by the last visitor, or I should probably not have found it. The ice was perfectly transparent, and I could see every stone and pebble on the bottom, shining very brightly, and seeming to nestle there in warmth and quiet,— strikingly in contrast with the confusion and cold which reigned above. The operation of cutting this hole was a most tedious one, and it must have occupied me at least three quarters of an hour; but at length the iron bar plunged through; and upon withdrawing it a crystal fountain gurgled out into the frost. My kettle was soon filled, and I set out to return.

My tracks were covered over, and again I was obliged to steer by the wind. I was getting on very well, having now the storm partially on my back; but my good fortune forsook me when I had reached about half-way. In the act of climbing over a rock, in order to shorten the distance, I missed my footing, and fell upon my face. The kettle slipped from my grasp, and, spilling its precious contents, went flying across the plain. With a philosophical resignation which I had the modesty afterwards to think quite commendable, in the circumstances, I followed the retreating pot, and, overtaking it at length where it had brought up against an elevation, I returned to the lake and refilled. This time I was more careful, and I reached the camp without further accident, except that I came upon the sea some distance above the hut; thus considerably increasing the length of my walk; and that, too, in the very teeth of the storm.

I had been absent two hours. Godfrey had lighted the lamp; and, after roasting in the saucepan a sufficient quantity of coffee to last two days, had then extinguished the flame. I found him seated on the keg shivering with cold, and uneasy about me. He was black all over with soot, and had been nearly stifled with smoke.

The lamp being relighted, the coffee was cooked in a little less than an hour; and having warmed up a few pieces of pork, mixed with almost the last remnant of our water-soaked bread, we left the suffocating atmosphere of our den, and carried the breakfast up to our hungry and impatient comrades. After shaking from our clothes the snow which had not been thoroughly ground into the fibres of the cloth, we assisted in dispatching the meagre meal; and were then glad to wrap ourselves in our blankets and buffalo-robes, to sleep and shiver through the remainder of the day and night. It was voted that we should do without supper. Those who were least unfavorably affected by the stone-moss, satisfied with some uncooked fragments of it the most pressing gnawings of hunger.

Meanwhile the wind hauled to the southwest, and continued to blow, and the snow to fall, with even greater vehemence. The cooks, Mr. Sonntag and John, turned out at daybreak; and they had even a more difficult task than had Godfrey and myself the day before. The temperature was several degrees lower, and the hut more incumbered with drift. The lamp and other fixtures were completely covered. Persevering however through every obstacle, our cooks, in about three hours, gave us a refreshing breakfast.

I do not wish to make any parade of our privations; but I should fail to convey any true idea of the day did I not say that it was passed in unmitigated misery. Our tent was made of thin hemp canvas: it was ten feet in length by eight in breadth; and into this were crowded eight persons. It was pitched upon a rock, and it faced the storm. We could not shift it without the certainty of having it more filled with snow than by leaving it standing as it was, with the door (which could not be closed tightly) exposed to the full force of the driving wind and the pelting drift.

Upon the bottom of the tent was spread one of our buffalo robes, and over this the other; we lay between them, each person having one foot and three inches of space. In order to economize room, (and without this economy we could not have all crowded together,) we lay, as the sailors termed it, "heads and points." Each man was wrapped up in his own private blankets, and under his head were placed his boots, coat, and any other little articles which he could collect together for a pillow. In some cases a stone was added to assist the elevation. The station of the cooks was next the door.

The moisture of our breath was condensed upon the cold canvas, and hung above us in a layer an inch thick of delicate frost crystals, which the least touch precipitated down our necks and among the bedding. By this means everything had become damp. The air in the crowded state of the tent was most unpleasant; in fact we had a cold steam bath.

All sorts of expedients were tried for killing time. First, after breakfast, we opened the bedding to give it an airing, and turned out to stretch our limbs; but we could not long endure the cold piercing wind, and one by one the party retreated to our shelter. The most hardy were not out more than two hours; and these, fearful of losing their way, did not go far from the camp. Later in the day we spread out our driest blankets; and, seated upon them, we tried to beguile ourselves with some rubbers of whist, interspersed with other games. Every one, except Mr. Sonntag, smoked his pipe; and those who kept journals embraced the opportunity to make spasmodic entries; — for the fingers and the pencil could not long keep company. Petersen had a sly joke for us now and then; and Bonsall entertained us from time to time with some original drollery.

Thursday, October 5th. Our condition is fast approaching the horrible. The storm has continued, without abating for a single moment, since Monday evening, and it still holds on with a steadiness that is most disheartening. Three days gone; three days away from the hut and from our preparation for the winter; and, worse than all, the food of three days consumed; — and nothing done! Our bedding, bad yesterday, is infinitely worse to-day; and, inactive as we are, we have a hard task to keep cheerful, with starvation staring us in the face. Were we doing something, this tormenting ghost could be frightened off. Bonsall has a copy of Ivanhoe, with which I spend the morning.

In the afternoon there is a lull in the storm. I have been out with Petersen to hunt; but it blew again harder than ever, and we were driven back.

We came upon a hare, but before my companion could elevate his stiffened arms the animal was out of sight, hidden by the sheet of blinding drift which whirled over the plain.

Friday, October 6th. The gale broke about midnight, and the morning dawned upon us bright as a winter's day could be. Nature looked as unconcerned as if her face had never been ruffled. The sun came dragging himself slowly up from behind the silver-peaked mountains, and the temperature rose to 20°.

How much are our emotions under the influence of our bodily comforts! Last evening our faces were gloomy, and our jests were tinctured with recklessness. This morning all is gayety and cheerfulness. We are stirring with the earliest daylight. The contents of the tent are spread down by the beach, upon some large rocks from which the snow has all been blown; and the frost and ice are scraped from the canvas.

Meantime others of the party tear off a portion of the north side of the roof of the hut, and then clear out the snow. This is a tedious and painful operation; for the shovelling, as before, must all be done with tin plates. At length the space is clear; the canvas is replaced and tightly bound down, and we collect moss to finish the thatching. More tedious still is this work than the snow shovelling; for the snow is much deeper than it was when we were driven home three days ago. The drifts are deep, and the walking laborious. We cross over the south bay, and find on the opposite shore, four miles distant from the hut, a good bed of turf.

The bags are filled, and the men go and come, one by one, across the ice.

While we were busy digging moss, a northerly wind sprang up very suddenly, and before any of us could reach the camp, the bedding was covered with fine particles of drifted snow. The different articles were hastily crowded into the tent in a worse condition than ever. — " Praise the fineness of the day when it is ended, and a woman when you have known her," says the Bible of the Vikings.

Notwithstanding the wind, we continued at our work, and brought in a considerable quantity of moss; and, although less than half the quantity that we want, we determined, in view of the coming storm, to make it suffice; and with the close of the day we finished our work. Petersen, as usual, has been out hunting, and brought home four ptarmigans.

Saturday, October 7th. Still blowing heavily from the north. We cannot expose ourselves long at a time; and after taking turns in clearing out the doorway of the hut, we carry stones to complete the internal arrangements. Petersen is occupied during the day in making a sort of open stove, or fireplace, of the tin sheathing which we have torn from the Hope. A pipe of the same material leads up through the roof. This ingeniously-contrived fireplace is large enough to hold two lamps, our saucepan, and kettle.

Sunday, October 8th. A gloomy Sabbath day in a gloomy place. We are kept within the tent by the bad weather. The wind is blowing more fiercely than ever from the northeast, and the minimum temperature during the day has been six degrees below zero. If Wednesday approached the horrible, the climax is reached to-day.

Stephenson, who had been complaining a little during several days, was taken sick in the morning. His old heart troubles, which were brought on by scurvy, and which endangered his life on many occasions on shipboard, have returned, and he has had, during the day, several fearful fits of dyspnœa. Poor fellow! I can do very little either to relieve or comfort him! Damp clothing and an atmosphere at zero are wretched cheer for a sick, — very sick man; and there are none but hard hands to soothe him. The cook makes for him a pot of tea, and I give him a few drops of tincture of colchicum.

Monday, October 9th. Clear and calm. We have a fine day for work; and although the temperature ranges from four to ten degrees below zero, yet we get our bedding a little dried. Even at the lowest temperatures a slow evaporation takes place, if the air is not already fully charged with moisture. We have labored diligently, and have completed the hut before night. The internal arrangements are quite simple; but their construction required much labor. On the south side, a space six feet wide has been elevated about eight inches. This is done with stones and sand, collected in the manner described in the last chapter. The elevation, which, after the Esquimaux, we call a "breck," is made as smooth as possible; and over it are spread our skins and blankets. Here five of the party are to sleep. The northwest corner of the hut is similarly elevated; and this space, five feet by six, is to hold the remaining three.

We move in late in the evening, and prepare to spend the first night in our new abode. Petersen, Sonntag, Bonsall, Stephenson, and myself occupy the south; and Godfrey, Whipple, and John the north side.

Petersen comes in at sundown with eight ptarmigans; and we celebrate our entry into our new quarters with a good stew of choice game and an abundant pot of coffee, cooked in our rickety fireplace with the staves of our blubber-keg, which was yesterday emptied of its contents. We have saved a small quantity of oil, and Godfrey rigs up an extempore Esquimau lamp. The hut is cold, but so much more comfortable than our tent that we have good reason to rejoice over the change. The light of the lamp dimly reveals those representatives of civilized comfort — beds, stove, walls, and rafters.

Long after the embers on the hearth had blackened, we smoked and talked and speculated by the dull light of the moss taper. Another gale was howling across the plain, but we bade it defiance. We were absolutely buried in a great snow-bank. The drift swept wildly above our heads, rattling over the moss roof, and ringing against our frail chimney.

Although accustomed to hardship, yet we could not feel cheerful, nor wholly forget that this cold, fireless, damp, vault-like den, promised to be for a little, very little while, our dwelling-place, and then our grave. John summed up our stores.

"There's three quarters of a small barrel of bread, a capful of meat-biscuit, half as much rice and flour, a double handful of lard, — and that's all." We had less than a pint of oil, and not a stick of wood except the staves of the bread-barrel and blubber-keg. A poor outfit for a winter which heralded its coming with such days as we had lately passed through. Yet courage did not forsake us, nor was there one word of lamentation. Placing trust where the heart bade us, we did not lose hope; and I feel sure that all of us retired to rest thinking of the future, — its duties and its trials, — prayerfully.

CHAPTER XVI.

THE HUT DISCOVERED BY ESQUIMAUX.

THUS, after twelve days of waiting and working, we were at length housed; but what should we do next? Hitherto all our efforts in hunting had resulted in failure. Only seventeen little birds rewarded our constant vigilance. Two or three foxes, and one hare, had been seen, but not a single bear: our traps had not been entered. Forty miles up the coast was the Esquimau Colony of Netlik. By going thither we might possibly get supplies, and by presents induce the people to bring something to us; but to undertake, in this stormy weather, to walk that distance, without protection or shelter of any kind, without the certainty even of finding the sea closed, and withal, in our reduced condition, would be a desperate adventure. Indeed, it could not be done. There did not seem to be any hope for us but in the *stone moss;* and this, poor though it was, some of us had not been able to eat.

These matters formed the subject of our conversation during the first day of our stay in the hut. The storm having continued unabated, we could not stir out of doors. The snow was banked up against the window, and there came in through the muslin pane only the faintest glimmer of light, which barely enabled us to see each other's faces. We could not afford the oil necessary to keep the lamp burning.

Late in the afternoon, as John was breaking up the staves of our blubber-keg, preparatory to starting the fire to cook us some coffee and a cake of meat-biscuit, an unusual noise was heard, coming from the direction of the beach. The doorway was filled with snow, and without much difficulty we could not get out; so we listened at the window for some minutes, expecting its repetition; but nothing further being heard, we concluded that it must have been the wind; and John went on with his work. He soon had a cheerful-looking fire crackling on the hearth, which threw out a little warmth into the damp apartment, and lighted it up with a strange unearthly glare. Wreaths of smoke, however, poured out through the cracks in the rickety stove, destroying whatever of comfort we might else have extracted from it. To escape this smoke we were compelled to draw our heads beneath our blankets. Our chimney needed some tinkering to make it draw.

To turn out in the storm and bring water from the lake, could not be attempted without too great danger; and we were therefore obliged to melt snow, of which there was abundance to be had by merely opening the door. The cook, intent upon preparing the supper, and we, in avoiding the smoke, soon forgot the sound which had startled us. Almost half an hour had elapsed, and probably the subject had passed from the mind of every one, when the sound was again heard; and this time in a manner which left no doubt that it proceeded from something living. One of us thought that it was the growling of a bear, and another that it was the barking of a fox; but after a few minutes had passed, without its being repeated, Whipple, who was half asleep in the corner, protested that it was "just nothing at all."

Nothing was heard for full five minutes more but the moaning of the wind and the rattling of the drifting snow; but our curiosity having been aroused, the door was opened, and the snow cleared away by dragging it down into the hut, until at length a small opening was made, through which we could see daylight. With the daylight came in a cold unwelcome blast and a sheet of feathery snow; and directly, too, an unmistakable human cry.

There were evidently two men calling to each other, and conversing loudly. The wind, however, made so much noise that we could not distinguish what they said. Conjecturing that they were Esquimaux, Petersen called loudly to them, "Huk! huk! huk!" After several repetitions, the hailing was heard and answered, and we soon distinguished footsteps approaching; but it was clear that the strangers were bewildered. This we could not at the time understand; but the cause was subsequently explained. The drift had left nothing to mark the position of our hut, except a slight depression in front, in the cleft by which we approached the door, over which the gable was so wreathed in snow as to appear like a bank of drift.

"Ma-ne! ma-ne!" ("here! here!") shouted Petersen at the top of his voice. The strangers were still puzzled; but soon their ears caught the direction of the sound as it was repeated, and with many expressions of surprise and gratification they hastily approached. Upon an invitation to enter, they threw themselves into the opening and crawled down, feet foremost, dragging along with them great quantities of snow.

They were a most un-human looking pair. Everything on and about them told of the battle they had had with the elements. From head to foot they were invested in a coat of ice and snow. Shapeless lumps of whiteness that they were, they reminded me of the snow-kings I used to make when a boy, which, but for their lack of motion, would have been to all appearance quite as human as our visitors. Their long, heavy, fox-skin coats, reaching nearly to the knees, and surmounted by a hood, covering, like a round lump, all of the head but the face, the bear-skin pantaloons and boots and mittens, were saturated with snow. Their long, black hair, which fell from beneath their hoods over their eyes and cheeks; their eyelashes; the few hairs which grew upon their chins; the rim of fur around their faces, were sparkling with white frost,— the frozen moisture of their breath. Each carried in his right hand a whip, and in his left a lump of frozen meat and blubber. The meat was thrown upon the floor; and, without waiting for an invitation, they stuck their whipstocks under the rafters; and pulling off their mittens and outer garments, hung them thereon. Underneath these frosty coats they wore a shirt of bird-skins.

They proved to be friends from Netlik, from whom we had parted nearly three weeks before. The sturdy, good-natured, and voluble Kalutunah, was one of them; and after we had cleared the ice away from his face, he hung around me, as he had done when I visited him in his hut, crying, "Doc-tee! doc-tee!" and laughing all the while as if it were great fun.

They had a long story to tell. They had left Netlik yesterday morning, each with a team of dogs and a sledge; had travelled over the ice, which they found good down to Cape Parry. There the water was open, and they were obliged to climb over the land. Coming down again to the sea they ran far out in search of bears. While thus engaged they were overtaken by the storm; and after having sheltered themselves in a snow-hut through the night, they became fearful that the ice might break up; and they made for the land, which they reached at a short distance above our camp. Running down the coast, with the design to seek shelter in the bay below us, they had discovered our boats and tent; and landing, immediately commenced seeking for us, when doubtless they were first heard. Not finding us, they went back to the sledges, picketed their dogs behind a protecting rock, and then travelled up and down the shore, confident that we must be somewhere near at hand.

Hardy fellows though they were, thirty-six hours' exposure had told upon them; and they were hungry and fatigued. Seeing John engaged at the fire, they requested him to cook for them one of their pieces of bear-meat; and being greatly annoyed by the smoke of our wood-fire they asked him to put it out and use their blubber. This he was glad enough to do.

It was not very long before we were rejoicing in a good and substantial meal at the expense of our guests. We were too nearly famished to see, in this procedure, any infringement of the delicacies of hospitality, — if such it can be considered in the circumstances. The presence of a good joint of bear's meat silenced all doubts on the subject. While the cook was preparing the stew our friends were chipping off kernels from the piece which remained. These they passed in turn to us; and we found the raw meat thus frozen quite palatable. The feast was enjoyed by all, and it was not ended until the bones were picked clean. The savage hunters ate the raw flesh as fast as they could split it off, until John served up his stew; when they abandoned the bloody joint for a few moments, to return to it again after they had consumed their cooked allowance.

Supper being over, we made for our guests the most comfortable bed we could, by levelling the pile of snow which was heaped up in the middle of the floor. Spreading over this a piece of india-rubber cloth, and another of canvas, we gave them a pair of thick blankets, and tucked them in for the night.

In order to leave the hut next morning it was found necessary to dig a tunnel through the drift, which now lay deeper than ever against the door. The snow was of course all drawn into the hut; and by this time so great was the quantity which had accumulated, that our quarters became very cold and uncomfortable. The tunnel when completed was about six feet long. The Esquimaux were stirring early, and, anxious to be off, were out as soon as an opening had been made; but the storm was now even worse than yesterday. It was snowing violently, and still blowing strongly from the south. I went out with them, to prevent their pilfering any of our small articles, at the depôt; and I assisted them in stowing under the boats their few articles of hunting equipment,—for since they intended to loose their dogs, every line, or piece of skin, or article of food, must be out of reach. The dogs were fastened by their long traces; each team being tied to a separate stake. They were howling piteously. Having been exposed to all the fury of the storm, with no ability to run about, they had grown cold; and as their masters told us, having had nothing to eat during thirty-six hours, they must have been savagely hungry. One of them had already eaten his trace; but we came out, fortunately, at the proper moment to prevent an attack upon the sledges.

Leaving the hunters to look after their teams, I returned to the hut. The blinding snow which battered my face, made me insensible to everything except the idea of getting out of it; and thinking of no danger, I was in the act of stooping to enter the doorway, when a sudden noise behind me caused me to look around, and there, close at my heels, was the whole pack of thirteen hungry dogs, snarling, snapping, and showing their sharp teeth

like a drove of ravenous wolves. It was fortunate
that I had not got down upon my knees, or they
would have been upon my back. In fact, so impetuous was their attack, that one of them had
already sprung when I faced round. I caught him
on my arm and kicked him down the hill. The
others were for the moment intimidated by the
suddenness of my movement, and at seeing the
summary manner in which their leader had been
dealt with; and they were in the act of sneaking
away, when they perceived that I was powerless
to do them any harm, having nothing in my hand.
Again they assumed the offensive; they were all
around me; an instant more and I should be torn
to pieces. I had faced death in several shapes before, but never had I felt as then; my blood fairly
curdled in my veins. Death down the red throats
of a pack of wolfish dogs had something about
it peculiarly unpleasant. Conscious of my weakness, they were preparing for a spring; I had not
time even to halloo for help — to run would be the
readiest means of bringing the wretches upon me.
My eye swept round the group and caught something lying half buried in the snow, about ten feet
distant. Quick as a flash I sprang, as I never
sprang before or since, over the back of a huge fellow who stood before me; and the next instant I
was whirling about me the lash of a long whip,
cutting to right and left. The dogs retreated before
my blows and the fury of my onset, and then sullenly skulked behind the rocks. The whip had
clearly saved my life; there was nothing else within my reach; and it had been dropped there quite

accidentally by Kalutunah as he went down to the sledges.

My principal object in mentioning this little incident is, to show the savage propensity of these dogs, which are to the Esquimaux more than the horse to us or the camel to the Arab. Savage they are, however, only when hungry. The night without food had developed all their latent wolfish qualities. Reclaimed wolves they doubtless are; and, as shown by the boldness of their attack when my back was turned and when I had nothing in my hand, and their timidity when I had possession of a slender whip, they have all of a wolf's cowardice. Their masters keep them in subjection only by intimidation; they will do nothing for a man they do not fear; and even the hunter who has been accustomed to them for years, and has fed them and driven them, has to watch them closely when they are hungry. His whip is then his constant companion. They are capable of no attachment to their master, be he never so kind, except in rare cases; and they will follow the man who last fed them. A little child or a disabled person is never safe amongst them in times of scarcity. A story was once told me at Proven, of a little boy, grandson of the governor, who started to walk from one house to another separated from it by about twenty yards, and who falling midway, was immediately pounced upon by more than a hundred dogs, torn to pieces, and devoured in an instant, under the eye of his mother, who had scarcely time even to scream. I was also told of an old woman, who met with a similar fate.

When Kalutunah came back to the hut, we inquired of him whether his people would undertake to supply us with some food, provided we would give them liberally of our wood, iron, needles, and knives. To this question he would not for a time give a direct answer. It was clear that he had something running in his head, for I could see his bright little eyes twinkling with mischief beneath their blubbery lids. There was no difficulty in perceiving what it was; and it was all embraced in a few short questions which he proposed, instead of answers to what had been asked of him by our interpreter. These questions were, — what we had killed with our mighty guns, and how much food we had brought from the Oomeaksoak, at the north.

The cunning fellow knew well what he was about, and our suspicions were aroused. I saw at once that it would not do to trust him. He was touching a subject upon which we were especially tender; for it was manifestly to our interest to exhibit as little as possible our deficiency in supplies. Although we had hitherto received nothing but kindness from these people, yet we had no reason to suppose that poverty would receive better treatment at the hands of savages than it frequently does at those of civilized men.

Especially important was it that they should be kept in ignorance of our want of fortune in the hunt; for they imagined that with our guns we could always command abundant supplies. When at Netlik some of them had expressed jealousy lest we should monopolize their hunting-grounds. It was certainly better that they should think that we had been busy building our hut, and had not yet had time to hunt. Petersen, naturally shrewd, and understanding well the character of the Esquimau, was quite a match for their cunning, even although he was at the disadvantage of having nothing to show when Kalutunah put the question squarely to him: "How will you live?"—"Live? shoot bear when we get hungry; sleep when we get tired; Esquimaux will bring us bear, we shall give them presents, and sleep all the time. White man easily get plenty to eat. Always plenty to eat, plenty of sleep." Such, as nearly as could be interpreted, were the spirit and substance of Petersen's reply.

Thus opened our negotiations. Their importance will be appreciated by the reader just in proportion as he may estimate the value which we placed upon our lives. As will have been seen, they were conducted upon this basis, namely: that, since with an Esquimau eating and sleeping and idling embrace the sum of human aspirations, it was in the circumstances an allowable policy, to encourage the belief that we asked for food only on account of our natural desire to sleep and be idle, and not from any want of ability on our part to capture with our own hands whatever we chose. Petersen managed the matter quite skilfully, and proved himself a very Talleyrand in diplomacy.

Plainly, the case stood thus. The hunt having utterly failed to supply us, we must get our food of the natives, or not at all; at least there seemed to be no other help for us except, as already observed, in the stone moss,—upon which we had very little expectation that any of us could live long. Kalutunah and his people coveted (and it was very natural that they should) our possessions; and they would take the shortest and safest road to get them. Although not generally inclined to cruelty, they are callous to suffering; and we knew very well that if the idea once entered their heads that we were dependent upon them, we should not get a pound of meat, and our hut would never receive a visit until they thought we had all starved to death. On the other hand, if they thought that we were lazy, and that we did not catch bears simply because we did not wish to do it; and that we preferred to take our ease and pay for what we wanted, they would supply us for a consideration. With them, although a drone is despised and often murdered to be gotten rid of, yet a great man is always a lazy man. He at least is the great man among them, who by skill and success in hunting, earns a right to the *otium cum dignitate*. Indolence then becomes respectable, as it does under like conditions everywhere.

CHAPTER XVII.

A TWO WEEKS FAMINE.

THE result of the negotiations recorded in the preceding chapter was to satisfy the Angekok that the Kablunet were not as poor as he had imagined; and that it was the policy of the tribe to cultivate friendly relations with them. Accordingly, we made with him a sort of treaty or compact, by which his people were to furnish us with as much food as we might want; and we, in return, were to supply them with wood, iron, knives, and needles, at rates subsequently to be fixed upon. With these terms both the contracting parties appeared to be well pleased; and the Angekok and his companion, after passing another night with us and receiving some valuable presents, took their departure for Saunders Island, where there was a settlement called Akbat (the Lumme Hill). They left with us enough meat (all they had) for one meal, and a piece of blubber, from which we tried out three pints of oil. Petersen manufactured, of a sheet of tin, a little flat lamp to burn with a cotton wick; and rigged it to the upright post which stood in the centre of the room as a support to the roof, now heavy with more than two feet of snow. This lamp gave us light enough to read by, and made the apartment look more cheerful.

It was almost two weeks before we saw the Esquimaux again. In the mean time our worst suspicions were aroused respecting their intentions towards us, and we began to entertain serious doubts of our own safety. This period is full of sad memories. It was a long interval of suffering; and to call up all the harrowing details of its history would give no more pleasure to the reader than to myself. I will therefore pass briefly over the record, giving only what is needful to complete the narrative.

Our work went on. The snow was cleared away from the doorway, and a trench nine feet long and two feet wide was cut through the drift out toward the sea. This trench was covered with blocks of snow; and, being made tight, gave us additional security against the winds. At its outer end a hole opened upward into daylight; and through this we obtained entrance to, and exit from the hut. This orifice was covered with canvas to keep out the snow.

That this rude contrivance for a doorway, together with the hut itself, may be better understood, I will describe it more in detail.

Let the reader suppose that I have just returned from a visit to the traps. First, I raise the flat canvas lid, then jump down four feet, then draw in my head and drop the canvas. I now crawl on all fours, through six feet of darkness, up a gentle slope, then three feet more down a rapid descent, when I come against the door; this I push open with my head; I pass through, the door shuts of itself, and I stand upright, taking care not to strike my head against the oar-rafters. I am now inside the hut. The floor, or aisle, on which I stand is three feet wide. To my right hand is the " breck," which is the bed and seat of four of my companions; my place is among them. To my left is the " breck " of three others. If this entrance is supposed to be late in the day, they are lying down side by side, a buffalo-skin under them, blankets over them, their heads close to my feet. Mr. Bonsall comes first, then Mr. Sonntag, then a vacant place, then poor sick Stephenson, and last comes Mr. Petersen. John, Godfrey, and Whipple lie in a row on the other side, at right angles to the direction of the four previously named. Before me is the post which sustains the roof, and supports our little lamp which has one feeble flame. Over this flame is suspended a square kettle, which we have made of our Borden's meat-biscuit can. We have abandoned the lake; and now, with this lamp and kettle, we melt from the snow all the water that we require, — at least all that we can afford. Beyond the post stands our open stove, in which may be seen the copper-kettle and the saucepan; but there is no fire there. We have fire only twice a day. Close behind the stove is the solid rock, which forms the eastern side of our hut. In a recess, in the further corner to the left, are stowed three clothes-bags; in the corresponding corner, to the right, are five more. Petersen's head is close to the stove; and close to Petersen's head stands a gun; the others are hanging outside on pegs, in the passage. The canvas and rafters overhead, and the walls all around, are white with a coating of frost and ice, — the condensed moisture of our breath. It is a cold, damp, dark, cheerless place. The temperature is not below zero at the floor, nor above 40° in the centre. The temperature outside ranges from zero to 20° below it. It is early winter yet, and the cold has not fully set in. This difference between the outside and inside record is owing to the heat radiated from our bodies. The warm breath, charged with the moisture which frescoes the walls and ceiling of our snow-palace with glittering crystals, heats it too. The reader will more readily appreciate this when he recalls the dimensions of the apartment into which were crowded eight men. Its average length (for the walls are not quite parallel) is fourteen feet, its breadth is eight feet, and its mean height is five feet.

I have said that we had fire only twice a day. This fire was not, however, intended for warmth, but merely for the purpose of boiling a pot of coffee, and of cooking whatever food we might have. Whilst we had fat we used the lamp which had served us in the field; but this failing, we burned whatever wood we happened to possess. I have already mentioned that we were using the staves of our bread-barrel and of our kegs. These could not, of course, last long; and, at length, there was no resource but our boats. The Hope was, accordingly, broken to pieces. It went to our very hearts to destroy this gallant companion of so many struggles; and we knew not how far the act might affect our future fortunes; but come what would, and regret the destruction as we might, there was no alternative. At first we used her tenderly, as if to prolong the actual dissolution,—tearing away such pieces only as did not affect her form; but, finally, the gunwale had to be sacrificed,—and then the Hope lay in the snow a hopeless wreck. We looked upon her now merely as a mass of lumber, and burned her up without compunction. The best pieces,—the thwarts, the keel, and in fact all that were likely to be of any service to the Esquimaux,— were saved, and carefully stowed away in one corner of the hut as merchandise, so as to be inaccessible to the thieving fellows whose skill and acquisitiveness were now to be our only dependence for the means of life.

It must not be thought that this insignificant supply of wood, altogether not more than a few arm-loads, gave us much fire. At most, we could use only a mere handful of splinters; and even these were poor, for the wood was water-soaked, and a large part of it could not be made to burn without constant blowing. In consequence of this there was so much smoke that we were almost stifled whenever meal-time came round; sometimes we were absolutely driven from the hut.

We were indefatigable in our efforts to add something to our stock of food; but day after day went by, and still it was the same monotonous story,— failure. Fox-traps were built along the shore, to the north and to the south, chiefly under the superintendence of Petersen. There were, I think, fourteen, and they ranged over nearly ten miles of coast. They were visited daily, when the weather would permit; but, except in a single instance, none of them were ever found to contain anything but drifted snow, which required them to be torn down and reconstructed. Several times they had been entered by animals, which had escaped in consequence of some defect of construction.

These traps were built nearly upon the same principle as a boy's rabbit-trap at home. Selecting a smooth, level rock, we arranged some flat stones of about six inches thick, so as to inclose on three sides an area six inches by two feet and a half. Over this inclosure were laid other flat stones; and between the two which closed up one of the ends, was inserted a peg projecting an inch within the inclosure. On this peg was loosely hung, by a loop, a small piece of meat; outside of this, on the same peg, was placed another loop made at the end of a cord, which was carried up through the rear of the trap, and over the top to the front, where it was tied around a thin flat flag of slate which moved freely up and down, being guided and held by two large blocks placed one on either side of the entrance. The operation of this simple machinery will be readily understood. The fox enters under the slide or trap-door, advances to the rear, seizes the bait, and attempts to back out; the bait is pulled from the peg, and with it the loop which supports the door. This support being removed the door falls, and the animal is caught. Everything now depends upon the cracks being tightly closed; for if the animal can get his little nose between two stones, he is sure to make his way out. It is also important that the space should not be large enough to allow him to turn round; for, in that case, the trap must be very perfect if he does not loosen the door and escape. This accident happened to us several times, — no doubt, to the great joy of the fox, but much to our discomfiture.

Not a day passed that we were not out with our guns and rifles. Petersen, accompanied by different members of the party in turn, watched the open cracks in the ice for a seal or a walrus; while others were scouring the land in search of hares and foxes. Of the former we discovered not one, although tracks were sometimes observed, and our search was most diligent. The animals being purely white, with only a few black hairs on the tips of their ears, could not be easily detected. They frequent the rocky places where they find shelter, and come down to the plain to feed on grass, moss, and lichen, which they dig up from beneath the snow. We hunted around and around the rocks at the base of the cliffs, where it seemed most probable that hares would be found, but to no purpose; we could never start one. The foxes (both the blue and white varieties) were repeatedly seen; but they were very timid, and could not be approached within a shorter range than two or three hundred yards. On one occasion Mr. Bonsall and myself had a tedious run for fully three hours after one, without success. Each of us had a gun, and we tried every art and stratagem. The little fellow was seen one moment far up the hill-side, seated upon a rock; and being thence pursued, he would leap down, and clambering around the face of the hill, would be next seen on the plain; where, again pursued, he playfully circle about us, as if the subject of slaughtering him was to us not the most serious business in the world. Bonsall hid behind a rock while I chased; and again I hid and Bonsall chased; but, although several times the secreted party seemed to be directly in the fox's path, yet he always turned at the proper moment to insure the safety of his neck, trotting gracefully away, snuffing the air, — the prettiest and most provoking of living creatures. He was about the size of a domestic cat, round and plump, white as the snow, with a long, pointed nose, and a long, trailing, bushy tail, which seemed to be his especial pride. It was quite evident that he was amusing himself; and he appeared to be conscious that he was doing it at our expense. He rolled and tossed himself about among the loose drift, now springing into the air, now bounding away, now stopping short, cocking his head to one side and elevating one foot, as if listening, seeming all the time to be showing off his "points" to enemies, for whom he cared not the value of the very smallest part of his very pretty tail. Tired and exhausted we gave up the pursuit and returned home. The fox followed us, always at a safe distance; and when we last saw him, as we looked back from the rocks above the hut, he was mounted on an elevation, uttering his shrill, sharp cry, which sounded much like mockery of our defeat.

Petersen had no better success at sea. He observed several seals, but all of them at a distance. One was fired at by him at the long range of two hundred yards, and was wounded; another was killed, or supposed to be, at a shorter distance; but the wounded one escaped and the other sank.

The place is barren and desolate beyond description. Kalutunah told us that the coast, from a little way below Cape Parry to the mouth of Wolstenholme Sound, is called "the barren ground." Even the poor pittance of stone-moss that we get, comes not without hard labor and much searching. Some of us are in pursuit of it almost every day. This service generally falls to the lot of Sonntag, Bonsall, and myself. Stephenson is an invalid, but when he can crawl out of doors we may count upon him, for he is full of spirit. The moss does not agree with John, Godfrey, and Whipple, as well as with the rest of us, and we seldom have their help; we therefore put them on watch alternately at the hut, and let one of them go with Petersen, and the other to the traps at Booth Bay, when they are able. The poor fellows, however, are mostly sick, and they seldom stir abroad.

We (the moss-gatherers) go out in the morning as soon as it is light. Each carries a tin-plate, a piece of hoop-iron (a relic of our kegs) bent in the shape of a horse-shoe, and a little bag, — which is a shirt with the neck and sleeves tied up. The plate is to clear away the snow, which is often more than two feet deep; the iron is to scrape off the moss. We travel always over much ground. Once we crossed the bay to the south of us, and were distant from the hut six miles. Sometimes our labor is rewarded with a good supply, — enough to last two or three days; sometimes we do not collect enough in five or six hours to give us a single meal. I have sought alone, for a whole day, without getting a pint. The greater number of the rocks have nothing on them, and the hard labor of clearing away the deep snow is unrecompensed.

We boil the moss with a handful or two of meat-biscuit, flour, or bread-dust, and thus eke out our supplies. It is disgusting at best, and is scarcely more nutritious than paper. When the Esquimaux left us, we had each thirty-six biscuits, besides three pints of bread-dust. The allowance to each man was one biscuit a day; but the temperature is so low, and our labor so hard, that this small quantity of food is not sufficient for our need. We vote to live better, and then starve if we must, — and so we double the ration.

Every day of this sort of life tells its tale in furrows in our cheeks; the stone-moss has given some of us violent diarrhœa and gastritis. We are all frightfully weak. Godfrey has fainted in trying to raise himself; and falling, he would have seriously injured himself against the wall, had he not been caught by John. The latter is scarcely able to walk; and besides he suffers much from hemorrhoids. Whipple is no stronger. Stephenson lies beside me, gasping for breath. His heart troubles have come back; and I never go out without expecting to find him, upon my return, a corpse.

What *shall* we do? Will the Esquimaux never come? —

Yes! here they are at last! Their merry voices sound loudly through the darkness of the night; and we are saved, — at least from our present peril.

CHAPTER XVIII.

SCHEMES FOR MOVING SOUTHWARD.

October 26th. THE Esquimaux have come and gone again; and we, having gone through the natural ravenous assaults of starving men upon their supplies, are now fattening on the juicy bear's meat they left us. They had gone down to Cape York on a visit to their brethren there, stopping on the way at Akbat, and hunting in the interval. Cape York is the most southern settlement of this people. The place is called by them Imnanak (the cliffs). They had upon their sledges the skins of three bears, and the greater part of the meat of the animals; but they were very chary of it, and we obtained only enough to suffice us for a few days.

We ate of our newly acquired food no more than was necessary to restore our strength. The deficiency of bulk we supplied, as before, with stone-moss. This moss, however, during forty-eight hours after the arrival of the sledges, was voted a nuisance; and we devoured the rich and wholesome food as only famished men could. These two days wrought a wonderful change in us. Our cheeks filled out; the dizziness with which we had all been affected vanished; and our normal strength was in a measure regained. The ghastly, haggard expression which our faces wore gave place to one of cheerfulness.

The evening after our savage benefactors left us figures in my memory as one of the pleasantest of my life; pleasant because it was cheerful, because all care was forgotten, and the moment was enjoyed for its own sake, without thought for the morrow, or fear of what was to come in the more distant future. We felt hopeful, strong, and self-reliant; and, more than all, we felt thankful in our very heart of hearts for the Providential gifts so timely sent us, teaching us our dependence upon the Great Universal Father, who, as he "suffers not a sparrow to fall to the ground without his notice," forsakes not even the weakest of his children in the solitude of the desert.

It was indeed a gladsome time. How curiously dependent is our spiritual upon our physical nature! Now that we had enough to eat, past and future perils and sufferings were alike forgotten, and we signalized our repast by doubling our ration of coffee. Petersen, ever careful, thoughtful, and generous, brought out from the middle of his bag a small package of cigars, — a present from Dr. Kane; and our senses inhaled new life with the rich flavor of a genuine "Havana." The men smoothed the bedclothes on the north side of the hut; and Sonntag, Bonsall, and myself took turns with them in a game of whist, and in reading some chapters from "The Fair Maid of Perth." The genial warmth of Scott was felt in that snow-imbedded hut, and our faces expressed the interest excited by his tale. The temperature was unusually warm, having risen to 44°; and it was far into the "wee sma' hours ayant the twa'," when we retired to rest.

The following days dragged their slow length along, and the same routine of duties and employments marked their progress. The Esquimaux came again, and brought to us a few small pieces of meat and blubber; and they went away promising to return with more. Other incidents occurred to occupy our attention. We caught two foxes; and as we owed one of them to one of the traps, we considered ourselves well paid for all our trouble in constructing, visiting, and reconstructing these. The prisoner so taken was small, and of a blue, or rather blueish-gray color; and his flesh made for us two scanty meals. Except in color, he appeared to resemble closely the white specimen already described. The other of the two just mentioned was shot by me in the night. I heard him running over the roof as I lay revolving schemes for the future; and, without stopping to dress, I hurried out of the hut with a gun. The night was so dark that the sight was not discernible, and I therefore fired almost at random. The first barrel missed its mark, but the second was more successful; and I could see the fox, badly wounded, hobbling down the hill over the snow. Fearful that the prize would escape, I gave chase, and overtook him after running about fifty yards; but the experiment had come near to costing me dearly. Having no boots, and only a pair of light stockings on my feet, these were found, upon my return to the hut, to be frozen, — their color resembling that of a tallow candle. The frost, however, had not penetrated very deeply; and, by the timely application of ice-cold water, of which there was fortunately a supply in the kettle, and light friction afterwards with the feathery side of a bird-skin, I escaped with a few blisters. This plan of treatment I learned from the Esquimaux; and on this, as well as many subsequent occasions, I had opportunity to test its efficiency.

Sunday, October 29th. I spent this day with Bonsall in wandering over the plain, searching for stonemoss; dedicating our thoughts to the absent. We knew how our friends at home were keeping the day, and we wondered whether or not they were remembering us in their devotions. We knew, too, that they must have been anxiously looking for us; and that, in a few days, they would begin to fear for our safety.

The temperature when we went out in the morning was thirty-two degrees below zero, and scraping off the snow was so cold a work that we obtained little moss.

At noon we halted nearly at the head of the south bay, where there is a pile of rocks above a low precipice from which we commanded a good view. Here we found Petersen, who had torn down a trap to clear it of snow; and who was just commencing to reconstruct it. He had visited all his traps, and rebuilt and rebaited them.

Petersen too had his thoughts in the south. His wife, his daughter, and his boy were engrossing his soul, while his body grew chilly at his unwelcome work. His face was sad and thoughtful; and as I came up beside him and lifted a stone for him, he said, sorrowfully, " I was thinking of Paul." Ah! pretty, gallant little Paul! it was well that you did not know that on your father's furrowed cheek lay a frozen tear.

We finished the trap, and involuntarily turned our eyes in the direction in which our thoughts had been flying. The sun, low upon the horizon, shone through a gray mist, with no more appearance of warmth than the rocks and ice and snow about us.

Far behind that dreary mist lay our home-world, gladdened by a genial sun — glowing in the gold and crimson of its autumn. The pictures which our fancy drew made such contrast with the realities of our situation, that we fell to scheming again for our deliverance.

I had a project which possessed at least the merit of tending in the direction of our duty: it was to hire the Esquimaux to carry us on their sledges to Upernavik. We would wait through November and set out by the moonlight of December, when, in all probability, the sea would be closed. Petersen declared this to be impracticable; but we agreed to renew its discussion in the hut, in our way toward which other plans were proposed; but none of them brought us to any conclusion, other than that it was necessary to do something soon.

We reached the hut, to find there an Esquimau just arrived from Akbat. It is two o'clock in the afternoon and the temperature has come *up* to twenty-seven degrees below zero.

Our new visitor is a sprightly little fellow; drives an excellent dog-team, of which he seems to be very proud; and is the most promising looking young hunter we have seen. He is dressed in the usual suit of bear and fox-pelts; but they are all new, and show evidence of care. He is evidently somebody's pet. Even among these poor savages the kindly care of female hands is manifest upon the favorite young fellows. He confesses his having a sweetheart in Netlik, and thither he is bound. Love's tokens pass everywhere — our Esquimau has a bundle of bird-skins to make an under-garment for his fair one.

We presented him with a small pocket-knife, and a piece of wood; both of which pleased him greatly. With the latter he at once spliced his whipstock. I gave him a couple of needles for his intended bride; and Sonntag added a string of beads for her. These attentions put him almost beside himself with joy; but he afterward seemed pained that he could offer to us no suitable return. He had nothing on his sledge (his hunting equipment of course excepted) but two small pieces of blubber, four birds, about a pound of bear's meat, a piece of bear's skin, and that inseparable companion of every Esquimau hunter, a small lamp. All these he laid at our feet; and soon he was dashing up the coast apparently unable to contain his impatience to show his treasures to the eyes whose approval he valued more than that of all the world beside.

October 30*th.* We have given up all thought of capturing seals; and we rely upon supplies from the Esquimaux, upon game from our traps, and upon the stone-moss. Mr. Sonntag, Mr. Bonsall, and William Godfrey are out after the last. I go with John to the north.

We have made two more traps. Petersen has gone as usual to the south. George Whipple has kept watch at the hut; he is not well. Stephenson has another relapse: but this is not as bad as his former attacks. The weather is fine. The air is calm, and the sky clear. The temperature at ten o'clock in the morning was at thirty, at twelve o'clock it rose to eighteen, and at three o'clock in the afternoon it stood at thirty-one degrees below zero; yet our hut is not uncomfortable.

One of my little household gods is "David Copperfield;" and I spent the evening reading aloud of the early struggles of the widow's son.

October 31*st.* The day differs from yesterday only in a slight change in the arrangement of the *dramatis personæ*. Petersen stayed at home to do some tinkering;—making of hoop-iron some knives for the Esquimaux. Bonsall and myself took his place. We found that one of the traps had been entered, but that the door had been caught in falling, and the animal had escaped. A fox had been sitting on another trap; but he was too cunning to venture inside. Mr. Sonntag visited the traps at the north, all of which he found empty. He built a new one and collected some stone-moss.

The temperature to-day has been almost the same as that of yesterday. At the same hours at which the thermometer was then noted, it has stood to-day at 27°, 26°, and 31° below zero.

Some fleecy clouds hang around the horizon; and they have been beautifully illuminated, for many hours, by the sun, only a small part of whose disk was seen above the ice at noonday. We could, of course, see even that part of it only by refraction. The god of day has gone to the south, and the long winter night is at length upon us.

Thus far we have avoided talking much of our prospects, for none of us had matured any plans. Indeed, whatever we might have projected, nothing could have been done hitherto, except what has already been accomplished; but, now that the sea is for the most part closed, a movement hence may be practicable.

The first proposal made, was that above mentioned, namely: to endeavor to live by whatever available means, during four weeks longer, and then to continue our journey over the ice southward. Many phases of this scheme were considered in turn. The alacrity manifested during our discussion was most gratifying. If the Esquimaux would not undertake to carry us southward on their sledges, it was proposed that we should purchase their teams; and if they would not sell as many as would be required to convey our entire party, that we should trade with them for dogs enough to transport one half of us, — the other half remaining, either to live with the natives until the former should bring succor, or to find their way to the brig.

A little calm reflection, and a few words from practical Petersen, showed that of all of our suggestions, the execution was too doubtful. In the first place, the distance to Upernavik is fully seven hundred miles by the tortuous route we must follow. We could make one journey to Akbat, thirty miles; a second to Cape York, from seventy to a hundred miles further; but then we should reach Melville

Bay, of which as it is in winter no one knew anything except that its shores were wholly uninhabited; it was, probably, not entirely closed, and the ice upon it must be rough; we should not be certain of finding game; and for so many persons the sledges could not carry a sufficiency of food.

If one half of our party should be left behind, they would probably be destroyed by the Esquimaux, as the force would not be strong enough to resist attack. It seemed too unpromising to undertake, in the dead of winter, to cross an icy desert of six hundred miles, with no other shelter than a snow-hut, and with no other resource for food than the precarious hunt. That the Esquimaux would not go with us appeared certain; and it was not probable that they would sell their teams. Nevertheless the plan is a favorite one with the party, and it is not easily abandoned. If it could be carried out in any shape, all of our objects would be attained. We should be in Upernavik more than six months before the arrival of the whalers on their way northward, in the summer. We dismiss the subject for the present, intending to talk of it to the Esquimaux when they shall come to us again.

All of our party are agreed that, come what may, we must endeavor to open communication with Rensselaer Harbor, and obtain a supply of food from the abundant stock of pork and bread of the Advance. If we can accomplish such a reinforcement of our stores as will sustain us during the winter, we may, in case our December scheme shall prove abortive, go to Cape York, and there await the arrival of the whalers, who always pass in July within hailing distance of that point.

Every day makes us feel more and more how dependent we are upon the Esquimaux; yet our confidence in them, never great, was shaken during the last visit but one we have received from them, and we must in some way speedily render ourselves independent of them.

The only conclusion upon which we agree, is that we must, in the first place, establish communication with the brig at Rensselaer Harbor. This is recognized by all of us as a necessity; but how it is to be effected we do not see. The danger of the attempt would be second only to that of our proposed southern journey. We are three hundred miles from the brig, and to travel that distance over the ice at this season of the year, is truly a grave enterprise. What shall we do?

CHAPTER XIX.

PLANS FOR OBTAINING SUPPLIES.

The subject of our miserable condition was resumed the following evening. Petersen volunteered to go, at the earliest opportunity, to Netlik, and to endeavor there to organize a caravan of sledges to proceed to the brig for provisions. I believe that there was not a member of the party who would not willingly have undertaken the dangerous task; but Petersen was clearly the best fitted by his experience for the service. Indeed, he was the only one of us who could talk with the natives.

Kalutunah, the very man whom we wished most to see, came next day, accompanied by a young hunter of Netlik, and by a woman with a child, which she carried in a hood upon her back. The little creature was not six months old; and yet, wrapped up in fox-skins, and lying close to its mother's back, its fur-covered head peeping above her left shoulder, it did not seem to suffer from the long exposure.

I was never more struck with the hardihood and indifference to cold, manifested by these people, than on this occasion. This woman had subjected herself to a temperature of thirty-five degrees below zero, with the liability to be caught in a gale; had travelled forty miles over a track the roughness of which frequently compelled her to dismount from the sledge and walk; she had carried her child all the way; her sole motive being her curiosity to see the white men, their igloe (hut), and their strange treasures. We must at least concede that she manifested extraordinary courage and endurance in the gratifying of her desire.

Kalutunah and his companion had each a sledge; and each brought some pieces of walrus-beef and blubber, for which we paid them liberally with wood from the Hope.

Petersen was soon in conversation with them, with respect to our contemplated journey to the south. Kalutunah had heard before of Upernavik, and he was greatly pleased with Petersen's description of its riches; its abundant wood and iron; its never-ending supply of seal, and walrus, and narwhal, and fox, and reindeer. He would like to live there; would like to take his family and all his people there; but it was impossible. No one could cross the great frozen sea — the "Melville Bay ice."

Kalutunah did not know when his people had communicated with the south; but there is a tradition to the effect that Innuit, (men,) that is, Esquimaux, live there; and that they once had intercourse with his own immediate tribe.

This fact has an important bearing upon the climatology of the region, and upon the physical aspects of Greenland and its adjacent waters. If the Esquimaux of the coasts bordering Baffin Bay on the north and south once held intercourse with each other, as is asserted by this tradition, then the intervening space (Melville Bay) was in a different condition from that in which we found it — that is, so completely ice-locked that no human being could live there. Kalutunah declared that unless there were on the way good hunting-grounds none of his people would undertake to cross the bay.

The Esquimaux, doubtless, once inhabited the whole coast from Cape Farewell to the extreme north point of Greenland: now, an unsurveyed ice coast-line sweeps around the head of the bay, for two hundred miles, being broken only at a few intervals by lofty capes — at least such is its appearance when observed from the sea at the distance of twenty miles, the nearest at which ships are able to approach.

This ice coast-line is formed by the edges of the great glacier masses which come slowly gliding down the valleys from the icy reservoir of the interior, the vast *mer de glace* of the continent. From it are discharged in this way into the bay enormous icebergs, which clog it, and make it what it now is,— an immense, impenetrable wilderness, which grows worse and worse, as it chills the air and extends into the water more and more with the lapse of each year and century.

The idea of passing this natural barrier seemed to Kalutunah as absurd as a scheme for flying to the moon would appear to us. It was a subject not to be seriously entertained for a moment. When reminded that his forefathers had done it, he merely replied, that then there was much less ice there, and that they had kayaks (canoes), and that the journey was performed in the Upernak, the midsummer, or season of thaw. The "Frozen Sea" is to his people what the tropics were to the Europeans before the days of De Gama, a place of death and destruction to all who should have the audacity to enter it. The fiery heat of the equatorial sun could not have been endued with more imaginary terrors than those with which the mind of this hardy son of the frost invested the ice-desert which lay bordering his hunting-grounds on the south.

He laughed outright when it was proposed that he should sell to us dogs with which to make the journey. He would not sell dogs for any purpose, or at any price; and for the best of reasons, namely, that they had none which they could spare. This I did not believe; for there were in the settlement more dogs than the owners had any possible use for, except to eat; and with a little additional exertion, they could seldom be reduced to such an extremity as to be obliged to kill their teams for such a purpose. We had, however, made up our minds to possess ourselves of a team if possible; for in any case it would be found useful. "Would not his people sell us as many dogs as we wanted if we would give them our boat, and all the wood and iron we had?" —"No!"—"They could not spare their dogs!" The truth lay in quite another direction, and was revealed by his tell-tale eyes, which said as plainly as so many words, "We are in a fair way to get all we want without troubling ourselves;" and he sucked in his cheeks in imitation of our lank faces, and then looked knowingly at the woman, who returned the salute with an expressive nod.

We were now unwillingly compelled to acknowledge, as Petersen had told us at first would be the case, that it was idle to think of making a mid-winter journey to Upernavik; and we settled down upon another scheme which, if it could be carried out, would accomplish our object. This was, to live through the winter by whatever means we could, and early in the spring go to Cape York, carrying our boat over the ice, and there await the arrival of the whaling fleet on their way northward. This plan involved many risks, but nothing else appeared possible for us. Not least among these risks was the liability to failure of our stores; and we must, therefore, procure for ourselves a sufficiency of food to insure us against starvation while our plans and the means of executing them were maturing. Accordingly the subject of continuing our journey was dropped, and one of more immediate importance was substituted.

The Esquimaux seemed to receive favorably the proposition of going to the ship; and said that, at least four sledges should accompany Petersen, provided we would give to each driver a fine knife and some wood. To this we readily agreed; and Petersen awaited only the arrival of the morning to start. To the woman and her baby was given a place in the corner; and what we now learned to know as the "Hosky's bed" (the whalers nickname the natives in the South, Hosky) was spread upon the floor for the men. Hitherto we had tried to keep them away from our own proper bedding, on account of certain uncompanionable little representatives of natural history which roam in droves over their persons; but our gallantry was now put to the test, as it would never do to turn a woman out upon the floor to sleep,— especially, since she had done us the honor to come forty miles to see us. We therefore sacrificed a blanket to the mother and her child, and crowded away from them as far as our limited quarters would allow. The tongues which had seemed never to tire of running were soon silenced by sleep.

This sudden, and I may also say, unexpected assent to our proposition was received with great joy on our part; and preparations were at once busily made for getting Petersen ready for his hard journey. The hunters told us what we had scarcely expected, that the sea at the north was closed, even at Cape Alexander; and, as if to prove this, they stated that a sledge had come from the village of Etah, which is fifteen miles northeast from that cape, bringing intelligence from Rensselaer Harbor. Some of the people of Etah had been to the Oomeaksoak. Our comrades at the Advance were very sick, (and here Kalutunah laid his head on his arm, and tried to make a sad face,) and Hans had had his hand injured by the explosion of a powder-flask. The relation of this last incident convinced us that what they said was true, since they could hardly cook up such a story.

We were aroused in the middle of the night by voices calling loudly down by the beach. We were used to such sounds now, and upon going out found there the young lover who had passed up the coast a few days before. He was accompanied by a widow, neither young nor beautiful, one of two women who had returned northward with Kalutunah after his first southern visit.

The new comers were invited into the hut, and

treated with the consideration due to them as guests. The facilities for the display of hospitality in the "Wanderer's House," as our den was fitly called considering who lived in it and who visited it, were poor enough. All who came seemed to have learned this, for they brought their own provisions. The widow carried in her arms a load of frozen birds, and the boy a chunk of walrus-meat. They did not seem fatigued nor cold, although they must have been exposed fully ten hours; and they were scarcely seated before they began to eat. They of course threw the hut into confusion, much to the annoyance of Petersen, who wanted to get some sleep preparatory to starting; but it was soon evident that sleep was out of the question, for several hours at least. The woman with the baby was asking question upon question, which the widow was doing her best to answer. The two hunters on the floor were sitting up, rubbing their greasy eyes, and trying to find space for a few words; while the young lover, who was a general favorite, was laughing and playing with Godfrey, who was indulging in some of his negro burlesques.

We tendered to the widow the use of our cooking apparatus; but she seemed disinclined to be troubled with it, and the food was eaten raw. The man, her companion, broke off piece after piece of his frozen walrus, and the widow skinned and devoured her birds with no less rapidity. Four lumme of respectable size disappeared in an astonishingly short space of time. She very kindly offered to share with us; and, singling out the astronomer who occupied the seat next to her, she made him the special object of her regard, chewing up for him a large lump of bird flesh; but Sonntag was compelled to plead a full stomach. So great a courtesy she did not expect would be declined under any pretence, and she seemed quite mortified; but nothing daunted, she passed the lump over to me; but no, I could not oblige her. With quite a desponding face she crossed the floor and tried Whipple. Not meeting with success in that quarter she came back to Mr. Bonsall, who was already quite a philosopher in making his tastes subservient to his physical wants. "Now for it, Bonsall!" cried Petersen. These words of encouragement had the effect to call forth a hearty laugh on all sides; which, being misunderstood by the widow, she hastily withdrew her offering of friendship, bolted it herself, and in offended silence went on with her work of skinning birds and swallowing them. We all felt that henceforth we should have an enemy in the widow.

This widow greatly interested me. She ate birds for conscience' sake. Her husband's soul had passed into the body of a walrus as a temporary habitation, and the Angekok had prescribed, that, for a certain period, she should not eat the flesh of this animal; and since at this time of year bear and seal were scarce, she was compelled to fall back upon a small stock of birds which had been collected during the previous summer.

This penance was of a kind which every Esquimau undergoes upon the death of a near relation. The Angekok announces to the mourners into what animal the soul of the departed has passed; and henceforth, until the spirit has shifted its quarters, they are not to partake of the flesh of that animal. This may be a bear, a seal, a walrus, a lumme, a burgomaster-gull, or any other embraced within their limited bill of fare.

The widow had one practice which, notwithstanding that it related to the same serious subject, caused us not a little amusement. Her late husband, for whose sake she refrained from eating walrus, met with his death last Upernak, (summer,) by being carried out to sea on a loose cake of ice to which he had imprudently gone to watch for seal. The tide having changed, the floating raft was disengaged from the land; and, in full view of his family and friends, the poor hunter drifted out into the middle of Baffin Bay, never to be heard of more. It happened that, during the evening, the name of this hunter was mentioned several times, always in terms of warm praise, and each time his widow shed a copious flood of tears. Petersen told us that all strangers were expected to join in this ceremony. Our first attempt, I fear, made a poor show of sorrow; but the second was perfect of its kind. The motions could not have been surpassed, even had the cause of grief been a rich banker, and the mourners his heirs. The tears were hardest to manage; but a sufficient quantity found their way to the surface to satisfy the bereaved one that her grief was appreciated by us, and she resumed her lively manner, so far forgetting our former discourtesy in our present respect for her sorrow, that she tried again to treat us to munched meat.

At length, to the great joy of Petersen, these ceremonies were ended; and when told that we wished to sleep, with an instinctive politeness which was as well appreciated as it was delicate, our savage guests crawled into their respective places, and in a few moments the hut was quiet.

November 3d. Petersen was off with the early morn, under the special charge of Kalutunah; on whose sledge rode, also, the woman and the baby. Godfrey went with him, and was carried on the other sledge.

We did not part from Petersen without many misgivings. He has a journey before him of three hundred miles; and he is in the hands of men in whom we have very little confidence; yet the great bribes that we have offered may be sufficient to purchase fidelity. He carries a letter from me to Dr. Kane informing him of our condition and wants.

Godfrey has gone mainly at his own request, and may be of service. In case the Esquimaux should fail to make the promised journey to the ship, then Petersen is to endeavor to purchase a team, and go with Godfrey alone. Failing this, he will try to make some arrangement by which we can join the natives in the hunt. Our chief difficulty is the want of dogs, without which the bears cannot be successfully pursued. It has long been one of our schemes to add our rifles to the sledge parties of the Esquimaux for mutual aid. This, however, would involve the giving up of our purpose to go southward, and the complete destruction of all our equipment; for, in order to carry out such a plan, we should be obliged to abandon our hut and take up our quarters at Netlik, or at Northumberland Island. Not being able to take with us our boat or any important part of our property, we should be left entirely dependent on the Esquimaux. The means now in our hands for advancing or retreating must be finally abandoned, for the moment we should be out of the hut it would be pillaged and torn to pieces.

In consequence of a light breeze from the south the boy and the widow remained with us. It grew calm in the afternoon; and the moon being full, and the air clear, they could travel as well by night as by day. They left us at eight o'clock in the evening.

Mr. Sonntag and John have gone with them, carrying many presents, with the hope of securing thereby a supply of meat, which would not otherwise be brought to us.

The weather is very fine, the temperature 30° below zero; and everything looks promising except in our poor hut. Stephenson is very sick, and I fear to leave him for an hour. The apartment has grown cold; the temperature is not above 20° anywhere; and at the floor it is below zero.

CHAPTER XX.

PETERSEN.

Our expectations with respect to our own personal safety and the success of our Cape York project were now centred in Petersen. If he should fail, there was no hope of carrying out, at the opening of spring, our recently formed resolution. Our confidence in him was great; and, for my own part, I entertained no doubt that if the object of his journey could be accomplished through human endurance and perseverance, it would be by him. Danger and exposure had long been familiar to him, and I felt well assured that one who had never before quailed would not be found wanting now. For this his whole life was a guaranty.

John Carl Christian Petersen was born in Copenhagen about forty-five years ago. Early in life he was apprenticed to a cooper; but growing tired of the restraints to which this situation subjected him, he shipped on board an Icelandic packet, and went in search of freedom and fortune.

Iceland pleased him less than Denmark; and, after a short stay, he returned home to engage himself soon after as cooper for the colony of Disco in North Greenland. At Disco and the adjacent settlements he lived during several years, marrying in that time a resident of the country, who made him an excellent and devoted wife, and by whom he had two children, a girl and a boy.

While at Disco, he met with a serious accident. On "King Christian's day," whilst engaged in reloading a cannon which had been fired in honor of the occasion, he was badly injured by a premature discharge of the piece. By this misfortune his hand and wrist were permanently stiffened to such an extent that he was no longer able to fulfil the duties of his station. He was therefore promoted to the post of vice-governor or assistant-manager of the settlement of Upernavik, the most northern of Danish stations in Greenland. To this place he removed with his family, and remained there until 1850, when Captain Penny, with the two ships "Lady Franklin" and "Sophia," bound for Lancaster Sound in search of Sir John Franklin, came into the harbor and offered to the vice-governor the post of interpreter.

Years of hard service had not destroyed his love of adventure, and the proffered appointment was promptly accepted. His qualifications for its duties were good. He had lived during nearly twenty years in daily intercourse with the Esquimaux, and was thoroughly master of their language. He was known on board every whale-ship that came to Baffin Bay; and having availed himself of the opportunities which his visits to them afforded, he had picked up from time to time a sufficient knowledge of English to enable him to act, during several years, as interpreter between his Danish comrades and the whalemen.

Those who are familiar with the history of the search for Franklin are acquainted with the services rendered by Petersen to the English expedition. The fleet returned home in the autumn of 1851, and he found his way from London to his native city, and thence, during the following summer, in the company's vessel, to Upernavik.

A few days after he reached home, Captain Inglefield, R. N., in the steamer Isabella, put into the port of Upernavik purposely to secure his services in the capacity in which he had proved so useful. Although gratified by this manifestation of the satisfaction which he had given to the Admiralty, his employers during the previous voyage, yet, having been for two years separated from his family, he was unwilling so soon to leave them again; and the tempting offer was declined.

After the lapse of a year, a similar proposal was made to him by Dr. Kane, and was accepted. He came on board of the Advance July 24th, 1853. His great familiarity with the climate and the movements of the ice, coupled with that quickness of perception which men often attain whose senses have been sharpened by necessity, made him a valuable auxiliary to our small force. His services as interpreter were often called into requisition during our stay at Rensselaer Harbor; and his genius for tinkering served us profitably in fitting out the sledge parties. The lamps, and other cooking apparatus used on these occasions, — which were so compact and simple, yet so serviceable, — were mainly of his invention and manufacture. He was, moreover, a good hunter; and he added, from time to time, something to our fresh rations, either by his gun or rifle, or from his traps.

He accompanied the disastrous northern sledge party of March, 1854, and was in consequence for a time broken down by scurvy and rheumatism; and when the autumn came, he was still an invalid. Yet, when Dr. Kane announced to the ship's company his determination to remain at Rensselaer Harbor, there to try the contingencies of another winter, Petersen was among the first to volunteer to go to the south, and attempt to carry to the nearest outposts of the civilized world news of the ill-starred fortunes of the **Advance**.

When the party whose history this book records was organized, he was chosen to pilot it through the ice-encumbered waters.

Long accustomed to every phase of arctic life, the various exigences of his perilous career had made him habitually cautious; but he was brave, as well as cool and prudent. I never saw in him any manifestation from which it could be inferred that he knew the emotion of fear in the face of danger. He was faithful as a friend, generous as a comrade, but with somewhat of the persistence of a frontierman's recollection of wrongs done to him. His general character; his knowledge of the region; his expertness as a boatman, hunter, and traveller; his acquaintance with the Esquimaux and their language; and his age, which was almost twice that of the oldest officer of the party, all conjoined to unite our suffrages upon him as leader and guide. With his devotion to the interests of our little party, for which he felt himself in a great measure responsible, the reader is already somewhat familiar. It would be impossible, however, for me to do full justice to his constant vigilance, or sufficiently to thank him for his services in the time of our need. It is with pleasure that I render to him now a portion of the tribute which is his due.

There were two things in the world which to him were the embodiment of all that was good and great: these were his native land and his boy. Denmark represented all that could be possibly wished for in a country or a government, and Paul every virtue possible in a son. Hour after hour, during the long winter nights, have I listened to his descriptions of the beauties of Copenhagen, the independent habits of King Frederick, the noble virtues of King Christian, and the glorious memories of his race and people. Many a long walk over desolate plains of ice and snow has been enlivened by his eulogies of the gallantry, intelligence, and beauty of his child.

Such was the man upon whom our faith rested in the crisis the issue of which we were awaiting.*

* Since the above was written Mr. Petersen has returned from a third Arctic voyage, — he having accompanied, as interpreter, the late expedition of Captain M'Clintock.

CHAPTER XXI.

INTERCOURSE WITH THE ESQUIMAUX.

THE three days which followed the departure of one half of our number were the most gloomy and uncomfortable that we had yet experienced. As already observed, the thermometer sank suddenly with the diminished sources of heat, and the mean temperature of the apartment was reduced nearly to zero. The walls and roof became more thickly coated with frost and ice; and by the feeble glimmer of the lamp we could see dense clouds of vapor streaming from our mouths and nostrils. We could not expose ourselves outside of our blankets without mittens on our hands, fur stockings on our feet, and all the clothing on our bodies which would be required for our out-door work.

Our previous routine of duties continued to mark the progress of the days; and the same fortune attended them. The traps were always empty; and we found little moss. The meat which we had obtained from the Esquimaux was nearly all consumed when Petersen left us; and we had only a mere mouthful for each of our two daily meals. Once more we were relying upon the stone-moss; and were, in consequence, growing again weak and sickly. The hours hung wearily on our hands. Our usual joint resources failed us. With our mittened fingers we could not manage the cards which had, heretofore, been one of our sure means of diversion. The circumstances were too depressing for us to feel our ordinary interest in reading aloud, or in listening; and the time was passed mostly in silence. Yet never had I appreciated the value of books as I then did. Bonsall's copy of "Waverley" was an unfailing friend. Upon leaving the brig I had selected from the narrow shelf which held the little library that I had learned to love so well during the last long winter, three small books, which I thrust into my already crowded clothes-bag. They were the before-mentioned volume of Dickens, the "In Memoriam," and a small pocket-Bible; all parting gifts from kind friends to me when leaving home; and all doubly precious, — for themselves, and for the memories which they recalled. They had become thoroughly water-soaked when the Ironsides filled off Cape Alexander; but I had dried them in the sun; and although they were torn, and their backs were loose, there was no part lost. I kept them under my head as helps for a pillow, and for their companionship.

I had brought, beside, two volumes of "Anatomy" and one of "Practice," as the most convenient form in which to carry waste paper for lighting fires. Nearly all of the "Anatomy" had been consumed during the journey down the coast; but I had saved the "nerves" and the "muscles;" and, in retracing the ramifications of the one, and the attachments of the other, I passed cheerfully many an hour that would otherwise have weighed heavily upon me. The "Practice" was now being fast sacrificed; but I got a start of the cooks, and kept ahead of them.

My great luxury during all this time was a short clay pipe, which I smoked almost continually. I had learned so to do, in self-defence, early in the cruise; for, without smoking myself, I found it almost impossible to bear the atmosphere of our tents or snow-houses; and being unwilling to occasion any feeling of restraint among my companions, I fought through the preliminary sickness, and could now smoke crumbled "pig-tail" with the veriest tar on earth.

On the evening of the sixth of November, Mr. Sonntag and John came back to us. Their arrival was most opportune, for we had eaten every ounce of meat which was on hand when they left us. They were brought by two Esquimaux, whose sledges carried a supply of food sufficient to last us for several days. They had a part of two bears' legs, several other small pieces of meat, and a bear's liver. This last the Esquimaux will not eat, but we were glad enough to get it. There were, besides, some pieces of blubber, about two dozens of lumme and burgomaster-gulls, and as many dried auks. All this provision had been purchased for fifty needles and a sheath-knife, — a small price where these implements are abundant, but an exorbitant one in the estimation of our Esquimaux. These native friends were getting to be very Jews in their bargainings. Heaven knows we did not grudge the poor creatures the few paltry things of which they stand so much in need; but, with us, the case was one of life and death; and, by keeping up the price, we prevented the market from being overstocked. A needle was worth to them more than a hundred times its weight in gold. Ours had become quite notorious, and by this time every woman in the tribe had at least one of them. Some of the women had nearly a dozen apiece. They were a wonderful improvement over the coarse bone instruments which they had hitherto used.

Mr. Sonntag and John had a hard journey. The track was rough. High ridges of hummocked ice lay across the mouth of Wolstenholme Sound, and through these they were compelled to pick a tortuous passage. On their way down they were obliged to walk a large portion of the time, because partly of the roughness of the road, and partly of the fact that there were four persons to one sledge. They were quartered in a double hut, one in each division of it, and were treated with great kindness and civility. They returned to us looking hale and hearty, and made our mouths fairly water with glowing descriptions of unstinted feasts. They had been living on the fat of the land, — upon bear, fox, and puppy, the best dishes in the Esquimau larder at this time of year. Yet food was scarce at Akbat, and hence they brought little.

The hunters, who returned with them, remained with us during the night; and next morning, after having received a few trifling presents, they started off to the westward to hunt. I asked them to take Mr. Bonsall and myself, to aid them with our guns, but they refused us. They were going in pursuit of the bear, and must have their sledges as light as possible.

I went down with them to the beach when they started, and I thus obtained a better opportunity than I had hitherto enjoyed of examining the travelling gear and hunting equipment of this singular people.

First, were the dogs. These were picketed, each team separately, on a level space between the pile of rocks below our tent and the shore; and as we approached them from above, they sprang up from the knotted heap in which they had been lying through the night, and greeted us with a wild, savage yell, which died away into a low whine and impatient snarl. They evidently wanted their breakfast, and it seemed to be their masters' intention to gratify them; for, going to their sledges, each one brought up a flat piece of something which looked more like plate-iron than anything else; but which, upon examination, I found to be walrus hide. It was three quarters of an inch thick, and was frozen intensely hard. Throwing it upon the snow a few feet in advance of their respective teams, they drew their knives from their boots and attempted to cut the skin into pieces; but the frost had been more severe than they had counted on, and the dogs seemed likely to come off badly, when, discovering the dilemma, I ran up for our hatchet and saw. With the aid of these instruments they reduced the skin to fragments, which were scattered among the teams, to be scrambled for with a greedy ferocity quite characteristic of an Esquimau dog.

During the ten minutes occupied with this operation the animals had become almost frantic. They tried hard to break loose; pulling on their traces, running back and springing forward, straining and choking themselves until their eyes glared and the foam flew from their mouths. I remembered my experience with two such teams four weeks before, and once more congratulated myself upon having escaped their wolfish fangs. The sight of food had loosened their wild passions, and they seemed to be ready to eat each other. Not a moment passed that two or more of them were not flying at each other's throats, and, clinched together, rolling, tossing, and tumbling over the snow. The masters seemed quite unconcerned, except when one of them would appear to be in danger of being injured, when an angry, nasal "Ay! Ay!" would for a moment restore discipline. A more fierce exhibition of animal passion I think I never saw. When at length the food was thrown to them, they uttered a greedy scream, which was followed by an instant of silence while the pieces were falling, then by a scuffle, and the hard stony chunks were gone. How they were swallowed or digested was to me inexplicable. The animals now became gentle enough, and lay quietly down.

The Esquimau dog is of medium size, squarely built; and, as was observed in a former chapter, is a reclaimed wolf, and exhibits the variety of color which, after a few generations, generally characterizes tame animals. Gray is often seen, and it was probably once the prevailing color. Some of the dogs are black, with white breasts; some are entirely white; others are reddish or yellowish; and indeed, there may be seen among them almost every shade. Their skin is covered with coarse, compact fur, and is greatly prized by the natives for clothing. There is much variety in form, but the general type has a pointed nose, short ears, a cowardly, treacherous eye, and a hanging tail. To this there are some exceptions; and most striking among those that I have seen, was a specimen brought home by Dr. Kane.

This dog, named by the sailors "Toodlamik," shortened into "Toodla," was taken from Upernavik, and survived all the disasters of the cruise to fall, at last, a victim to a Philadelphia summer. His skin, stuffed and set up with lifelike expression, now graces the gallery of the excellent museum of the Philadelphia Academy of Natural Sciences. He differed from his kind in having a more compact head, a less pointed nose, an eye denoting affection and reliance, and an erect, bold, fearless carriage. I must express a doubt, however, as to his purity of blood. From the beginning to the end of the cruise, he was master of all the dogs that were brought to the ship. In this connection it is worthy of remark, that, in every pack, there is one who is master of the whole, — a sort of Major-General; and in each team, one who is master of his comrades, — a General of Brigade. Once master, always master; but the post of honor is gained at the expense of many a lame leg and ghastly wound, and is only held by daily doing battle with rivals. These could easily gain the ascendency in every case, but for their own petty jealousies, which often prevent their union for such a purpose. If a combination does take place and the leader is hopelessly beaten, he is never worth anything afterward; his spirit is gone forever, and the poor fellow pines away and finally dies of a broken heart.

Toodla was a character in his way. He was a tyrant of no mean pretension. He seemed to consider it his especial duty to trounce every dog, great or small, that was added to our pack,— if the animal was a large one, in order, probably, that he might at once be made aware that he had a master; if a small one, in order that the others might hold him in the greater awe. It was sometimes quite amusing to see him leave the ship's side, in pursuit of a strange dog, his head erect, his tail gracefully curled over his back, going slowly and deliberately at his mark, with the confident, defiant air of one who feels his power and the importance of his office. There were often combinations against him, no doubt induced by the very desperate nature of the circumstances; but he always succeeded in breaking the cabal; not, however, I am bound to say, always without assistance; for the sailors, who were very fond of him, sometimes took his part, when he was unusually hard pressed. A brave dog was Toodla!

Leaving the dogs, we went to the sledges to get them ready for starting. While the preparations were being made, I examined one of them minutely. It was, almost without exception, the most ingeniously contrived specimen of the mechanic art that I have ever seen. It was made wholly of bone and leather. The runners, which were square behind and rounded upward in front, and about five feet long, seven inches high, and three fourths of an inch thick, were slabs of bone; not solid, but composed of a number of pieces, of various shapes and sizes, cunningly fitted and tightly lashed together. Some of these were not larger than one's two fingers; some were three or four inches square; others were triangular, the size of one's hand; while others, again, were several inches long and two or three broad. These pieces were all fitted together as neatly as the blocks of a Chinese puzzle. Near their margins were rows of little holes, through which were run strings of seal-skins, by which the blocks were fastened together, making a slab almost as firm as a board.

These bones are flattened and cut into the required shape with stones. The grinding needed to make a single runner must be a work of months; but the construction of an entire new sledge, I was afterwards informed, was unheard of in the present generation. Repairs are made as any part becomes broken or decayed; but a vehicle of this kind is a family heirloom, and is handed down from generation to generation. The origin of some of the Esquimau sledges dates back beyond tradition.

Upon turning over the specimen before me, I found that the runners were shod with ivory from the tusk of the walrus. This also had been ground flat and its corners squared with stones; and it was fastened to the runner by a string which was looped through two counter-sunk holes. This sole was composed of a number of pieces, but the surface was uniform and as smooth as glass.

The runners stood about fourteen inches apart,

and were fastened together by bones, tightly lashed to them. These cross pieces were the femur of the bear, the antlers of the reindeer, and the ribs of the narwhal. Two walrus ribs were lashed, one to the after-end of each runner, for upstanders, and were braced by a piece of reindeer antler, secured across the top.

On this rude yet complicated and difficult contrivance was to be stowed an equally rude equipment. This, such as it was, had been placed under our boat, in security against the dogs in case they should gnaw themselves loose during the night. First, one of the hunters drew out a piece of seal-skin, which he spread over the sledge, and fastened tightly by little strings attached to its margin. On this he placed a small piece of walrus skin, (another meal for the dogs,) a piece of blubber, and another of meat. This last was his lunch; and, although he was bound upon a hunt which might last during several days, it was all that he would get until he should capture fresh provision. If this good fortune should not happen to him, he would not return home until on the eve of starving.

During his absence he would not cook any food; but he would want water. He therefore carried a small stone dish which was his "kotluk" or lamp, a lump of "mannek" or dried moss, to be used for wick, and some willow blossoms (na-owinak) for tinder. These last were carefully wrapped up in a bird-skin to keep them dry. He had also a piece of iron-stone (ujarak-saviminilik) and a small sharp fragment of flint. These were his means for striking a spark.

Let us follow him in his future proceedings: he grows thirsty; he will halt, scrape away the snow until he comes down to the solid ice, in which he will scoop a small cavity. Then he will get a block of fresh ice from a neighboring berg, and, starting his lamp, (using the blubber for fuel,) he will place this block close beside the flame, having previously set the lamp beside the cavity. It is a slow operation; but by and by the water will begin to trickle down into the hole, and when he thinks there is enough melted to satisfy his thirst, he will remove the fixtures, and, kneeling down, will drink the soot-stained fluid. If he grows hungry he will break off some chips from his lump of frozen walrus-beef, and cut a few slices from the blubber, and make of these his uncooked meal; but he will not have any fire to warm himself. No people in the world have less of this than these children of the ice-deserts.

Each of our visitors carries with him an extra pair of boots, another of stockings, (dog-skin,) and another of mittens. These he will use if he should have the misfortune to get on thin ice and break through.

Having placed all the above-mentioned articles upon the sledge, the owner threw over them a piece of bear-skin, which was doubled so that when opened it would be just large enough to keep his body from the snow, if he should wish to lie down to rest. He then drew out a long line, fastened one end of it through a hole in the forward part of one of the runners, ran it across diagonally to the opposite runner, passed it through a hole there, and so on to and fro, from side to side, until he reached the other end of the sledge, where the line was made fast, and the cargo was thus secured against all danger of loss by an upset. He then hung to one **upstander** a coil of heavy line, and to the other a lighter one; and tied them fast with a small string. The former of these coils was his harpoon line for catching walrus, the latter, that for catching seal. His harpoon staff was a heavy piece of ivory, — the horn, or rather tooth, of the narwhal. It was five feet long, two inches in diameter at one end, tapering to a point at the other.

All being ready, the dogs, seven in number, were next brought up, led by their **traces**. The harness on them was no less simple than the cargo they had to draw. It consisted of two doubled strips of bearskin, one of which was placed on either side of the body of the animal, the two being fastened together on the top of the neck and at the breast, thus forming a collar. Thence they passed inside of the dog's fore-legs, and up along the sides to the rump, where the four ends meeting together were fastened to a trace eighteen feet in length. This was connected with the sledge by a line four feet long, the ends of which were attached one to each runner. To the middle of this line was tied a strong string which was run through bone rings at the ends of the traces, and secured by a slipknot, easily untied. This arrangement was to insure safety in bear-hunting. The bear is chased until the sledge is within fifty yards of the prey, when the hunter leans forward and slips the knot, and the dogs, now loose from the sledge, quickly bring the bear to bay. Serious accidents sometimes happen in consequence of the knot getting foul. The hunter tries in vain to untie it, and before he can draw his knife and cut it, (if indeed he should be fortunate enough to have a knife,) man, dogs, sledge and all are among the bear's legs, tangled inextricably, and at the mercy of the infuriated monster.

The dogs were cold and eager to be off. They were hitched to the sledge in a moment; the hunter with his right hand threw out the coils of his long whiplash, with his left he seized an upstander, and pushing the sledge forward a few paces, he at the same moment shrilly sounded the familiar starting-cry "Ka! Ka!" — "Ka! Ka!" which sent the dogs bounding to their places, and dashing down over the rough ice-foot. The hunter guided his sledge among the hummocks, restraining the impetuosity of his team with the nasal "Ay! Ay!" which they well understand. Having reached the smooth ice, he dropped upon the sledge, let fall his whiplash upon the snow to trail after him, shouted "Ka! Ka!" — "Ka! Ka!" to his wolfish team, and was off at a wild gallop.

I watched the sledges from the rocks below the hut until I grew cold. They moved gracefully over the heavy drifts, and wound skilfully among the hummocks. Sometimes they were lost to view for a moment in a valley or behind a wall of broken ice. At length they appeared only as dark specks upon the white horizon. Even when they were almost lost to sight, a cheerful voice reached me through the clear air; and as I turned away, "Ka! Ka!" — "Ka! Ka!" rung in my ears. — Happy, care-defying creatures!

I dropped through the door of our wretched hut; crawled through the dark passage and rolled myself up in my blankets to get warm; half wishing, all the while, that I were a savage; and thinking for the moment how happy I would be to exchange places with the men whom I had just watched. They were going out into the desert, laughing at and defying cold, wind, and storm; caring for nothing, lamenting nothing, fearing nothing; in their own minds, creatures of a predetermined fate.

CHAPTER XXII.

FAILURE OF OUR PLANS.

The Esquimaux left us at eight o'clock in the morning; at one in the afternoon we had made the round of the traps and were all again assembled together. Visiting the traps had by this time become almost a merely mechanical operation, performed with only a vague hope that something might possibly be found; and it was useful chiefly for exercise. So accustomed had we become to disappointment, that we went from trap to trap, re-baiting and re-setting, and often re-constructing them, as if it were a part of our duty to do these things for their own sake, without expectation of reward.

To-day Mr. Sonntag and John rested. Whipple was still unwell, and did not venture out. Stephenson had recovered from his late attack of sickness, and was able to sit up, but not to go abroad. This left now upon the active list only Mr. Bonsall and myself. Bonsall visited the north and I the south traps with the usual fortune.

Upon our return, a cheerful cup of coffee with some tender steaks of young bear's meat, temporarily dispelled the gloom which had for several days reigned in our hut. The temperature of the apartment came *up* to the freezing-point; and we were in the midst of a joyous feast, talking cheerfully of our future prospects, and looking hopefully to the time at which our absent comrades should come back to us, with the wished-for relief, when we were startled by the unmistakable crunch of human footsteps upon the snow.

We listened. A slow and measured tread, which was unaccompanied by any other sound, told us that some one was approaching. Who could it be? The Esquimaux did not so come. Their voices always first announced their presence. I looked around upon the faces of my companions, and read there a confirmation of my own fearful suspicion, — " It must be Petersen!"

Yet it might not be; and, willing to catch at the faintest ray of hope, I hailed in Esquimau, " Kina?" — " Kina-una?" (" Who? — Who's there?") There was no answer save the solemn footfall.

The man, whoever it was, halted close to the hut. A moment, and the sharp creak of the canvas cover over the doorway was heard; then the man dropped through the orifice, uttering a deep moan. I opened the door; and there in the dimly lighted passage lay Petersen. He crawled slowly in; and, staggering across the hut, sank exhausted on the breck. Godfrey was only a few paces behind him, and came in immediately afterward, even more broken. Their first utterance was a cry for " water! — water!"

I asked Petersen, " Are you frozen?" — " No!" — " Godfrey are you?" — " No! but dreadful cold, and almost dead." Poor fellow! he looked so.

They were in no condition to answer questions;

but they rather needed our immediate good offices. Their clothing was stiff, and in front, was coated with ice. From their beards hung great lumps of it; and their hair, eyebrows, and eyelashes were white with the condensed moisture of their breath. We aided them in stripping off their frozen garments; and then rolled them up in their blankets.

Long exposure to the intense cold, fatigue, and hunger, had benumbed their sensibilities; and with the reaction which followed came a corresponding excitement. We gave them to drink of our hot coffee, and this combined with the warmth of the hut soon revived them; but the violence of the change produced a temporary bewilderment of mind, and the sleep which followed was troubled and restless. Their frequent starts, groans, cries, and mutterings, told of the fearful dreams of cold, starvation, thirst, and murder by which they were distressed.

It was not until the following morning that we obtained the full particulars of their journey; but Petersen told us, while he drank his coffee, what it was necessary that we should know at once. They had walked all the way from Netlik, where an attempt had been made to murder them. The Esquimaux were in pursuit, and if not watched would attack our hut.

So the Esquimaux had at length shown their colors! Growing impatient, they had resolved upon getting possession of our property by the shortest means. What could be their scheme? They would surely not venture to attack eight of us, armed as they knew we were with guns; yet it was impossible for us to know how numerous they were, or how much they might rely upon their superiority in this respect. The idea at once suggested itself, that, with a combination of forty or fifty persons, and an effort well directed, they might surprise us; and, dashing in a body from the rocks above upon the slender roof of our hut, they might bury us beneath the ruins, and harpoon us if we should attempt to escape. We did not fear a direct attack.

A watch was accordingly set and kept up during the night. The sentinel was armed with Bonsall's rifle, and was relieved every hour. The remainder of our fire-arms were hung upon their usual pegs, in the passage, having been previously discharged and carefully reloaded. The iron boat was drawn up in front of the hut.

The night wore away. Mr. Petersen and Godfrey awoke, ate again, and fell back into their sleep. The sentry marched to and fro along the level plain, a few rods to the eastward of the hut; and the creak, creak of his footsteps was distinctly heard as he trod over the frozen snow. Inside the hut all was quiet, save now and then a low whisper, the heavy breathing and occasional delirious outcries of the returned travellers, and the noise made by the periodical changing of the watch. Scarcely an eye except those of Petersen and Godfrey was closed in sleep. We were all too busy with our thoughts, and too much agitated by our anxieties.

As I took my turn at the sentry's post, I was impressed with the strangeness of my situation,— keeping guard over the lives of eight poor, starving, shivering men; and against what? Not wild beasts, for in the whole region around there was no evidence of their existence; indeed, it did not seem possible that any such things could live in the desolation about me: not against tempest and storm, for the sky was without a cloud, and the air was hushed in the profoundest silence; but against creatures human like ourselves! As I looked around upon the bleak rocks, and out upon the frozen desert — all wrapt in night and still as death, — and thought of the thronged world at the south; and reflected, that "*here* where men are few, as well as *there* where they are many, the common wants and common sufferings of poor humanity are made to serve the purposes of cruel rivalries and selfish greed," I could not suppress a sigh over the hopelessness of attempting to find anywhere "on earth, peace."

At intervals, during the middle hours of the night, noises were distinctly heard in the direction of Fitzclarence Rock; and although we could not at any time discover the speakers, yet it was evident that we were closely watched. The savages were hovering around us; and, hiding behind the bergs and rocks, along the coast, and down in Booth Bay, were awaiting their opportunity; but they never came within view. They doubtless saw our sentry, and, growing cold with watching, they sneaked homeward. A party went to Booth Bay next morning, and discovered there numerous fresh tracks.

CHAPTER XXIII.

PETERSEN'S ADVENTURES AMONG THE ESQUIMAUX.

WE took the earliest opportunity to get from Mr. Petersen and Godfrey a full account of the journey which had resulted so disastrously to all our hopes.

It will be remembered by the reader, that they left us on the morning of the third of November; and were, therefore, absent four days. They reached Netlik in about nine hours from the time of starting; and were there comfortably quartered, one in each of the two huts. Everything went "merry as the marriage-bell" during the day following; and the travellers were well-fed and well-treated. The very best food was given to them, the choicest cuts of young bear, the most juicy lobes of liver, and the tenderest puppy chops. The hunters all went away early in the morning, as Kalutunah said, to hunt, in order that they might have a better stock of food to leave with their families, as well as to take on the journey to the brig. This excuse for delay seemed reasonable enough.

Very few of them however came back at the close of the day; and of those who did return, Kalutunah was not one.

The next day passed, and still he did not show himself. Petersen grew uneasy. The moon was one day past its full, and there was no time to lose. Everything else which happened was calculated to inspire him with confidence. Many hunters came in, mostly strangers to the settlement; and all was bustle and activity. Sledges were coming and going continually; dogs were howling, snarling, and fighting; some of the women were running to and fro, between their huts and their stone houses, or rather their stone meat-graves; others were actively sewing boots and mittens. Petersen flattered himself that he was to have a caravan in earnest, and that the whole tribe was to accompany him.

Kalutunah did not return until toward the evening of the sixth. He was accompanied by several sledges; and among the drivers was a man named "Sip-su." This fellow had been at our hut. He was the largest and best built man of the tribe that we had seen; but his face wore a fierce expression, foreign to the countenances of his companions. While they always appeared to be in a good-humor, ever laughing and gay, he was seldom seen even to smile; and on all occasions he maintained the most dignified reserve. A few stiff hairs growing on his lip and chin, coupled with an unusually heavy pair of eyebrows, heightened the savage effect of his face. Sip-su was a genuine barbarian.

He made it his boast that he had killed two men, members of his own tribe. They were unsuccessful hunters; and, being a burden upon his people, he took it upon himself to rid the settlement of the nuisance. He waylaid them among the hummocks, and mercilessly harpooned them.

There were now collected together about a dozen sledges, and the huts were crowded with people. Petersen's patience was, by this time, well-nigh exhausted; but he knew that the Esquimaux usually do their work in their own way. He had made up his mind that they intended to go in the morning; but as the moon was very bright he thought that he might venture an attempt to hasten the departure by a few hours; but, to his surprise, his request was answered with a surly statement that they did not wish to go with him at all, and that they had never had any intention to go. At this announcement the people in the hut laughed heartily.

This was too much for human patience; and Petersen demanded, with something of indignation in his tone, to know what they meant by thus cheating him with false promises; but they deigned no other reply, than that they could not pass Cape Alexander, — as they called it, "the blowing place."

All these proceedings, so different from anything that he had before seen, were calculated to excite suspicion that they foreboded mischief; but Petersen was not a man to be frightened at shadows. He went at once over to the other hut, and telling Godfrey what had happened, cautioned him to be on his guard. He then returned, resolved to put on a bold front and to make a strong effort. As he came into the hut its inmates set up a fiendish laugh. This excited less his fear than his anger. He told them that they were a set of lying knaves;

and that, if they did not keep their promises, his people would come with their guns and kill them all, and destroy their dwellings. His threats were, however, thrown away, for they only laughed the more.

Seeing all his schemes thus imperilled, he demanded that they should sell him a team of dogs, since they had more than they wanted, — he would pay them well. No direct answer was made to this demand; but Sip-su put to Kalutunah a question, which was, in effect, "Don't you think we can get his things in a cheaper way?"

Petersen no longer doubted as to their evil intentions toward him, more especially as they all importuned him to lie down and sleep. He knew, however, that they were of opinion that he carried, somewhere about his person, a pistol; and he felt confident that he could use this opinion as a talisman to keep him from harm, at least for a time. They thought, indeed, that each one of the white men carried one of these instruments; and having seen some of their marvellous effects on former occasions, they had settled down into the belief that they were magical wands, with which the "Kablunet" thrust danger aside. This idea we had always endeavored to strengthen; and, although Petersen had no pistol about him at this time, yet, as the Esquimaux did not know the fact, he might rely upon their fears.

He had left his rifle outside; for, if brought into the hut the moisture of the warm air would be condensed by the cold iron, and the powder being thereby dampened, the weapon would not be serviceable. In order to keep the natives from handling it, he had told them that the instant they touched it they would be killed; and thus far his warning had been respected.

How long he would be able to hold these imaginary terrors over them, he did not know; but he was determined to push the matter just far enough to find out, if possible, what was the nature of the conspiracy which he had reason to believe was directed, not only against Godfrey and himself, but also against their comrades at Booth Bay.

He accordingly seated himself carelessly upon the breck. His whole demeanor thus far had been such, that none of his suspicions were revealed; and he felt that they looked upon him as a cat looks upon a wounded mouse, with only the difference that he must be disarmed. This task was undertaken by Sip-su. Satisfied that this was their object in trying to get him to lie down, he threw himself upon the breck and feigned asleep. This procedure required presence of mind; but it did not seem to him to augment greatly his risks, since he knew that they would hardly venture to attack him until they had exhausted all their arts in endeavoring to get the pistol which they supposed him to carry.

The Esquimaux, like many other people, find it difficult to keep their tongues tied, or to practice prudence; and scarcely had Petersen shown the first symptom of being asleep before all their voices broke loose at once, and in an instant the story was told. Men and women, boys and girls, were discussing it. Petersen and Godfrey were to be killed on the spot, and the hut at Tessuisak (Booth Bay) was to be surprised before Mr. Sonntag and John could return from Akbat. In both cases Sip-su was to lead the assault, and Kalutunah was to act as his second in command.

Sip-su was just beginning to put into execution the first part of the plan of operations, by instituting a search for Petersen's pistol, when Godfrey came to the window and hallooed to his chief, to know if he was alive. He was satisfied, from what he had seen and heard in the other hut, that foul play was intended.

Petersen awoke from his sham sleep, and, having exchanged words with Godfrey, made some excuse and went out. He found a crowd of men, women, and boys around his rifle. It was fortunate that he had impressed upon them the idea that it was dangerous to touch it. Seeing them assembled about the gun, he called to them to know why they were not afraid to go so near; and they all withdrew.

Having secured his rifle, he told them that he intended to go in hunt of bears (Nannook); and drawing from his pocket a handful of balls, he remarked, as he dropped them one by one into his other hand, that each of them was sufficient to kill a bear, or a man, or any other animal. They would have persuaded him to stay; but he had already had enough of their treachery, and he resolved to walk to Booth Bay. This, although a dangerous experiment, was clearly more safe than to remain.

Conscious that their guilty intentions were rightly interpreted, the Esquimaux clustered around him, declaring, with suspicious eagerness, that they "would not hurt him," that "nobody meant him any harm."

It was late when, with Godfrey, he started toward our party. The night was clear and calm, but the cold was terribly intense. At our hut the temperature was forty-two degrees below zero. The distance to be travelled by them would have been, by the most direct line, forty miles; but more nearly fifty by the crooked path which they must follow. Even the three days of feasting at the Esquimau settlement had not restored the physical strength of which they had been deprived by their course of life at the hut; and, reduced as they were in flesh, it seemed to them scarcely probable that they could make the exertion necessary to enable them to rejoin us.

The Esquimaux sullenly watched them from the shore as they moved off; and when they had gone about two miles, the former hitched their teams, and, leaving the settlement, were soon in full pursuit. The wild, savage cries of the men, and the sharp snarl of the dogs, sounded upon the ears of our poor comrades like a death-knell. In their previous anxieties, they had not looked forward to this new danger. The ice-plain was everywhere smooth; there was not in sight, for their encouragement, a single hummock behind which they might hope to shelter themselves.

On came the noisy pack, — half a hundred wolfish dogs. Against such an onset, what could be done by two weak men, armed with a single rifle? The dogs and the harpoons of their drivers must soon finish the murderous work. Petersen was, however, resolved that Sip-su or Kalutunah should pay the penalty of his treachery, if at any moment within range of the rifle. At this stage of desperate expectation, the sledges, at the distance of about half a mile from the fugitives, suddenly turned to the right, and were driven seaward.

It was now evident that the Esquimaux were not bold enough to meet the chances of an encounter, in which one of them must become a victim of the dreaded rifle; and consequently, that in an open field there was no reason to fear their close assault; but it might be their intention to lie in wait among the hummocks or behind a berg, and thus to gain the advantage of an ambush. The rough ice was therefore avoided as much as possible by the travellers, although by this course their journey was seriously prolonged. Still, it was not always practicable to keep away from the hummocks; and Petersen's sufferings were augmented by the exposure of his hand, which he was obliged frequently to bare, in order to be prepared to use his rifle at any moment of need. Whatever the purpose of the savages, however, they did not show themselves.

Upon reaching Cape Parry, both Petersen and Godfrey were so far exhausted that they could scarcely walk; and there remained nearly one half of their journey to be accomplished. At times they felt drowsy, and almost lost consciousness; but to halt would in all probability be fatal to them. Sustaining each other, they slowly and steadily continued down the coast.

The morning twilight at length appeared in the southeast; and after weary, painful hours, the sun's rays, shooting from beneath the horizon, showed them that noon had arrived; yet there still lay miles between them and the hut. Benumbed by cold, exhausted by fatigue and hunger, and parched by thirst, they might have yielded to despair; but their faces were toward the south; the warm hues of the sky re-inspired them with thoughts of home, and these brought hope and courage to their hearts.

After an uninterrupted walk of twenty-four hours, their heroic energy triumphed. I have already told the reader of their sad condition when they came upon us in the night.

CHAPTER XXIV.

SUPPLIES OBTAINED WHEN LEAST EXPECTED.

November 8th. WE built, this day, a wall in front of our hut. The blocks, of which it was composed, were cut with our little saw from a solidified snow-drift.

As the wall had a degree of resemblance to a military defence, our poor snow residence bore somewhat the aspect of a baby fort. Bonsall called it Fort Desolation; John grumblingly declared that Fort Starvation would sound much better.

The hut and the locality had already several names. The Esquimaux called it "Tessuisak," meaning "The place where there is a bay." Those which our people gave it from time to time, some seriously, some playfully, express the fluctuations of our spirits. We christened it "Hopes Checked," when we were first driven ashore. "The Wanderer's Home" followed soon afterward, when the Esquimaux began to come to us. When they stopped with us more frequently, on their way to and fro between Netlik and Akbat, we changed it to "The Half-Way House." Once, when we were talking of home, and the hut was warm and cheerful, and we were praising our country and our country's great men, we named our dwelling "The

Everett House." Then, again, we had bright dreams of moving on in our course, when the spring-time should return, and the sun should come to gladden the eye and to guide us southward, and we called the place " Hopes Deferred." " Desolation " and " Starvation " were fitting names with which to close the series, for we really seemed now to be at the lowest ebb of our fortunes. We were at the end of our plans, and, in two days more, we should be at the end of our provisions. We saw nothing further.

We were destitute — helpless. The only human beings within three hundred miles were seeking our lives. Of what value, now, was the question, *What shall we do?* The damp and chilly air; the blackened embers on the hearth; the frost-coated rafters overhead; the ice-covered walls around; the feeble flicker of our lamp, going out for want of fuel; the almost empty shelf, where we kept our food, — all took up the question for us, and sent to our hearts the scarce unwelcome answer, " Die! " — Why not? Life was not then of so much worth that we should plot and plan to save it, when all its purposes had been destroyed, — Upernavik, Cape York, the whalers, all were beyond our reach.

The reader will readily appreciate our condition at this time, morally, as well as physically, better than I can describe it. We had been so long hoping almost against hope; so long living in a state of uncertainty, neither being able to die, nor yet foreseeing how we should live; so often tortured almost to starvation by that mocking substitute for food, *stone-moss;* and now we were at last so beset by crafty savages that our feelings very naturally, and perhaps not inexcusably, assumed somewhat the character of recklessness. Yet in our calmer moments we felt that we were not forsaken. More than once succor had come to us when we had least reason to expect it, and we could not deny ourselves the satisfaction of believing that it was sent to us by the direction of a higher than human hand.

We labored diligently, during the 8th and 9th, to get our hut in a condition to guard us against the possibility of surprise by the Esquimaux, for whom a sharp look-out was incessantly kept. We also set to work again to gather stone-moss.

The sun was now so far beneath the horizon that we had twilight at noonday; and, at that time, stars of the first and second magnitudes were seen dimly twinkling in the gray sky.

The wall which we built about our hut was intended as a protection more against the wind than against the Esquimaux; for even the least breath of air, at the low temperature then prevailing, made it impossible for a sentry to hold his place upon the plain. Inside of this wall were brought the last remains of the Hope, which hitherto had lain, half buried in the drift, down by the beach. The pieces were broken into convenient size; and were buried under the loose snow. We also secured our tent.

November 10*th*. Again the Esquimaux appear to us more as our good angels than as our enemies. Under extraordinary temptation, and, doubtless, at the evil instigation of a bad leader, these poor savages had proposed the death of Petersen and his companion; but this day two of them, Kalutunah and another hunter, came to us, and threw at our feet a large piece of walrus-beef and a piece of liver. The latter was not yet frozen; and the animal from which it was taken had, therefore, been recently caught.

We were talking about them, in no spirit of love, when they arrived; and, as they came up the hill, various were the expressions of opinion as to what ought to be done with them. One said that we should detain them, and hold them as hostages until their people should have performed their promises; and that their dogs should be seized, and used in the interval; but, apart from any consideration of justice, such a proceeding would scarcely have been safe. Another hinted that fourteen dogs would save us from starvation; for, if we should not succeed with them in the hunt, we could kill and eat them. Again, apart from any question how far our necessities overruled the old law of *meum* and *tuum*, it was certain that such a step, whatever its immediate advantages, would bring us ultimately into open, and probably, to our party, fatal hostility with the entire tribe. Perhaps, as the present of food seemed to indicate, we had not exhausted all of our means of negotiation; and, until driven to the last resort, we could not justifiably use the strong hand upon our neighbors' property. Great allowances were obviously to be made for the tribe, upon whom we had no claims except upon grounds of humanity too general for their uninstructed minds. The success or failure of our schemes could be of no consequence to them; and there remained no principle upon which to sustain the seizure of the men and teams, unless it should be one which would warrant this act as a measure of precaution for our present safety, which was not in peril from the visitors; or as a measure of confiscation and bodily punishment, which we were not in a position to enforce.

At first Kalutunah was shy; and he brought his harpoon into the hut with him, which he had never before done. Although evidently relying mainly upon his gifts and smiles to conciliate us, he was yet unwilling to trust himself unarmed in our midst. Desirous to reassure him, we gave to him presents, and jested with him as though our relations were undisturbed; but although apparently his apprehensions were greatly relieved, he did not for a moment lay aside his harpoon. After remaining an hour he left us at about nine o'clock, and dashed off seaward upon the ice, on a moonlight hunt for bears.

Petersen spent the day in making knives for the Esquimaux, in order to be prepared for the amicable relations which seemed about to be reëstablished, and for the promotion of our endeavors to obtain a team of dogs. The knives were made of hoop-iron, a relic of our kegs. The pattern was that of an ordinary sheath or butcher's knife. The handle was of wood from the keel of the Hope, and copper nails from the same source furnished the rivets. Through the skill of the workman the result was very creditable, although his only tools were an old file, one end of which was used as a punch, a hatchet, a small saw, and a pocket-knife.

November 11*th.* There came to us this day, with four sledges, six Esquimaux, of whom three were residents of Akbat. They were all on their way to Netlik. One of them was our old friend of sentimental memory, the widow, who carried, as usual, a bundle of frozen birds under her arm. She was as voluble as ever, had much to tell, and many questions to ask. We were compelled to cry with her only once.

All of the visitors were at first shy; which proved that if they had not shared the late conspiracy, it was, at least, known to them. Finding themselves, however, treated in the accustomed manner, they were soon at their ease. Each of them had brought something for barter; and in a short time there was piled in one corner of our hut such a supply of food and fuel as we had not seen for many a long day. The aggregate was about one hundred pounds, of which three fourths were flesh. We had walrus, bear, seal, and birds; and with economy this store would be sufficient for us during five or six days. But one meal was necessarily devoted to our guests, who consumed as much as would have served ourselves during one third of that time. We witnessed most reluctantly such excess of indulgence at our expense; but it would have been no less impolitic than uncivil to check it.

At the end of three hours the party set off northward, apparently well pleased with the share which they had received of our riches; but they would not sell any dogs.

November 12*th.* Esquimaux are coming from every quarter, and are flying about in every direction. We have a new arrival from Northumberland Island, — a man whom we have not before seen. He appeared at about noon, and added to our stores a walrus flipper, about fifty little auks, and some pieces of blubber. In return, he demanded a staff for a harpoon, a knife, and three needles. He is the first of these people who has not stipulated for payment upon delivery of his goods.

Regard to our health and strength induced us to profit by this sudden accession to our stock of provisions; and we ate three substantial meals: a degree of luxury which we had not enjoyed since leaving Rensselaer Harbor.

Our new friend, named Kingiktok, (the Rock,) is a sober, civil fellow, who says very little except when questioned. We fancied him immediately, and sought his friendly confidence by the gift of a few needles for his wife, a pocket-knife for his son, and a whipstock for himself. As if to express his gratitude he said that he was our friend. This he repeated several times with so peculiar an emphasis, that we began to doubt whether his object was to cover a treacherous purpose, or to intimate that he desired to distinguish himself from others who were hostile to us, and whose inimical designs he could disclose. Petersen, who had not previously given much attention to him, now endeavored to elicit from him whatever information he was disposed to impart; and thus we obtained the statement that himself and his brother Amalatok (with whom the reader has already been made acquainted on page 104), were the only persons in the whole tribe who were not hostile to us. No circumstance of this communication surprised us as much as, that an Esquimau should be the bearer of it.

To enable the reader to see more of the workings of the uncivilized people with whom we were in contact, I will give briefly a part of what we learned from Kingiktok.

The wife of his brother Amalatok is believed by the tribe to be a witch, a reputation which is not belied by her looks. What has caused this stigma upon her, Kingiktok refused to tell; but he said that she had been condemned to death, and that Sip-su had declared himself her executioner.

The style of execution in vogue, is not more creditable to the tribe than it is comfortable for the victim. The executioner awaits an opportunity, creeps behind a lump of ice, and plants his harpoon in the back of the condemned, when the latter is least expecting it. The prospect of such a fate for Mrs. Amalatok, added to the reproach cast upon her, had naturally aroused the watchfulness and vindictiveness of her lord and his brother, who were not altogether without courage. Their national habits had trained them to the vigilance and readiness needful to such an exigence. Feuds are apparently, in many cases, not only irreconcilable between the original parties, but hereditary. Forgiveness of injuries is certainly not a virtue which stands very high in their estimation; and thus it happens that the lying in wait for an adversary is a long established practice, upon which the settlement of private quarrels must often depend. Unfortunately for Amalatok and his brother, and for the witch-wife, who watches for herself as closely as she is watched,

Sip-su carries with him the voices of the greater number of his tribe; and, consequently, the brothers never venture to sleep in the villages; though visits are interchanged with the inhabitants, who do not hesitate to call at the hut of Amalatok on their way to the outer hunting-grounds. On all such occasions the parties are very civil to each other, and the visitors are hospitably feasted.

An Esquimau seems to have a repugnance to killing even an enemy, unless he can do it by stealth. I have often been amazed that these men should have the courage to attack, with their slender harpoons, the huge and fierce polar bear; and yet that, according to their standard, Amalatok and Sip-su, who feared to meet each other in open fight, but sought every day to take a mean advantage of each other, were far from being cowards.

The feud with Sip-su unlocked the speech of Kingiktok, who told us that, from the beginning, the former had done all that he could to persuade the tribe that the white men were unable to catch the bear, the walrus, and the seal; and that, if left to their fate, they must die; in which case the tribe would get all their wood and iron. This view of the case was for a time opposed by Kalutunah, who insisted that the white men could kill anything with their *auleit* (guns) or *boom*, as they more commonly called our weapons, in imitation of the sound made by their discharge. The public judgment, however, sided with Sip-su; and, accordingly, the Esquimaux waited and waited, and were surprised upon visiting our hut, to find us alive. They grew impatient; but their jealousies interfered in our behalf. When Kalutunah returned from us with a new harpoon, a whipstock and a knife, and some needles for his wife, domestic rivalry stimulated the visits of others of the village. Provisions came to us, and prizes were carried off. Kalutunah himself was determined not to be outdone, as he plumed himself not only upon his reputation as a hunter, but also upon his equipment which, in fact, was the best we had seen. Thus this rivalry fed us.

Sip-su continued to abstain from this competition, until his wife, envious of her neighbors, left him no alternative but domestic rupture; to avoid which he condescended to make a visit to us. He brought, however, only a trifling supply, for which he demanded a large price; and as we could make no distinctions without disturbing our standards of trade, he carried home with him only a single needle and a very small piece of wood. He had yielded his principle and his dignity, and had gained no thanks from his wife. It is not to be supposed that his previous inclinations respecting us were rendered more amiable.

When Petersen fell into the hands of the Esquimaux, Kalutunah went to inform his rival, Sip-su, who lived near Cape Robertson, at Karsooit, which was fifty miles away. It was this journey which occasioned the delay already mentioned. In the mean time, the news was spread by other hunters, and there was a general assemblage of the people. A plan was arranged substantially, as recorded in a previous chapter; but Sip-su was timid in the presence of the magical "auleit;" and he deferred the execution of his design, until it was frustrated by the awakened suspicions of our comrades. Incensed at their escape, the disappointed savage led the pursuit, with the hope of setting the dogs upon them; but again his courage failed at the critical moment.

With every allowance due to the inventions and exaggerations of an enemy, we found this narrative too nearly in accordance with the results of Petersen's observations to admit of our doubting its substantial truth.

From Kalutunah we had received numerous benefits and manifestations of friendliness; and it is on that account gratifying to know that when he concurred with others for our destruction, he yielded only to what was to him extraordinary temptation. He was young in authority; the majority of his people were against him; his rival had the popular side; and it might even have seemed a duty to secure to the tribe, at what he was accustomed to regard as a trifling price, the vast treasure of wood, iron, and needles possessed by strangers of another race, between whom and himself there was no formally recognized tie but that of interest.

The time, we hope, is not very remote, when, through the fraternal aid of Christian men, he and his benighted kindred shall learn not only to encourage the feeble virtues which they now possess, but also to resist successfully the promptings of those savage passions of which we had so perilous a demonstration. Perhaps in the diplomacy and the wars of civilized people, there may be found motives for looking charitably upon the wrong-doings of the ignorant and undisciplined Esquimaux.

CHAPTER XXV.

GOOD CHEER.

KINGIKTOK left us early the following morning; and in the evening eleven other members of the tribe came up from Akbat, on their way to Netlik. This was the most lively as well as the largest party that had yet visited us. Kalutunah was one of the number, and was as good-natured and voluble as usual. He brought to us the quarter of a young bear, and received in payment one of Petersen's hoop-iron knives; but the shrewd fellow had learned to distinguish iron from steel; and he did not seem to prize his present very highly. He had before seen one of this kind of knives; and, having used it in trying to chip off some kernels from a piece of frozen liver, he had bent the instrument double. He at once suspected the quality of our gift. He tried to cut with it, but the result was not satisfactory. He then deliberately bent it in the form of a letter U; and, throwing it on the ground, he pronounced it, with a characteristic grunt of indignation, "no good." He was contented when we gave him a piece of wood with which to patch his sledge.

The bear's leg, which we thus added to our stores, was Kalutunah's share of a hunt from which the people of Akbat had returned the day before. Kalutunah was a guest on the occasion, and, as such, was entitled, by Esquimau rule, to the choice of pieces when the animal was caught.

Our visitors were four men, three women, and four children. Two of the women were the two widows who have previously figured in this narrative. Each of them was accompanied by a child, — one of whom was about four, and the other about three years old. The latter belonged to the sentimental widow; and its name, being interpreted, signifies " a mother's only child." The mother's fondness for this stay of her old age, was quite touching; but it took much from the poetry of the scene when we saw her strip off its furs and turn it loose to root among our bedding, with the accumulated blubber and soot of three years sticking to its skin.

One of the hunters had with him his wife and two children. He was " moving;" and he carried all of his domestic utensils, together with his entire family, upon his sledge. The utensils were not very complicated. He was going to Netlik, where he intended temporarily to quarter in Kalutunah's hut, if he should find room there; and, if not, in a snow-house. One of his children was a girl three or four years of age, the other a boy of about seven. He informed us that one had died not long before, of a disease which, from his description, I judged to be pneumonia, — a very common and very fatal complaint among the Esquimaux in the spring and autumn.

Our hut was very much crowded, there being nineteen persons within it; but we made it a point never to turn strangers away from our door. Kalutunah said, on his arrival, that his party could build a snow-hut and sleep in it; but this we would not permit them to do.

Two Esquimau lamps were burning cheerily all the evening; two Esquimau pots hung over them, suspended each from a rafter, and sent up wreaths of warm steam; and our own lamp was for two hours in full blast in the fireplace. These together made much heat; and, added to this, we had the warmth given off by our nineteen bodies. The result was to elevate the temperature from 29° to 60°. The hut was warmer than it had ever been before; but it was, altogether, less pleasant than when the temperature was below the freezing-point. When the thermometer stood at 28°, we were most comfortable. We had grown so used to low temperatures that 60° was much too warm for us; but this was, in itself, a comparatively trifling discomfort. The air had become very impure. We had no ventilation except through our small chimney, which, although sufficient to purify the atmosphere on ordinary occasions, was now quite inadequate for that purpose. To make matters worse there was a general thaw. The frost overhead melted, and, after hanging in long rows of soot-stained beads on the under side of the rafters, fell, drop by drop, into our faces and upon our clothing. A clammy sweat covered the walls, and here and there trickled to the ground in spasmodic streamlets. We ought to have called the place Fort Misery, — for it was a miserable place at the best of times.

At eight o'clock in the evening the interior of our hut presented an unusually cheerful scene.

We were in the midst of a plentiful feast; this time not at our expense, — at least, not at the expense of our provision stores. Kalutunah had brought in a huge chunk of walrus-meat — a flipper weighing in the neighborhood of fifty pounds. It was frozen hard, and was covered with snow. He threw it on the floor in the middle of the hut; and, around it, were soon grouped the inmates. On the edge of the brecks two women had installed themselves, — one on each side of the door. These were watching their lamps and kettles. By the side of each lay a cake of frozen snow; from which, from time to time, for the last hour, she had been breaking off pieces and depositing them in her kettle, — melting them into water for her people to drink. Having satisfied their thirst, she then attempted to heat the portion which remained. This she could not boil by the feeble flame of her lamp, but she had its temperature, in a little while, elevated to about 190°, which would answer to cook with. The hunters splintered off, with our hatchet, some pieces of meat, and passed them to the women, through whose management they were soon stewing finely, and smelling lusciously. Kalutunah was very fond of soup; and the sentimental widow was doing her best to gratify his taste. The woman who attended to the other pot was in like manner serving her lord who sat near her.

If the reader will follow me into the hut he will see there a succession of *tableaux* which may be novel to him. The two above-mentioned hunters sit facing each other, and facing the lump of frozen beef, which lies upon the ground. Kalutunah has the sentimental widow at his left, and the other hunter has his wife at his right. Godfrey kneels in front of the fireplace, attending to our lamps, which burn there. He is cooking some coffee, and frying some steaks of bear-ham. The hum of the kettle and the crackle of the blubber in the pan are cheerful sounds. Petersen sits in his corner by the stove. He looks very demure; and, although he talks nearly all the time, it is easy to see that he is doing it against his will, and that he would much prefer to be quiet. The Esquimaux are continually asking questions, and he has to answer for all of us; and since he has found that the Esquimaux will not sell us any dogs, nor go to the ship, nor hire their teams to us for that purpose, he is not inclined to be communicative with them. The children are crawling about over the brecks; the rest of us are mixed up indiscriminately, white men and red men; some sitting on the edge of the breck; some lying at full length upon it; all leisurely eating; — leisurely, I say, for the meat is so icy that it is chipped off with difficulty, and we obtain it only in little crisp pieces which make the teeth fairly ache with cold. The writer of this sits behind Kalutunah, from whom he receives alternate mouthfuls.

An hour later and the soup has been drunk; the coffee has passed around; the stew and the fry have disappeared; but the feast is far from ended. Scarcely an impression has yet been made upon the walrus flipper; but the warmth of the hut has partially thawed it, and the knives penetrate it more readily, and strips can be cut off. These now fly about in all directions. Everybody has one. The strip may be three inches, or it may be a foot in length; its width two inches, and its thickness one inch. The feeder takes one end of it in his mouth, and seizing, between his teeth, a convenient portion, he cuts it off close to his lips, and then swallows it as quickly as possible, and repeats the process. Having taken two or three bites of meat he then takes one of blubber. The red men have taught the white men how to flourish the knife, and what is the proper motion to insure safety to the lips. The walrus-meat is very juicy, and is also very dark. The faces and hands of all of us are covered with blood; and but for the beards on the faces of some of us, it would be difficult to distinguish the civilized men from the savages. The children have each a strip of beef and blubber, and are disposing of these equally with the best of us. The seven-year-old stands with his back against the post, straddling across one corner of the flipper, rapidly shortening a slice which his father has given him. His body is naked to the waist, as indeed are the bodies of all our guests. His face and his hands are red with the thick fluid which he squeezes from the spongy meat, and which streams down his arms, and drops from his chin upon his distended abdomen, over the hemispherical surface of which it courses, leaving crimson stains behind.

Still an hour later and there is nothing left upon the floor but a well-picked bone; and we have wiped our hands with the bird-skins which the widow has torn from the lumme of which she has made her supper. As usual, she had her feast alone; and with little assistance she has consumed six birds, each as large as a young pullet.

We have now established the most friendly relations. When does not good cheer make good spirits? Mr. Sonntag sits behind me; and, true to his profession, is questioning one of the hunters about their astronomy. Godfrey is amusing the women and children with a negro song, keeping time with an imaginary banjo. I am seated beside Kalutunah, and we are teaching each other scraps of our widely different languages. Bonsall is at my side, looking on, and helping. I try to get the savage to articulate YES and NO, and to teach him of what Esquimau words they are equivalents. He pronounces "ees" and "noe," after several efforts, and says, inquiringly, "tyma?" (right?). I nod my head and say "tyma," to encourage him; whereupon he laughs heartily at my bad pronunciation of his word.

We make an effort to count. He gets "*une*" for ONE, and an immensely hard "*too*" for TWO; but he cannot manage the *th*, of THREE. In return he teaches me to count in his language. I cannot quite pronounce as he does; but he pats me on the back in a very encouraging manner, as much as to say "well done," and repeats "tyma" to me over and over again. We go on through the series with much laughing and many tymas; with thumps on my back from him, and from me reproachful punches in his ribs, and encouraging twitches of his left ear; until, at length, we have reached ten. His people do not count further, and Petersen tells me that any number beyond ten, whether much or little, is called by a general name.

Sonntag's investigations in astronomy show some curious results. He and Petersen have been asking questions about the sun, moon, and stars. It appears that these heavenly bodies are spirits of departed Esquimaux, or of some of the lower animals. The sun and moon are brother and sister. The story of their origin is this:—

In a distant country there once lived an unmarried woman who had several brothers. Being once at a festive gathering, she felt herself suddenly and violently seized by the shoulders. This she well knew was a declaration of love, for such is the custom of her people; but who the man was she could not discover, since the hut was quite dark. There being to her knowledge no men in the village, beside her brothers, she at once suspected that it must be one of these. She broke from him, and, running away, smeared her hand with soot and oil. Upon returning to the hut she was seized again, and this time she blackened one side of the face of her unknown lover. A lighted taper being brought soon afterward, her suspicions were confirmed. She then cut off her breasts, and, throwing them at him, exclaimed "if thou holdest rightly eat that." Seizing the taper she now ran out of the hut, and bounded over the rocks with the fleetness of a deer. Her brother lighted a taper and pursued her, but his light soon went out, yet he still continued the chase, and, without having overtaken her, they came to the end of the earth. Determined not to be caught, the girl then sprang out into the heavens. Her brother followed her; but he stumbled while in the act of springing, and, before he could recover himself, the object of his pursuit was far away from him. Still bent upon gaining the prize, he continued the race; and, from that time until this, the sun has been going around and around, and the moon around and around after her trying still to catch her. The bright light of the sun is caused by the taper which the maiden carries; while the moon, having lost his taper, is cold, and could not be seen but for his sister's light. One side of his face, being smeared with soot, is therefore black, while the other side is clean; and he turns one side or the other towards the earth as suits his pleasure.

That cluster of stars in "Ursa Major," which we designate as "the dipper," they call a herd of "*took-took*," (reindeer). The stars of "Orion's belt," seen far away in the south, are seal-hunters who have lost their way. The "Pleiades" are a pack of dogs in pursuit of a bear. Other clusters and other stars have other names. The *aurora borealis* is caused by the spirits at play with one another. Rain is the overflowing of the heavenly lakes on the ever-green banks of which live the happy spirits who have taken up their abode in the skies, where sunshine and summer are eternal. These happy spirits have abundance to eat without the trouble of catching it.

The Esquimaux are close observers of the movements of the stars. We went out toward midnight to look after the dogs, and Petersen asked Kalutunah when his party intended to go. He pointed to a star which stood almost directly over Saunders Island, in the south; and, carrying his finger around to the west, he pointed to another star, saying, "when that star gets where that one is we will start."

Our guests being tired, we fitted up for them such accommodations as were within our power, and they were soon asleep. With so many to provide for we were obliged to remit somewhat of our fastidiousness; yet we would not allow them to touch the inside of our blankets; nor could we lie down with them; and we therefore passed the night awake, solaced by an extra cup of coffee, and a fresh supply from Bonsall's tobacco-box. Refreshed by our recent meal, and encouraged by the sight of materials upon the shelf for a dozen more, we experienced new life and resolution.

CHAPTER XXVI.

FURTHER PLANS.

I TAKE up the narrative again on the 16th of November. Two eventless days have passed since the Esquimaux left us. We have in the interval grown much stronger. Our daily ration per man has been about two pounds. This has not been sufficient to satisfy our appetites, which have craved vegetable food; but it is ample to sustain us in health, and to slowly recuperate our lost energies.

The absence of all vegetable food is a source of suffering to us which can hardly be appreciated by those who have not had a somewhat similar experience. Our stomachs, hitherto used to a more bulky diet, do not readily become accustomed to the new order of things; so that, while eating enough for health and strength, we are always hungry.

The natives live upon an exclusively animal diet; but they consume it in larger quantities than could be afforded by us. Their daily allowance of food I should estimate at from twelve to fifteen pounds; about one third of it being fat, — the blubber mainly of the walrus, the seal, and the narwhal. In times of plenty, they eat more than that quantity; in times of scarcity, less. Being exceedingly improvident, and having rarely stores reserved sufficient to supply them during two weeks, they are often in want. At such times, however, it must be conceded that they exhibit a commendable spirit of cheerfulness and philosophical resignation; and when they are again successful in the hunt, they make up for lost time by a series of stupefying feasts. I have seen an Esquimau, upon returning from a long and exposed hunt, or when about to commence a difficult journey, eat at a single meal, prolonged through several hours, fully ten pounds of walrus-flesh and blubber.

It is in his generally large consumption of food that the Esquimau hunter finds his shield against the cold. I do not believe that he could live upon a vegetable diet. Taste, with the pleasures which it brings, has very little to do with his meal; and he takes food through his capacious jaws with much the same passiveness as that of a locomotive when receiving coal from the shovel of a fireman; and the cases are parallel. In the latter, the carbonaceous coal is burned up in the furnace to make heat, to make steam to start the wheels. In the former, the carbonaceous blubber and flesh are burned up in the lungs to make heat, to make steam, to start the hunt. Feed the locomotive on willow-twigs, and on a frosty morning it will be very likely to cease its operations; feed the Esquimau hunter on wheat bread or maccaroni, and he will quickly freeze to death.

The same laws govern the Esquimaux and the white men; and exposed as we were to temperatures so low, living chiefly in an atmosphere varying from zero to the freezing-point, and subjected during a part of the day to a temperature ranging from zero to sixty degrees below it, we found ourselves continually craving a strong animal diet, and especially fatty substances. The blubber of the walrus, the seal, and the narwhal was always grateful to us; and in its frozen condition it was far from unpleasant to the taste. I have frequently seen members of the party drink the contents of our oil-kettle with evident relish. One of our number was especially notorious for his depredations in this quarter; and, as the manufacture of oil from blubber was attended with the consumption of an amount of fuel which we could ill spare, we were compelled to pass a formal vote, guarding the oil-kettle by excluding it from the *cuisine*.

At the time of which I write we were all in good health, except Stephenson; and his troubles were not immediately caused by our mode of life, although they were greatly aggravated thereby. I have explained in a former chapter that his disease, which was a functional derangement of the heart, (pericardial effusion,) was originally the result of repeated attacks of scurvy, from which he suffered while on board the Advance. Although the cause was entirely removed, the return of its unpleasant consequences was from time to time threatened; sometimes with fearful results. The remaining members of the party had all, like him, been more or less affected by the scurvy while on shipboard; but every trace of the disease had by this time disappeared from our systems, and we were in as good condition as men could well be who were living so irregularly; subsisting upon a diet varying so much from week to week and from day to day in quantity and quality.

In view of this fact, I think I hazard nothing in saying, that probably no climate in the world has less tendency to develop scurvy than that of the Arctic regions, provided that the proper kind of food is used by the residents in it. This food must be chiefly animal, largely fat, abundant in quantity, and mainly free from salt. The Esquimaux are exempt from the disease, although they disregard all of our ordinary hygienic laws; and I am satisfied that, with our present knowledge and experience, scurvy need not be the formidable scourge which it was in former times, — if, indeed, it need be known at all on board of vessels wintering in the Arctic seas. Altogether the climate is one of remarkable healthfulness; for, were it otherwise, living as we did in our close hut, we must have been attacked by disease.

Our newly acquired physical energies fitted us for again attempting something, either for the success of our southern scheme, or for our deliverance. Petersen again proposed to renew the attempt to go to the ship, provided that we could obtain a team of dogs. His plan was, to start when the moon should have returned, and, avoiding Netlik, go directly to Northumberland Island, where there was reason to believe Kingiktok or Amalatok would join him; thence proceeding northward, with all dispatch, he would reach the Advance, and return before the moon should have set. He would need one companion, and would go well armed; and he thought that he could make the journey to and fro in twelve days. His proposition was favorably received, and Bonsall's offer to accompany him was accepted. There were several reasons to make this satisfactory; the most prominent being the facts that he was, Petersen perhaps excepted, the most hardy man of the party; and that, to as great a degree as any member of it, he possessed those necessary qualities for such an emergency,— courage, caution, and energy.

An old man whom we had not before seen, arrived the next day, from one of the settlements far up Whale Sound. He brought us a small addition to our store of provisions; and he received from us some presents. He had been hunting bears, and had a long story to tell, which he did with the usual accompaniment of violent gesticulation, about his having followed the track of a Nanooksoak (large bear) down into Booth Bay, where he lost it on account of the darkness. He asked to be allowed to remain until it grew lighter, when he would continue the pursuit. The request was of course granted; and, having given him a supper, which, as to quantity, is best described by saying that it was an Esquimau one, we put him to bed.

This man was the only member of the tribe that I had seen who possessed what could properly be called a beard. He had upon his chin and upper lip a respectable growth of hairs, which were silvered with age. They probably did not show themselves until long after the man had arrived at years of maturity; for the faces of the young men, and indeed of the greater number of the middle-aged who visited us, were as innocent of beard as a woman's.

Shunghu (for such was the name of our visitor) had scarcely fallen asleep, when there was another arrival — a man, a woman, and a child. The man called himself "Tattarat," (Kittywake-gull;) he came from Imnanak (Cape York), and was moving northward with his family. He told us that the people of Akbat, and the only family besides his own then living at his settlement, were preparing to do likewise. This was in consequence of the failure of the southern hunting-grounds. The sea to the westward of Cape York was completely closed; and the unusual severity of the season was likely to render a residence south of Netlik, during the winter, extremely hazardous. They had not, for many years, known such a winter. It had set in a "half-moon" earlier than usual. This report confirmed our own conclusions, and our residence at Booth Bay was clearly the result of this freak of nature. Had the season remained open two weeks longer, we should, in all probability, have reached Upernavik!

The favorite hunting-grounds of the Esquimaux of this coast, are about Cape Alexander; at which place, and immediately south, southwest, and west of it, the sea is always more or less free from ice. When the distance from their permanent residences, such as Netlik, Akbat, &c., to this water, becomes inconveniently great, in consequence of the gradual widening of the land-belt, they move up toward this cape, and camp in snow-houses, which they build at some eligible spot upon the land, or upon the ice, within a few hours travel of the usual resorts of game. It does not often happen that they are compelled to do this; although for the sake of the interchange of friendly greetings, the inhabitants of the southern settlements generally move northward for a short portion of the winter season. They return before the ice breaks up, and while they can still travel.

This early moving up from Cape York looked unpromising for us, and the **knowledge** of the fact did much to shake our faith in the practicability of our resolution to go thither.

Our visitors remained with us through the night; and, at eight o'clock next morning, at which time there was a little increase of light, they went out in search of the bear whose tracks Shunghu had discovered the evening before. They returned, unsuccessful, after an absence of about two hours. A light wind had covered the tracks with **drift**.

We now made a proposal for the purchase of dogs; but for a time we despaired of having better fortune than on former occasions. At length, the exhibition of an old harpoon and Bonsall's shining hunting-knife was effective, and the hunters promptly offered, each, two dogs. Tattarat received the harpoon, and Shunghu the knife, and both parties were well pleased with the bargain. Tattarat would have sold us another animal, but he had only four left, and had a heavily laden sledge to drag to Netlik. Shunghu also would have disposed of two more, but the remainder of the team belonged to his son, and he could not part with any of them without first consulting the boy. Our visitors left us at noon.

The history of the next few days will have little interest for the reader, except as it points to our future plans and proceedings, and I therefore resort again to the more condensed diary form.

November 19*th*. A southerly gale kept us within doors this day. The wind was accompanied by light squalls of snow and heavy drift. The outside temperature reached as high as twelve degrees below zero; and a sensible effect was soon produced upon the atmosphere of the hut.

Petersen commenced the manufacture of a sledge for his contemplated journey; such of us as could, helping him.

The dogs did not seem to be satisfied with their change of quarters. They were howling piteously all day, and trying to break loose. We fed them on walrus-hide.

November 20*th*. The sledge was nearly finished this evening. The runners were made of the thwarts of the Hope, and the cross-pieces of wood from the same source. There remains only to put soles on the runners, and to lash the whole together. This last is the work of an hour, and is not required immediately. The soles involve greater difficulty; we have nothing suitable for them. Hoop-iron and a piece of moderately hard wood are all that can be made available.

We are again getting short of provisions, and look anxiously for the Esquimaux.

November 21*st*. Breakfasted on our last piece of walrus-beef. Petersen brought from the traps a fox which served us for supper. This was a piece of unlooked-for good fortune, for we had given up all hope of getting anything from that source. Stephenson, who has been cheered and comforted by our tea, received to-day the last of it.

November 22*d.* Light snow and a southerly wind. The thermometer stands outside of the hut at zero, and inside of it at 40°. The temperature has been gradually rising during the past three days.

Toward evening it began to snow violently, and soon afterward a furious gale howled across the ice-fields. The wind brought in an unusually high flood-tide, which, together with the increased warmth, indicate the existence of a large body of open water not far away.

We had for breakfast this day one bird, which was cut into four pieces. The half of one of these would scarcely give a mouthful to each person, so we tossed up for the quarters. The unlucky four contented themselves with their coffee. Another unexpected fox furnished us a supper.

November 23*d.* Breakfasted this morning on a soup made of some rejected bones. Afterward the traps were visited, but there was no fox to-day.

The snow was knee-deep over the plain, and the traps were filled with drift. It was a tedious task to put them in order again. This cold work gave us an appetite to attack a piece of spoiled meat, which some cunning savage had palmed upon us for fresh. Being frozen, its condition did not affect our olfactories; and its bad taste was partially destroyed by some citric acid, a small vial of which I had brought with me, to use, if occasion required, as an antiscorbutic.

November 24*th.* Breakfasted on a cup of coffee. Later in the day we boiled together some blubber and stone-moss, which made us all sick.

In the afternoon two Esquimau hunters arrived from Akbat. We bought of them three birds, upon which we supped. They had nothing else upon their sleds. They would not sell any dogs, and they remained but a short time. One of them said that he had a sledge at home which he would gladly trade for ours, and promised to return with it the following day; but we have become so well accustomed to Esquimau promises that we have very little faith in them.

Petersen shod, with some strips of hard wood, the runners which he had made.

CHAPTER XXVII.

PREPARATIONS FOR ABANDONING THE HUT.

The reader will fail to appreciate the events which have been narrated, and the apparently shifting purposes of our party, unless he recalls from time to time the motives and circumstances which were explained in the opening chapter of this history. After full deliberation, and with the advice of the person most experienced in arctic ice, we had set out in the belief that the separation of the brig's company was important to the preservation of its members. To secure the main object of our journey we had constantly striven; and our hope was not suffered to relax while there remained apparent the slightest possibility of its accomplishment. When forced to think of replenishing our stores from the brig, in which there was abundance of salt food for her entire company, we still avoided a re-union of the parties, trusting to our ability to complete the execution of our principal design. It was no time for judgment upon the abstract prudence of such ventures as we were making. Our undertaking was, from its first step, confessedly a desperate one, the result of desperate circumstances; and it must be prosecuted while we could flatter ourselves with the least ray of promise on the side of its ultimate success. We promoted every favorable suggestion, keeping up our spirits by mutual encouragement, until perseverance ceased to be justifiable.

During the progress of Petersen's labors upon the sledge, we reviewed our means of judgment; and endeavoring of course to avoid the extreme of rashness, we estimated anew the force of the various considerations proper to our situation. We were entirely out of food, and the movements of the Esquimaux warned us of harder times coming. When we arranged our plans for going to Cape York, we had relied for assistance upon the natives at that place; but they had now all gone away, or were about to go. The conclusion was forced upon us, that we could not winter at Booth Bay; and this last resort failing, we were compelled to accept the consequence, that our ultimate object was hopeless. A return to the brig upon one side — inevitable death upon the other — were now, beyond all question, the only alternatives.

The return to our comrades at Rensselaer Harbor was first proposed while we were picking bones for breakfast on the 23d; and the wisdom of that proposal was confirmed in our minds next morning, when it was discussed over our coffee, and moss and blubber soup.

Our plan was to set out as soon as the moon should give light enough to guide us on the way, it being now almost as dark at noon-day as at midnight. We would obtain two more dogs, thus completing a team of six, which it was thought would readily drag our sledge laden with the very trifling cargo required, and with Stephenson who was unable to walk. We would make directly for Northumberland Island, stopping once on the way and camping in a snow-house. For each person, therefore, a pair of blankets would be needed.

This plan was of course to take precedence of that previously arranged, by which Petersen and Bonsall were to be the principal actors; but, like that, its execution was dependent upon the Esquimaux. We could do nothing without more dogs.

Preparations for departure were immediately commenced. That all of us would live to reach Rensselaer Harbor seemed highly improbable; yet there was some comfort in looking forward to a struggle which would relieve us from our present uncertainty, and speedily decide our fortunes.

Our real wants were many; but it is scarcely necessary to say that these could be only meagrely supplied. Our clothing was wholly insufficient for such a journey as was contemplated. Only three of our number possessed complete suits of fur. Each of us had, fortunately, a coat or "Jumper" as we called it, (the Esquimau hooded Kapetak,) of seal or reindeer-pelts; and three of us had pantaloons of the same material; but the pantaloons of the other five were of cloth or canvas, now well worn. Only skin clothing is adequate to resist the intense cold and piercing winds of the arctic deserts.

We had no effective resource but our buffalo robes. It will be remembered by the reader that when we first took up our quarters in the hut, these were spread upon the "brecks;" and there they had remained ever since. For nearly two months they had served as a thin pad to cover the stones and gravel on which we slept. To these they were found to be in places tightly frozen; and their edges were glued by ice to the walls, so that it was not without some difficulty that they were removed. We were obliged to cut away several kettles full of ice before they would let go their hold upon the stones. This ice was formed by the vapor which had been condensed upon the walls, and which, melting from time to time as the temperature of the hut became elevated, trickled down to a lower and colder level where it was again frozen. A large lump had thus accumulated close behind Mr. Bonsall, and one corner of his blanket had become imbedded in it. We called it by way of distinction, "Bonsall's glacier." We had also a "Petersen's glacier," and a "John's glacier." Petersen's was at his feet, and John's was at his head.

When taken up, the robes were found to be coated on the under-side with frost, in consequence of which many pebbles adhered to them. It was, therefore, necessary to suspend them from the rafters for a few hours before they were in a suitable condition to be worked upon.

We slept now with two thicknesses of blanket between our bodies and the stones and pebbles, and we were not much benefited or refreshed thereby.

The "buffaloes" being partially dried, we commenced our tailoring operations on the twenty-fifth, after a breakfast of strong coffee. John was master-workman. The skins were spread over a breck, and he cut out the garments after a style peculiarly his own, — a mixture of the fashions which prevail at Paris and at Netlik. The pieces as they were cut out were taken by different members of the party, and we were all soon engaged, with "palm and needle," sewing up the seams of stockings, pantaloons, and mittens. It was cold work, but we should not so much have minded this had we not been gnawed by a merciless hunger.

Three of the party whose education in this department of useful art had been sadly neglected, were put under the tutorage of Petersen. One of these got on well enough, for he had had a little previous experience; but the two others had a sorry time of it. If their fingers had not been so stiff and benumbed they would, doubtless, have succeeded better; but, as it was, they could never get the awkward "palm" in proper contact with the but-end of the needle; in consequence of which the latter frequently slipped from its thimble, and made ugly holes in their hands. By common consent, a less difficult task was assigned to them, that of scorching coffee for the journey. As the browned beans were poured out of the saucepan, they were ground in a canvas bag by pounding with the hatchet.

As the temperature of our hut was 25°, the sewers were often obliged to stop in their work, and strike their hands upon their backs to maintain the requisite degree of suppleness.

Coffee was now even a greater luxury to us than it had been before; and we drank it from time to time through the day. Fortunately we had plenty of it; and now that we were about to abandon the hut, much more than we should need. It had all been well soaked in the sea, and was a little brackish; but we had become used to that. It did much to supply the place of food; and, although possessing no nutritive qualities itself, yet its well-known power of arresting the wasting processes of the animal economy, aided greatly to support our strength. Its stimulating qualities were also useful. Our experience at this period convinces me that, to men living on short allowance of food, in a cold climate, where special stimuli are required, there is nothing as valuable as coffee. To arctic travellers, spirits, in any form, are in almost every case worse than useless; while coffee is always grateful, and always beneficial.

At the close of our first day's tailoring we supped on walrus-hide fried in oil. Before retiring to rest Petersen astonished us by producing from his bag a "ship's biscuit," which he divided into eight parts, giving one to each of us. It was chiefly useful in reviving past recollections, and in exhibiting a characteristic trait of our kind-hearted guide. It softened the expression of more than one very long and very wrinkled face; and Petersen was, by acclamation, voted a "good fellow." The biscuit was the half of a daily allowance, in times when such evidences of civilization were less strange to us than now.

Next morning, for breakfast, we boiled, instead of frying, our walrus-hide, and found the process a decided gain over the latter method. The skin was from a half to three quarters of an inch thick, and tough beyond conception. To chew it was quite impossible; and in order to eat it we were obliged to cut it into thin slices, like chipped beef, and swallow it as we best could. It was heavy food.

Shortly after the completion of this wretched meal, four sledges, with four hunters, five women, and seven children, arrived from Akbat. The children were of all ages and sizes, from the babe at the breast to a chattering girl of fourteen years. Our hut was more crowded than it had ever been before, there being in all twenty-two persons, having five square feet to each. We could not all have lain down at one time. The annoyance of packing we could easily pardon, for we obtained from the party four dozens of lumme, a few pieces of dried seal meat, and some strips of dried seal intestine imperfectly cleansed. Better almost than the food were two dogs, which we purchased of the party. We had now a team of six.

These Esquimaux were moving northward. One of the hunters was the old man from Cape York, of whom Tattarat had spoken; the others were of Akbat, at which place only two families now remained. They told us that the hunting-grounds at the south were closed up; that they were on their way first to Netlik; and that thence they would probably continue up the coast toward Peteravik, a place which we understood from their account to be near Cape Alexander. The young hunter who promised us the sledge was one of the number; but he had changed his mind. Being afterward further questioned, it turned out that he owned no sledge at all, and that even the one which he drove was borrowed!

Much to our gratification our visitors remained only a few hours. The women and children, however, took a short nap; and all partook of a hearty meal before setting out on their journey.

The four hunters came back next day. It was at once evident that they were bent on mischief; for they not only attempted every moment to pilfer from us, but they seemed glad when they discovered that they were annoying us. Soon after their arrival there came another party from the south. These also were moving; and they entered at once into the spirit of mischief which possessed their predecessors. Among the last arrivals was a very ugly and disagreeable woman whose thieving propensities exceeded anything of the sort that we had yet seen. Nothing was too small to escape her notice; and upon going down to her sledge when her party were about to leave, we found a most heterogeneous collection of odds and ends, most of which seemed to be of no possible use. Prior to this we had missed two of our tin drinking-cups. She was charged with the theft; but she strenuously denied having taken them, until we threatened to search her sledge, when she ran off and brought them to us; and, as if for a peace-offering she threw at our feet three birds. She had evidently, with her woman's instinct, penetrated our special weakness. We were always open to bribes of that sort.

The whole party became at length so troublesome that we were compelled to drive them away, in order that we might get on with our preparations; for we were **losing** much valuable time. They did not, however, leave us; but they continued to hover in the vicinity. We suspected them of designs upon our dogs; two of which it will be remembered we had purchased of them on their former visit. Our first four purchases had become reconciled to their new quarters; but the last two seemed to prefer going with the teams to which they had belonged. They tried hard to break loose; and this their owners seemed to be doing all they could to encourage. A watch was accordingly set, and kept up until all was quiet; when our sentry, believing that the rogues had gone, came inside. No sooner was he within the door than the dogs set up a cry, and in an instant footsteps were heard. We rushed out as quickly as possible, but not in time to save both of the dogs. One of them and his captor were bounding away. Luckily for the man he was almost immediately hidden by the rocks; for Bonsall's English rifle was going quickly out at the door-way, and in a moment more an ounce ball and the thief would have had a race for speed. The Esquimau ideas of honesty are of the Spartan order. They never steal from one another; but he is the best fellow who can contrive to take most from the pale-faces.

Everything was ready by the evening of the 28th; but the sky had looked threatening all day, and a storm fell upon us a little before midnight, the time we had fixed upon for starting.

The air **became** calm on the following day; and, as soon as we were satisfied that the storm was broken, we began our final preparations. Our equipment consisted of eight blankets, our field lamp and kettle, two tin drinking-cups, ten days' coffee rations, a small bag of blubber, (about eight pounds,) and another bag containing two days' food. This last was two dozens of birds which had been previously boiled, boned, and cut into small pieces. These were now frozen into a solid lump. We had no more. Our expectation was to reach in two days Northumberland Island, and there to obtain fresh supplies.

In consequence of the severity of the cold, the sled was lashed together in the hut, and then taken out through a hole cut for the purpose in the roof. A few minutes sufficed for the packing, and our five dogs were then harnessed. Stephenson was assisted out of the hut, and down over the rough ice-foot to the smooth field, where he took the place assigned to him on the top of the cargo. Then slowly and silently we moved away from the scene of so many days of weary waiting, suffering, and disappointment.

CHAPTER XXVIII.

DARKNESS AHEAD!

OUR movements were like those of men returning from a long journey rather than beginning one. The insufficient food upon which we had been subsisting during the last few days, had so much reduced us that, at the end of the first hour, many of us were more fatigued than we had been, on former occasions of similar labor, at the end of a day. Our progress, slow at the beginning, became slower every moment. The exercise did not warm us as it had done when we were in more vigorous health; and we grew chilly in spite of our exertions. Face, hands, and feet seemed to be pierced by a multitude of torturing needles. The frost penetrated our bodies as if they had been inanimate; and the blood which coursed through our veins felt almost as if it were half congealed. Against the intense cold our imperfect clothing offered a very inadequate shield. The thermometer, when we left the hut, indicated forty-four degrees below zero. The air was fortunately quite calm; and the moon, shining with an intensity which it can exhibit only in an arctic atmosphere, gave us sufficient light. The snow-crowned mountains of Northumberland Island were dimly visible above the northern horizon. These were the distant, uninviting landmarks towards which our steps were directed.

We should have made much better headway had we possessed a better sledge. The wooden sole was so rough and soft, and made therefore so much friction, that the dogs could not drag the load without our assistance. Having no ropes with which to attach ourselves, we took turns, two at a time, at pushing against the upstanders.

In this manner we had made about eight miles when Stephenson, seeing the difficulty which beset us, insisted on being allowed to dismount and walk. This it did not seem possible that he could do, and his request was not granted; but shortly after, when not observed, he rolled from the sledge, and declared that if he could not walk he would go no farther. I raised him up, and gave him the support of my arm. We proceeded thus together for about a mile, when he suddenly fell by my side and fainted away.

We were at the moment close beside a small iceberg, which, on its eastern side, was hollowed out in the form of a crescent. Across in front, from wing to wing, lay a heavy snow-drift inclosing a small area. Into this protected place we carried our sick comrade; and, after wrapping him in our blankets, we built about him a rude shelter with blocks of snow, which were cut from the hard drift. Godfrey started the lamp to cook for him some coffee. He did not speak for several minutes. His first words were: " Leave me and save yourselves. I can never reach the ship, and had better die at once."

We were in a dilemma. Go on without Stephenson we would not; and go on with him it seemed that we could not. What should we do?

The difficulty resolved itself. Although we had not made, on this our first march, more than one half of the distance we expected, being only half way to Cape Parry, and less than one fourth of the way to Northumberland Island, yet we were all thoroughly exhausted; and without rest it did not seem possible that we could go much farther. We determined, therefore, to camp; and accordingly such a snow shelter was constructed as, on former occasions of similar exposure, we had found to afford a safe protection; but we soon discovered that we could prevent ourselves from freezing only by constant activity.

It was clear that we must move on; for to run about with the view of keeping warm, or rather I should say, with the view of keeping alive, would be only to wear ourselves out without accomplishing anything in the direction of our purpose.

I proposed to my comrades that Stephenson should be left in my care. I would undertake to get him back to the hut; and would rely upon their reaching Northumberland Island, and sending supplies to us, through our friends Amalatok or Kingiktok. The necessity for the adoption of such a course was evident, if the journey was to be continued; and I was anxious, at whatever hazard, to avoid turning the party back. I saw nothing better for poor Stephenson, and at the same time for the success of our undertaking.

My proposal had scarcely been made before the party declared, that, with even the reduced cargo, it would be impossible ever to reach Northumberland Island without rest; and rest it was clear could not be obtained in the interval. In view of this fact it was decided, without much delay, that we should return in a body to the hut, and fall back upon our original plan of sending Petersen and Bonsall with the sledge. Several of us were already severely nipped by the frost; and all felt themselves to be losing rapidly what little strength they had.

The cargo was re-stowed; the invalid, wrapped in blankets, was placed upon it; and our melancholy faces were turned southward, toward our only shelter. Poor as this refuge had always been, it was now worse than ever. A pile of frozen sods and snow was heaped upon the floor, and the cold air was streaming in through the orifice from which these had been taken.

We reached it — how or when I doubt if any one of us distinctly remembers. I have often tried to bring to recollection some phenomenon which would indicate the period of the day. I cannot even remember the direction of the shadows which our bodies cast upon the moon-lit snow. I know that we did not all arrive together. As we moved slowly forward, first one, and then another, and another of the party fell behind; and it was at least an hour after the sledge had reached the hut before the last one, no longer able to stand upright, came crawling over the plain, upon his hands and knees. More than one of us thus finished the journey; and it has always appeared to me as a remarkable exhibition of the instinct of life that we toiled on in our stupefied unconsciousness even of danger. Stephenson's fainting fit evidently saved us; for, had we gone two miles farther and then turned back, or had we still gone forward, there was perhaps not one of us who would not, unconscious of the risk, have stopped by the way for a short nap, through which he would have passed into the sleep which knows no waking.

We had just sense enough left to enable us to appreciate each other's wants, and to give assistance, the stronger to the weaker; to close up temporarily the hole in the roof; to carry in our frosted blankets, and to spread them upon the breck underneath those which we had left behind. We knew when we awoke next day that these things had been done; but none of us retained more than the most vague impression as to the manner of their execution. The intense cold, operating upon our feeble and overtaxed bodies, had made wild work with our mental faculties.

We lay down in the darkness; and, through hours uncounted, slept and shivered away the effects of our unfortunate journey.

When we awoke we had lost our reckoning. Whether it was the first or the second day of December we could not agree; but, since the majority were in favor of the first, it was so declared. The stars told us the time of day. It was nearly noon.

Although stiffened and sore with the cold and our severe exertions, we were rejoiced to find that none of us were seriously injured by the frost. I had slightly frozen both my hands and feet while engaged in trying to restore life to Stephenson. We were very hungry; and, above all, feverish and thirsty. Our first duty was to make a fire and melt some water. The little that we had left in the kettle was of course now frozen into a solid lump.

Fire was not produced without difficulty and serious alarm. The person to whom had been intrusted the box containing our tinder, brimstone matches, and flint and steel, had no recollection of the place where he had put them. Godfrey had used them at the berg where we camped, but what had become of them since, no one could tell. That the box was out upon the ice, seemed highly probable. I do not remember to have heard, at any other time, such expressions of despair as followed the dawning of this conviction. We had nothing else with which to make a spark, for it was hopeless to think of producing such a result at so low a temperature by the friction of two pieces of wood. Our alarm was, however, unnecessary; for the box was found upon the floor. Some one struck it with his foot, and we knew it by its rattle. Godfrey now remembered having rolled it up in the blankets when we stowed the sledge, and it had fallen unnoticed upon the ground when these were brought inside the hut.

The lamp was soon lighted; and, having collected together the few remaining splinters of the Hope, we made a fire, and for breakfast cooked some strong coffee, and warmed one half of what remained of the provision which we had taken with us on our journey. The other half was reserved for Petersen and Bonsall, who left us immediately after our repast was finished. I went with them down to the beach in company with Mr. Sonntag; and, after bidding them God-speed, watched them as they moved slowly up the coast. They both walked at first; but after they had gone about a mile one of them dropped upon the sledge. Soon afterward they were hidden from view behind the hummocks; and I turned toward the hut with Petersen's last words ringing in my ears: "If we ever reach the ship we will come back to you, or perish in the attempt, as sure as there is a God in heaven."

If they ever reached the ship!

The four following days were the most wretched of our hut-life. We could not elevate the temperature above zero. The roof could not be made as tight as it was before. We had not strength enough to remove the pile of sods and snow which lay in the middle of the floor. We were, during the greater part of the time, in darkness, not having oil sufficient to keep our lamp burning more than two hours of each day. The wood of the Hope was all consumed, and we had no fuel but the thwarts of the Ironsides. Our food was walrus-hide.

There was not, in such a place, under such circumstances, much to encourage hope; and the travellers were scarcely out of sight before all manner of speculations, respecting their probable fate and ours, were passing from mouth to mouth. One was fearful that they would be waylaid by the Esquimaux; another thought that they would freeze on their way to Northumberland; and all were agreed that, if they should reach the brig, there was scarcely a probability that they would be able to return; and from what the Esquimaux had told us, and from what we had every reason to expect, the party who had remained in the vessel must be too much broken down by scurvy to send us aid. For my own part I could give little substantial encouragement to anybody, for the reason that I could find little for myself. Even if our two comrades should return to us, should we be alive to profit by their devotion? Yet we were still six living men, and there was the old proverb.

The traps were visited as they had been formerly, and on the second day after the departure of the sledge Mr. Sonntag brought in a fox, which he had found dead in one of them. This trap was one of the farthest from the hut, and not having been visited before during several days, the animal had frozen. Its skin was torn from it in an instant, and it was devoured before it was half cooked.

We grew weaker each day. Happily, Stephenson improved. Although, like the rest of us, he lost strength, yet he had less palpitation of the heart; and he recovered so far as to be able to move about.

The pieces of young walrus-skin which we had been using for food were consumed on the third day; and we were forced to resort to some scraps of old hide, which were so tough that they could scarcely be cut, and on this account had been rejected by our dogs.

The traps were examined in the afternoon, but this time there was no fox.

On the day after, the fourth since our friends had left us, I made as much of the circuit as my strength would permit, and with the same fortune. I reached the spot where, with Petersen and Bonsall, I had, a few weeks before, talked of our homes in the south, and schemed for our deliverance; but the sun was no longer in sight to warm the sky, and to put a glow into my heart. The moon had usurped his place; and her silver face seemed to reflect nothing but the coldness of the ice-fields which lay beneath her.

I looked on every side with a yearning for something outward to lighten the heavy weight which oppressed my spirits; for darker times, and times of greater responsibility, I knew were near at hand; but desolation and the silence of death were everywhere around me; and better than ever before, better probably than ever again, I felt what it was to depend upon one's self and God.

Then came a reaction which will be readily understood by the intelligent reader. I arose from the rock upon which I had been seated, and again fixed my eyes upon the sea. The stern silence which had been almost maddening, became now a source of inspiration. In the reflux of thought which followed, I forgot the cold moon, the leaden stars, the frowning cliffs, the desolate waste, the chilly glacier; forgot my loneliness; and I was back again in the world of life and power and action. The frozen sea grew into a fertile plain; the hummocked ridges were resolved into walls and hedges; and a southern panorama of sunny fields spread itself before me. A crack which meandered to the southwest, which had recently opened with the tide, and from which were curling up wreaths of " frost-smoke," favored the illusion. Clusters of little hummocks suggested herds of cattle and flocks of sheep. Larger masses were converted into trees; and a long bank of snow, whose vertical wall threw a dark shadow on the plain, was the margin of a dense forest. Farther away, a pinnacled berg became a church with spire and belfry; another wore the appearance of a ruined castle; while still farther to the southwest, where the stream seemed to discharge itself into the ocean, stood a giant fort, under whose bristling guns lay a fleet of stately ships.

Around all that I saw were clustered home associations, and objects which, years before, had suggested to my boyish mind the serious purposes of life; and I turned away with renewed strength to fight the battle through, and with renewed determination to behold again those scenes which my imagination had grouped together on the desolate sea.

CHAPTER XXIX.

PLOTS AND COUNTER-PLOTS.

I HAD not returned from my walk more than two hours, before three Esquimau hunters, with as many sledges, arrived from Netlik. One of them was Kalutunah. Their visit seemed to have been prompted by curiosity, for they brought nothing to trade; and they came into the hut with only two small pieces of meat, which were scarcely more than sufficient to furnish to themselves a moderate meal. One of these pieces was appropriated without ceremony to the use of our party, notwithstanding that the proceeding was protested against by the hunters, with a multitude of sullen "Na! na! na-miks!" Men in our condition were not likely to be deterred by a mere verbal negative. An equivalent for the meat was afterward given to them, and they appeared to be satisfied. Both pieces were soon cooking.

I now repeated to Kalutunah a request which had been made on previous occasions, viz: that his people should take us upon their sledges and carry us northward to the Oomeaksoak. His answer was the same as it had been hitherto. It was then proposed to him and his companions that they should hire to us their teams; but this also they declined to do. No offers which we could make seemed to produce the slightest impression upon them; and it was clear that nothing would induce them to comply with our wishes, nor even to give us any reason for their refusal. In fact they thoroughly understood our situation; and we now entertained no doubt that they had made up their minds, with a unanimity which at an earlier period seemed improbable, to abandon us to our fate and to profit by it. In this view we were confirmed by a discovery which one of our men made upon going down to their sledges. They had brought with them several large pieces of bear and walrus meat, which they were evidently determined that we should not obtain; and to insure this they had buried the pieces in the snow. For this procedure they might well have had motives which it was not for us to question; for example, provisions might be scarce at their settlement. Upon inquiring of Kalutunah if such was the case, he informed us that they had, the day before, captured a bear, three seals, and a walrus. They had, then, plenty, and could not possibly have been actuated by the necessary selfish prudence which I had in charity attributed to them.

The question to be decided became a very plain one. Here were six civilized men, who had no resort for the preservation of their lives, their usefulness, and the happiness of their families, except in the aid of sledges and teams which the savage owners obstinately refused to sell or to hire. The expectation of seizing, after we should have starved or frozen to death, our remaining effects, was the only motive of the refusal. The savages were within easy reach of their friends, and could suffer little by a short delay of their return. For their property compensation could be made after our arrival at the brig. For my own part, before attempting to negotiate with Kalutunah, I had determined that his party should not escape us in case of failure in our application to them for aid.

My comrades were not behind me in their inclinations. Indeed, it is to their credit that in so desperate an extremity, they were willing to restrain themselves from measures of a kind to give us, at the time, far less trouble than those which I suggested. Being unwilling that any unnecessary harm should come to the Esquimaux, I proposed to put them to sleep with opium; then, taking possession of their dogs and sledges, to push northward as rapidly as possible; and leaving them to awaken at their leisure, to stop for a few hours of rest among our friends at Northumberland Island; then to make directly for Cape Alexander, with the hope of getting so far the start of Kalutunah and his companions, that before they could arrive at Netlik and spread the alarm, we should be beyond their reach.

This plan met with the unanimous sanction of the party; and we prepared to put it into immediate execution.

In the way of this there were some difficulties. Our guests were manifesting great uneasiness, and a decided disinclination to remain. Many threatening glances and very few kind words had been bestowed upon them; and they were evidently beginning to feel that they were not in a safe place.

It became now our first duty to reassure them; and accordingly, the angry looks gave place to friendly smiles. The old, familiar habits of our people were resumed. Many presents were given to them. I tore the remaining pictures from my "Anatomy," and the picture of the poor foot-sore boy who wanted washing, from "Copperfield," and gave them to Kalutunah for his children. Such pieces of wood as remained to us, were distributed amongst them. Each received a comb. This last they had sometimes seen us use, and they proceeded immediately to comb out their matted hair, or rather, to attempt that work; but forty years of neglect, blubber, and filth had so glued their locks together, that there was no possibility of getting a comb through them. The jests excited by these attempts to imitate our practices did more to restore confidence than anything else.

At length was reached the climax of our hospitalities. The stew which we had been preparing for our guests was ready, and was placed before them; and they were soon greedily devouring it. This proceeding was watched by us with mingled anxiety and satisfaction; for, while the pot was over the fire, I had turned into it, unobserved, the contents of a small vial of laudanum. The soup of course contained the larger part of the opium; but being small in quantity it had been made so bitter that they would not eat more than the half of it. In order to prevent either of them from getting an overdose we divided the fluid into three equal portions; and then with intense interest awaited the result, apprehensive that the narcotic had not been administered in sufficiently large quantity to insure the desired effect.

After an interval of painful watchfulness on the part of my companions, the hunters began to droop their eyelids, and asked to be allowed to lie down and sleep. We were not long in granting their wish, and never before had we manifested more kindly dispositions toward them. We assisted them in taking off their coats and boots, and then wrapped them up in our blankets, about which we were no longer fastidious.

Our guests were in a few minutes asleep; but I did not know how much of their drowsiness was due to fatigue, (for they had been hunting,) and how much to the opium; nor were we by any means assured that their sleep was sound; for they exhibited signs of restlessness which greatly alarmed us. Every movement had therefore to be conducted with the utmost circumspection.

To prepare for starting was the work of a few minutes. We were in full travelling dress, coats, boots, and mittens, and some of us wore masks; the hunters' whips were in our hands, and nothing remained to be done but to get a cup from the shelf. The moment was a critical one, for, if the sleepers should awake, our scheme must be revealed. Godfrey reached up for the desired cup, and down came the whole contents of the shelf, rattling to the ground. I saw the sleepers start; and anticipating the result, instantly sprang to the light and extinguished it with a blow of my mittened hand. As was to be expected the hunters were aroused. Kalutunah gave a grunt and inquired what was the matter. I answered him by throwing myself upon the breck, and crawling to his side, hugged him close, and cried, "Singikpok," (sleep). He laughed, muttered something which I could not understand, and without having suspected that anything was wrong, again fell asleep.

This incident convinced us that we could not much rely upon either the soundness or the long continuance of the slumbers which we had secured, and that in order to prevent our guests from getting to Netlik before we should be beyond their reach, we must resort to other expedients. They must be confined within the hut, and the possibility of their escape prevented until relief could come to them from their companions at the settlement. This could only be accomplished by carrying off their clothing.

I slipped from the side of the sleeping savage, and sought for a little package which had dropped from my hand in the excitement of extinguishing the lamp. This package contained some of my journal-entries, some scientific notes, some records respecting the Esquimaux, and other important papers, and I could ill afford to lose it; but nowhere could it be found, nor was it safe to seek long. Everything was ready; my companions were impatient to be off; the cups thrown from the shelf were scattered about the hut, endangering every movement. If the savages should detect us in the act of leaving, I knew that their fate was sealed. The risks were too great, the moment was too critical, to admit of delay. I abandoned the search.

We crawled noiselessly out of the hut, carrying

with us the boots, coats, and mittens of the sleepers. Stephenson was fortunately better than he had been for weeks. I gave to him the rifle, and stationed him with it on one side of the door. I took the double-barrelled shot-gun and occupied the side opposite. All of the fire-arms being now under my control, it was my intention, in case the Esquimaux should discover us, to await their coming out of the hut, and, under cover of our guns, compel them to mount the sledges and drive us northward.

Mr. Sonntag went down with the other men and prepared the sledges for starting. The dogs were greatly frightened by the sudden and novel treatment to which the strangers subjected them; and it was not without much trouble that they were harnessed. Meanwhile one of the men brought up the greater portion of the meat which was found buried in the snow; and having placed it in the passage, (it was sufficient, with economy, to last the prisoners five or six days,) we tore down the snow wall in front of the hut; and, with the frozen blocks, barricaded the doorway. Sonntag cried to us that all was ready. Leaving the sentinel's post I took Stephenson by the arm, and supported him to my sledge. Mr. Sonntag and John had one, and Whipple and Godfrey the other, of the remaining two. The poor dogs, howling in terror, dashed off at the first crack of the whip, and once more Fort Desolation was at our backs.

CHAPTER XXX.

MOVING NORTHWARD.

THE dogs gave us much trouble. Unaccustomed to us, or to our voices, and startled by our sudden appearance among them, they seemed to be too much frightened to submit to control; and, setting off at a furious pace, they dashed helter-skelter over the plain, some running one way, some another, their tails down, their ears up,— all uttering their peculiar wild cry, and all, seemingly possessed with the one idea of breaking away from their strange-looking drivers. My team twice took me back nearly to the hut, before I succeeded in getting any mastery of them; and, weak as I was, they had by that time nearly mastered me. Meantime John and Godfrey were having a similar contest with their respective teams, which had carried them out among the rough ice half a mile from the coast.

At length my brutes' heads were turned from the hut, and we were dashing at a ten-knot speed after the other sledges. I thought now that my trouble was over; but no sooner had I overtaken my companions than my wolfish herd flew past them; and then wheeling short around, some to the right, some to the left, they turned the sledge over backward, rolled Stephenson and myself into a snow-drift, and beat a hasty retreat. I caught the up-stander as I tumbled off, and was dragged several yards before I could regain my feet, and throw myself upon the sledge. At this moment the dogs were plunging through a ridge of hummocks. The point of one of the runners caught a block of ice. All but two of the traces snapped off; and away went the dogs back toward their narcotized masters. To secure them again was of course impossible. The two animals which remained were hastily attached, one to each of the other sledges; and leaving the third sledge jammed in the ice we continued our course.

As we proceeded the dogs became more accustomed to our voices, and we made good headway. Cape Parry was reached without further accident. Here we halted, in a cave on the southern side of the point, for the purpose of making some repairs, and refreshing ourselves with a little rest and a pot of coffee.

The cave gave us a good protection against a light wind which had sprung up during our journey. It was about forty feet in depth, and twelve in height; and being on a level with the sea it had a smooth, glassy floor. The dogs were picketed near its mouth; and, after being fed, they huddled quietly together; and, well reconciled to their new masters, they gave themselves no more uneasiness. Godfrey had broken his whipstock in his efforts to control their refractory tempers, and John had whipped his lash half away. Without repairing these, it was impossible to proceed with the teams, and fully two hours had elapsed before we were ready to continue our journey.

I was preparing to start with Mr. Sonntag to pick a track through the hummocks which lay across the little bight into which we had come, when three men with a sledge hove in sight around a point of land, about a hundred yards from our camp. They were at once recognized as our late prisoners. They had been able to extricate from the ice the sledge which we had been forced to abandon; and, refreshed by their food and sleep, they had quickly attached our fugitive dogs and started on our trail.

Each party discovered the other at the same moment, and both were equally surprised. The Esquimaux were of course in our power; but the surest way to guard against the hostility of the tribe, in consequence of our act of aggression, seemed to be to strike terror into these men; for a savage despises nothing as much as weakness, and respects nothing as much as strength.

Seizing the rifle, I sprang over the ice-foot and ran out to meet them. Sonntag was at my side with the gun. The Esquimaux stopped when they saw us approaching, and held their ground until we came within thirty yards of them, when, halting, I brought the rifle to my shoulder and aimed toward them. They turned away and, throwing their arms wildly about their heads, called loudly to us not to shoot. — "Na-mik! na-mik! na-mik!" I lowered my rifle and beckoned to them to advance. This they did cautiously, assuring us at every step that they were friends.

By this time Whipple had come up, and each of

us seized a prisoner. I took Kalutunah by the collar, and, after giving him a hearty shake, in token of my displeasure, I marched him before me to the mouth of the cave; then facing him around toward his sledge, I pointed to it with my gun; and, turning toward the north, I told him, of course chiefly by signs, that if he took the whip which lay on the snow at his feet and drove us to the Oomeaksoak, I would give him back his dogs, sledge, coat, boots, and mittens, but that if he did not do this, he and his companions should be shot forthwith; and, suiting the action to the word, I pushed him from me, and made a feint to level my gun. He sidled away a few paces, crying, "Na! na!— Na-mik! na-mik!" over and over again, as fast as his tongue could utter the words, making gestures all the time with his right hand, in imitation of driving dogs; and with his left pointing northward. It being now evident that he understood both my demand and the penalty in case of non-compliance, I rested the stock of my gun upon the ice and nodded my approval of his decision. I then beckoned him toward me, and, pointing to the dogs, sledges, &c., I gave him to understand that we would consider all those things as ours until the terms of the contract were complied with on his part. He approached with his old-fashioned familiarity, and expressed his satisfaction by an overwhelming volley of "tyma," (good or right). He was evidently convinced that the tables had turned, and that I was doing him a great favor, in negotiating instead of using the dreaded weapon.

Our prisoners were a sorry looking party. They had arrayed themselves in our blankets, cutting holes in the middle of them for their heads. If not the original inventors of the Spanish *poncho* they are none the less entitled to credit for their ingenuity. One was dressed in red, another in white, and another in blue. One of them had discovered and appropriated an old pair of discarded boots; the others had wrapped their feet in pieces of our blankets. None of them seemed to have suffered from the cold. They had been awakened by the dogs running over the roof, as we had feared would be the case. The opium did not seem to have had more than a brief effect.

The cunning fellows had found means to light the lamp; and discovering that we had taken their sledges and had abandoned the hut, they had evidently resolved not to be altogether losers by the operation; and, in a business-like manner, they had proceeded to collect whatever they could carry away. In addition to the presents which we had made them, they had upon their sledge several tin-cups and tin-plates, a spoon, an old russia cap, a part of my lost manuscript records, and some other small articles; the useful and the useless all piled together. These things had been carried under their arms until they found the sledge. They had left the hut expecting to walk to Netlik or they would doubtless have taken more.

As a proof of our disposition to trust them we restored their clothing; and as they slipped into their jumpers, and tied on their moccasins, I could not but reflect that this was a strange way to make people happy. A more grateful set of fellows I had never seen. Our plan had succeeded better than was anticipated; for they did not attempt to touch dogs, sledge, or even a whip until they were bidden.

We were soon under way; and, running around the cape, we headed in for Netlik. The time occupied in reaching it was greatly protracted in consequence of our being obliged to walk or run during at least one third of the time, in order to prevent ourselves from freezing.

We were first made aware that we approached the village by the howling of an immense pack of dogs, which grouped themselves together on the white hill-side, and set up their wild concert, that could be heard at the distance of several miles. As we neared the shore, a crowd of men, women, and children came down over the ice-foot to meet us.

The savages, to the number of about fifty, assembled around us the moment we came to a halt. Among them I recognized many familiar faces. Everybody seemed greatly surprised to see us, especially under such auspices. They were all eager for news,— why we came, and why we had been brought, seemed to be the prevailing questions.

Feeling that it was still necessary to maintain the tone of authority with which we had commenced the adventure, we met all their advances with reserve. Without giving time for an invitation, we told Kalutunah that three of us would go to each of the two huts; and, having stopped there long enough to eat and sleep, we would continue our journey. For the benefit of the assembled multitude, just so much of the Cape Parry pantomime was repeated as was necessary to draw from Kalutunah and his two companions a renewal of their pledges, with which they were no less prompt than on the previous occasion.*

Our situation required the use of whatever advantage could be drawn from the superstitious fear which the savages had of our weapons. The Esquimaux outnumbered us as eight to one; we were half dead with cold, hunger, and fatigue; we could not even feel assured that our guns were in a condition to be discharged; and with much of our prestige destroyed by preceding events, we had good reason to doubt our ability to maintain ourselves in case of any general excitement of the people into whose midst we had been thrown.

The dogs were given in charge of the boys, and we proceeded to the village. Mr. Sonntag, taking with him John and Whipple, was conducted to the hut of the chief, while I, with Stephenson and Godfrey, was taken by Kalutunah to his own mansion.

The settlement was now greatly enlarged by the people who had come from the south; and as I walked up from the beach I observed several snow-houses grouped around the two stone hovels which constituted the permanent portion of the village.

---

* In relation to the knowledge of fire-arms, the reader will observe a great difference between the Esquimaux of Smith Strait and those mentioned in the reports of the later English Expeditions to the north coasts of America. The former had, with a few exceptions in cases where communication had been held with the whale and discovery ships about Cape York, no practical acquaintance whatever with the terrible weapons of the white men, previous to the arrival of the Advance; and although a vague account of our guns must have spread through the settlements, yet we owed our safety to the fact that the "charm" of novelty had not been dispelled before we were thrown among the savages without other protection than the threats narrated in the text.

In these snow-houses the moving families which we had recently entertained in our hut at Booth Bay were temporarily sojourning.

Kalutunah, in order the better to keep out the wind, had lengthened with snow the covered entrance to his hut, so that we were obliged to crawl fully twenty feet before we emerged into the dimly lighted apartment. It was completely deserted, the inmates having gone down to meet the sledges; but they were close behind us with others drawn by curiosity, and all came pouring in until the place seemed likely to be more tightly packed than it was when I visited it in September. The discomfort which would thus be caused, and the embarrassment to be anticipated in case any hostile feeling toward us should spring up, induced me to request Kalutunah not to admit any other persons than the ordinary inmates. He hesitated, manifestly regarding my procedure as an invasion of his authority, and he looked for a moment as though he would ask "is not my house my own?" The exigence, however, appeared to justify a little forwardness on my part, which being clearly expressed with the aid of a hint towards the "boom," the intruders retired from the hut and from the passage, leaving only about a dozen persons within. Fortunately several of these were small children.

Oh the luxury of that savage den! Ten weeks before, when I visited it, it was to me the embodiment of all that was most repulsive; now it was a real "weary man's rest." Our enfeebled bodies had just been exposed during fifteen consecutive hours, in travelling between forty and fifty miles.

So great was the exhaustion of one of the party that he fell from debility alone the moment he went into the cold air. We were in a fit condition to appreciate the blessings of a place where we could lie down without the certainty of freezing; and we indulged in no close criticism of our surroundings.

We received all manner of kind attentions from our host. The women pulled off our boots, mittens, coats, and stockings, and hung them up to dry. My beard was frozen fast to the fur of my coat; and it was the warm hand of Kalutunah's wife that thawed away the ice. Meats of different kinds were brought in and offered to us in the only styles known to the Esquimau *cuisine*, that is, parboiled and raw; or as Stephenson more elegantly expressed it, "cooked with fire," and "cooked with frost;" but our fatigue had destroyed our appetites, and the warmth of the hut soon so overcame us that we fell asleep in the very act of taking food from the hand of our hostess. Now that the stimulus under which we had been acting was removed, scarcely anything could have prevented us from sleeping at the end of the first half-hour of our stay in that close, warm place. The hut was warmer by 120° than the atmosphere to which we had been so long exposed.

I lay down among a promiscuous collection of half-clad and un-clad men, women, and children; and my first consciousness was of some one pulling at my feet. It was the mistress of the establishment, who had prepared for us a plentiful meal; and we were soon doing such justice to the boiled steaks of bear, and the frozen steaks of seal, as need not have shamed an Esquimau hunter. Another long nap followed this feast; another feast followed the nap; and so on alternately through greater or less stages, until we had recovered from our fatigue and were strengthened by our good fare. We then signified to Kalutunah that we were prepared to start; and in a few minutes he had everything ready for us. The stars told us that we had been resting about twenty-seven hours.

Taking leave of the good people of Netlik, we clambered down over the ice-foot, and then mounting the sledges, we followed the path among the hummocks which Kalutunah's son picked for us, until we were clear of the bay, when, waving adieu to the young Esquimaux who had followed us, we continued our journey over the frozen sea.

CHAPTER XXXI.

OVER THE FROZEN SEA.

Our course was toward Northumberland Island, which, as the crow flies, is about twenty miles from Netlik; but as we were obliged to make several *détours*, in order to avoid the extensive ridges of broken ice which lay parallel with the axis of the channel, the distance actually travelled by us was nearly thirty miles.

Our destination was reached in about six hours. The natives of the island came out to meet us. We found here, as at Netlik, two substantial stone-huts; to each of which three of us were conducted, and placed in charge of the mistress of the establishment.

These two huts belonged to the before-mentioned brothers, Amalatok and Kingiktok; and each hut being occupied by only one family, our quarters were neither as distressingly close, nor as uncomfortably warm as the huts of Netlik. Kingiktok fulfilled graciously his duties as host; and his wife in concert with the witch-wife of Amalatok exerted herself to make us comfortable. Our boots, stockings, coats, and mittens were hung to dry; and then food and water were given to us. The food was the flesh of birds and was abundant in quantity; and, although served as usual, namely, parboiled and frozen, it was very acceptable. The water was melted snow; and, having been prepared in a pot which had probably never been cleansed, and being drunk from a seal-skin dish which could not be cleansed, was not, on the other hand, to be commended.

Northumberland Island is, during the breeding season, a favorite resort of the little auk; and with a providence which I had not seen among the Esquimaux in other places, the people here seem to have collected the birds in great numbers. Soon after our arrival one of the women brought into the hut a solid cube of them, a foot in diameter. This was the contents of one of their *caches*, made during the last summer. The birds had been thrown in as they were caught, and they were now all frozen together *en masse*. We were at liberty to break them off with a stone, one at a time, and, after removing the skin, to eat them in their actual condition, — or to wait until the women should have cooked them. We practised both alternatives. The pot would not hold more than half a dozen birds at one time, and it was replenished as fast as emptied. Our stay was prolonged in consequence of a light wind which had sprung up from the northeast.

This halt and abundant feeding did much to restore our strength, and we were in no haste to start, for every hour added to our gain of physical energy. Knowing that we should be compelled, either to camp in a snow-house upon the ice-fields, or to perform a long journey to reach again an Esquimau hut, we had reason to be thankful that the wind had come to detain us; for, although our drivers were as much as ever disposed to obey us, yet it would have been highly impolitic to restrain their eagerness to push forward.

We learned at this place that our friends Petersen and Bonsall had been there before us; and, having made a long halt, had gone northward under the guidance of Amalatok.

We parted from our savage hosts as soon as the wind had died away; and we headed up the strait which separates Northumberland from Herbert Island; but our progress in this direction was arrested by an impenetrable barrier of hummocks, which obliged us to alter our course to the eastward. The light was not sufficient to enable us to see the condition of the track far in advance, and after proceeding a short distance on our new route we found ourselves in a sort of *cul de sac*, almost completely surrounded by rough ice. In every direction there was to be seen only a succession of apparently endless ridges of crushed tables, piled up in many places to the height of thirty or forty feet.

The Esquimaux have a great horror of these rugged barriers, and always avoid them where it is possible to do so, even at the expense of greatly increasing their distance; but there was clearly now no course for us but to attempt to penetrate through the wilderness in the direction of Herbert Island, which appeared to be about seven or eight miles from us. Retreating a few paces we discovered a narrow lead, which was entered; and we followed its numerous tortuosities for about a quarter of a mile. Here it was found to end, and we were all compelled to dismount and clamber over a jagged pile of ice, beyond which we were disappointed in not again finding a lead. For several hours we toiled on, winding in all directions, seeking the smoothest, or rather I should say the least rough, places. Of course we could not ride.

At length, after having travelled, as we supposed, about ten miles, and having made in linear distance about three, we came upon a moderately level plain, and resumed our places upon the sledges. By holding a northeast course, to avoid the rough barrier which we had passed, we reached, at length, the island for which we had been steering. During this trying journey across the channel Stephenson bore up bravely, and astonished all of us by his endurance.

Upon meeting the shore we mounted to the land-ice, and ran at good speed over its level surface, along the base of the sloping *débris* which lay under the weather-worn cliffs. An hour's comfortable travelling brought us to the north side of the island, where, descending again to the field-ice, we struck out across the north arm of Whale Sound, directly for the main land, the distant mountains of which, dimly illuminated by the moon, loomed up in the north and northeast. The landmark toward which our drivers were steering was Cape Robertson. Near this cape we knew that the village of Karsooit was situated; but we feared that it was so far to the eastward that it could not be reached by us without going too much out of our way, and we therefore looked forward, with no little disrelish, to camping in a snow-hut. It soon became evident to us, however, that our drivers were leading us toward the village; and, seeing that we were growing cold, they gave us the encouraging assurance that *igloe* (huts) and *koona* (women) were before us.

Our track was now almost as smooth and level as a floor, except that here and there it was made gently undulating by the unequal snow-drifts. Our dogs galloped swiftly over it. The islands sank rapidly behind us, and the land in front grew more distinct. We were encircled by an ice-horizon, and there was not within sight a single object to break the uniform smoothness of the white field, except an occasional berg which threw its long dark shadow upon the glistening plain.

I was struck with the character of the snow. The temperature was lower than it had been on any previous occasion of our exposure, and the intense cold had so hardened the crystals that we seemed to be travelling over a bed of sand. The sledges did not move with their accustomed freedom. To overcome the friction which retarded our progress, our drivers resorted to an ingenious, though simple, expedient. Halting at short intervals, they capsized their sledges, and, dissolving in their mouths a piece of ice or snow, they moistened their fingers and applied them to the under surface of the runner. Thus was instantly formed a thin film of ice.

We halted once for a meal. One of the sledges was unlashed, and a piece of bear-meat and another of narwhal-blubber were produced. The latter of these was of the consistency of well-hardened butter, and was pared off in delicate slices; but the meat was so solid that we could not without difficulty break it to pieces. We made, nevertheless, a good repast, and being thereby greatly refreshed we proceeded on our way. It is astonishing how soon one grows hungry in those low temperatures.

Our progress was also much retarded in consequence of our being obliged frequently to dismount and walk, or rather to run, in order to keep ourselves from freezing. Although at such times we were supported by the up-standers, which we grasped with our hands; yet, even with this assistance, it was sometimes found necessary to check the dogs, in order to accommodate their movements to our ability.

Towards the latter part of the journey we became seriously alarmed, in consequence of a light wind springing up from the northeast. To face a strong breeze in such a temperature was quite impossible. The first puffs which came cut our faces severely, and chilled us through and through; but fortunately we were soon under the shelter of the high cliffs of the main-land.

The coast reached, we headed up a narrow inlet toward the village. As heretofore, our coming was proclaimed by the howling of dogs, and very soon a bright light was seen glimmering on the white hill. Never did light glow with a brighter welcome. A faint cheer broke from our party as it burst into view. We had travelled at least fifty miles.

The sledges halted close to the beach, and three of the party were immediately conducted into the hut where the light had been discovered. The rest of us were taken about half a mile further, to a similar shelter. These dens were the very counterpart of those in which we had been quartered at Netlik. They were packed full of human beings, and were hot, close, and foul. The comforts, however, far outweighed the discomforts, and we were duly thankful for the change. We suffered most annoyance from the heat. Passing from a temperature of 50° below zero to one of 75° above it was a severe trial to the animal economy; and we could do nothing else than accept the good offices of our hosts, who proposed immediately to divest us of our clothing. To their astonishment, however, we persisted in retaining some portions of our artificial covering.

A large seal, which had been recently caught, lay in the middle of the floor when we entered. And to it we did ample justice. Our drivers came in, each with a seal-skin tub, and carried off the refuse portions for their dogs; but soon afterward joined us in the feast.

After finishing the meal, and taking a short nap, I paid a visit to the other hut. It belonged to our old enemy, Sip-su. The gruff savage had not relented in the least, and he showed no disposition to oblige his uninvited and unwelcome guests. Although he had evidently been astonished and intimidated by the unceremonious manner in which he had been treated by his visitors, it was clear that he was not mollified.

Our halt here was not as long as our two former ones; and, when well refreshed, we started again on our journey. Our route lay along the crooked coast, and passing in quick succession dark capes, white glaciers, broad bays, and narrow inlets, we brought up, at the end of five hours, in a double hut which stands on the shore of a small bay to the south of Cape Saumarez.

The ride was exhilarating, and in all respects pleasant. We were not exposed long enough to grow either tired or cold. We had four sledges, — an old hunter named Ootinah having joined us at Karsooit. The track was quite smooth, and the dogs, as fresh at the end as at the beginning of the journey, kept up a constant gallop. Encouraged by the familiar cries of their masters, they would now and then dash off at a furious pace, each team striving to outstrip the others. We averaged in speed about six miles an hour, and must have made sometimes, for a short distance, fully ten. The snarling of the dogs as one team after another shot ahead, the crack of the whips, the merry laughs and the encouraging " Ka! ka! — Ka! ka!" of the drivers, and the creaking of the sledges, still ring in my ears; and they are the more pleasantly remembered, because they bring this day into striking contrast with that which followed.

We quitted the double hut after a few hours. The Esquimaux told us, before starting, that our next halt would be at Etah, which we knew to be the most northern of the native villages. To reach that village we must pass "the blowing place," (Cape Alexander.) We therefore had before us a day's journey of sixty miles, which we had some reason to dread; for the Esquimaux, whenever alluding to Cape Alexander, did it with a shrug and a shiver. Besides, our experience of the cape in September, when our boats were nearly swamped, was fresh in our recollection. We had grown so inured to the cold that we did not fear exposure, during any reasonable period, to any temperature, especially now that we had recovered so much strength; but neither we nor our drivers could live long in a December wind. The Esquimaux of the arctic wastes are as fearful of a gale as are the Bedouins in their desert. It pelts the one with a cloud of snow, and it buries the other in a cloud of sand; and both of these make frequent victims

CHAPTER XXXII.

ROUNDING CAPE ALEXANDER AGAIN.

The first twenty miles of the distance were passed rapidly and comfortably, and the monotony was most pleasingly broken by a chase after a bear, and by another after a fox. The fox escaped to the shore, and the bear to some rough ice. Our drivers were anxious to continue the pursuit, and it was not without some difficulty that we prevailed upon them to relinquish it. Although the chase was pleasant and exciting while we were on smooth ice, we had no taste for bouncing over the hummocks at the speed of a pack of wild dogs in pursuit of prey.

As we neared Cape Alexander we had a foretaste of what was in store for us. When many miles to the south of it we were overtaken by a light southerly wind, which increased as we advanced; and almost at the very moment when we caught, through the thick atmosphere, the first faint glimpse of the great vertical rock which as a monster fortress seemed to guard the entrance to the Polar Ocean, a squall struck us. It gave us a cheerless salute; and being mixed with a cloud of fine drift, and coming directly into our faces, it cut us terribly.

Unable to bear up against it we hauled close under the coast, where we were sheltered during our passage around the head of a small bay.

The cold gust which came down upon us from the cape was only an eddy; for, when outside of the little bay and away from its protecting icebergs and islands, the wind was found, as before, to be blowing steadily from the southward. There was something cheering in this, for the storm was, at least partially, at our backs.

The wind soon rose to a moderate gale. The irregular coast eddied it back into our faces; and to escape the suffering occasioned by these frequent blasts we drew further away from the land. The ice, at a short distance from the shore, was found to have been in places bared of snow by the almost constantly prevailing winds; and over the glassy sheet we were absolutely driven before the gale. The dogs, seldom stretching their traces, ran howling from the sledges, which crowded upon their heels.

It was a wild scene. The night was dark. The moon had gone far down behind the mountains, and we had no other light to guide us than the pale glimmer of the stars. The shadows of the cliffs, whose mighty crests towered a thousand feet above our heads, lay coldly upon us, and intensified the midnight gloom. The patches of snow which hung upon the abrupt angles of the giant wall; the white sheet which lay upon its lofty summit; the glaciers which here and there protruded through its clefts, brought out in bold relief the blackness of its deep recesses. The air was filled with clouds of drift, which sometimes wholly obscured the land, and which swept fiercely before us over the icy plain.

At length a dark line was seen to cross our path; wreaths of "frost smoke" were curling over it, and these revealed its character. "Emerk! emerk!" (water! water!) was the cry which simultaneously broke from the drivers. The headway of the sledges was stopped as quickly as possible, and we brought up at only a few yards from a recently opened and rapidly widening crack. Already it was twenty feet across.

We mounted to the top of a pile of hummocks and peered into the darkness. Cape Alexander was only a few miles in advance. The ice in the shallow bay on its southern side was severed by numerous cracks; while beyond, starting from the foot of the cape, a broad sheet of water spread itself to the westward. Its dark surface, agitated by the wind, was covered with white caps; and here and there a frosty surf was breaking over a small berg or vagrant floe. The pieces of ice which lay along its margin were in motion, and their hard faces were grinding tumultuously together. The clamor made by these, the ceaseless beating of the surf, the moaning of the wind, the rattling of the drift, the piteous wailing of the dogs, were so loud that we could scarcely hear each other speak; and the force of the gale was so great that we were almost blown from the pinnacle to which we had climbed.

Our situation seemed almost desperate. To cross over the land was impossible, for there was no break in the cliffs by which we could ascend. To turn about and hunt for a **land-passage**, would have been certain death, for we could not face the storm. Our drivers, more **hardy** than we, were for going back. Rendered almost **frantic by suffering**, we were in no condition to hear such a proposition, and again the pistol did its work of intimidation. We had caught a glimpse of the white ice-foot hanging above the water at the base of the cliffs; and by this we were determined to attempt a passage.

Returning to the land, we ascended the ice-foot by a ladder made with our **sledges**, and then ran rapidly along its level surface. In a few minutes we were beyond the crack which had baffled us; but coming soon afterward to **a small** hanging glacier we were obliged to return to the field-ice. We had gone only a short distance over this before we met another chasm. Running along its margin, eagerly seeking an opportunity to cross it, we came at length opposite to a point of ice, which, projecting beyond the general line of fracture, narrowed the chasm to about four feet. It was impossible to ascertain in the darkness whether or not this projection was fast. There was not a moment to lose. Every instant diminished our chances of a passage; for the floe was moving off, and the crack was widening. Already we had consumed much time in fruitless searching. Resolved to take the risk, I sprang upon the supposed tongue; but when too late I discovered that it was loose. The treacherous raft sank beneath my weight, and I went down into the cold sea.

I struggled to gain the opposite side. In the effort the lump of ice which was still under my feet tilted, and losing my equilibrium I fell backward, and should have gone completely under had not Stephenson been standing close to the spot whence I had sprung. Reaching forward as I inclined toward him, he caught me under the arms and drew me out.

I owe my preservation to the timely aid of my former patient; for although there was but little danger of my drowning, with so many persons at hand to render assistance, my life would not have been worth an hour's purchase, if I had remained long enough in the water to become thoroughly wetted, and had then been landed on the ice, in a gale of wind, with the temperature below the freezing-point of mercury. As it was, my skin-clothing turned the water, and only a little penetrated through the opening between my pantaloons and boots. Falling upon my knees, and elevating my feet, I drained this out as well as I could; and Mr. Sonntag having in the mean time found a better crossing, I joined the sledges as the last resisting dog was thrown over the crack.

Our faces were once more turned toward the coast. My clothing was soon so stiffened with ice that I could scarcely run, and the water which had trickled down into my boots burned like melted lead.

We were soon back upon the ice-foot; and following its numerous windings we reached at length the open water. Here we were rejoiced to find a smooth surface and abundant room for a passage. In occasional places the "foot" was ten yards in width, but more frequently from one to two yards;

and sometimes where there was an unusual protrusion of the cliff it was scarcely wider than the sleds.

We continued to wind along this varying ledge without interruption until we came to the outer extremity of the cape, where a sharp rock projected into the water. Here for the space of several feet the belt was not more than fifteen inches wide, and it was sloping. The word "halt" was passed along the line, and men and dogs crouched behind the rocks for shelter. The wind was still blowing furiously, lashing the waves against the frozen shore at our feet, whirling great sheets of snow down upon us from the overhanging cliffs, and howling like an army of demons. We could not face the storm of drift, which pelted mercilessly upon our backs, and to go forward appeared to be impossible; yet this we must try. Advancing to the point, I discarded my mittens, and, clinging with my bare hands to the crevices in the rock, I moved cautiously along the sloping shelf. Twenty feet vertically below me, the water, black as ink, except where it was breaking into surf, yawned to receive any victim whom an inadvertent step might precipitate into it. I shall not soon forget the emotions of joy and thankfulness with which I found myself safely landed upon the broad belt at the further side of the dangerous place.

Now came the troublesome operation of getting over the dogs. These were driven forward by their masters, and being seized by their collars, were one by one dragged around the point. Then the sledges were pushed along the shelf, and were there held on one runner until the dogs could stretch their traces, when, bounding forward in obedience to a fierce "ka! ka!" the animals whirled them into safety before they could topple over the precipice. The teams, each accompanied by its driver, having all been thus brought over, the remainder of the party followed. Except some frost-bites upon our fingers, the scars of which we will carry with us to our graves, the passage was made without an accident.

Continuing on our course, tortured at every turn with anxiety lest we should ultimately reach a spot where the ice-foot was gone altogether, we were at length gladdened by a glimpse of the broad ice-field of Etah Bay, and by the discovery that this limited the open water.

Since first coming within view of Cape Alexander we had travelled fully fifteen miles, at least one third of which distance was upon this unsafe shelf above a foaming sea. All of us had been more or less frozen in the interval.

The ice-foot grew wider as we advanced; and at length we were opposite to the before-mentioned plain. To this we descended, and then headed for the native village of Etah, which was from fifteen to twenty miles distant. The track was smooth, the wind greatly lightened the draught, the whips were not spared, and after a rapid run we reached our destination, more dead than alive.

CHAPTER XXXIII.

REACHING THE BRIG.

WE found Amalatok at Etah, and we were told by him that Petersen and Bonsall had, as at our other halting-places, preceded us; that they were accompanied by several sledges; that they had passed Cape Alexander over land;* that after having rested they had continued their journey, and had reached the brig in safety; but that being broken down and unable to return, and the crew of the Advance being sick, Dr. Kane had intrusted to the Esquimaux some provisions which they were then bringing to us.

We could readily credit all of this story except the latter part of it; for some partially consumed pieces of pork lay strewn about the hut, proving conclusively that the savages had been false to their promises, and that they had not intended to come near us. We afterward learned that Dr. Kane had promptly loaded four sledges with pork and bread, and that, as the drivers of them had received many valuable presents, it was thought that their faithfulness had been secured; but that the

* Our guides did not know of the mountain-pass through which Amalatok had led Petersen and Bonsall.

bread had been thrown away before they were fairly out of sight of the brig, and the pork had been appropriated to their own uses.

The wisdom of our course in leaving Booth Bay was now clearly evident, although our journey was yet far from finished. The distance from Etah to Rensselaer Harbor was much greater than any single march that we had yet accomplished. Dr. Kane estimates it at ninety-one miles; and adopting his allowance for the necessary deviations from a straight line of travel, this estimate is probably not excessive.

I showed my frosted feet to the wise doctors of the tribe; but they only shook their heads. Such rude restoratives as I could command were applied, but without avail. Wherever the water had touched the skin the frost had gone in deeply, and life could not be restored. The pain was very severe; and it was evident that if I staid in the warm hut long enough to allow the frozen parts to become thawed, I should not be able to finish the journey to the brig. Tired and exhausted as I was by so long an exposure, my suffering was too great for sleep; and after we had been housed four hours, I awoke Mr. Sonntag, and giving up to him the charge which hitherto we had shared, I apprised him of my determination to start immediately for the vessel, and requested that he would not mention my absence to the party until they had thoroughly rested.

Taking Ootinah with me I crawled noiselessly out of the hut, and then explained to him my desire to go on at once. He quickly comprehended both my situation and my wants; and with a disinterestedness which I never saw in any other member of his tribe, (for he did not ask for pay,) he promptly signified his disposition to accede to my request, and proceeded to harness his team. This man had been my driver since leaving Karsooit, and he seemed to have formed an attachment to me. He had, during the last hour of our last march, rendered me important aid by pounding my stiffened limbs with his whipstock. I remember his services with gratitude.

We were soon under way, but we had not gone far when voices were heard behind us; and long before reaching Cape Ohlsen I was overtaken by my comrades, each one having now a separate sledge. Appreciating the motive which had induced them to follow, I nevertheless regretted their promptness; for with so short a rest after so hard a journey, I felt sure that they were running a useless risk.

After crossing the narrow channel which lies off Cape Ohlsen, we rounded the north cape of Littleton Island, and held off from the coast of the main land, in order to avoid as much as possible the heavy hummocks which lay near it. Cape Hatherton and Refuge Harbor were soon at our backs, and we arrived at length opposite Anoatok. Here, contrary to our wishes, we were detained for some time. Passing close alongside of a grounded ice-berg, the sharp senses of the dogs discovered a walrus which was blowing in the crack at its base. Halting their teams, the hunters seized their weapons and watched for his reappearance; but the animal had been frightened away, and did not again show himself. While the Esquimaux were thus engaged, we crouched into a recess of the berg for shelter, (for the wind was still blowing from the south,) and we availed ourselves of this opportunity to strengthen ourselves with a meal of frozen meat and blubber. Prior to this halt, a dash after a bear, the trail of which fortunately ran for several miles directly in our course, gained for us almost as much as was here lost.

We were now about ten miles from the coast, to make which was an absolute necessity; since by following the outer line of the hummocked ridges we were getting further and further from the land. We had all good reason to dread the effort which it must cost to reach the shore, for nowhere could we detect any level ice, and we must therefore walk.

One of the party, a young hunter named Myouk, pointed out to us a track by which he had passed on his way to the brig, and which had been selected by daylight. I undertook to act as guide, and for a time experienced no difficulty in following the track; but coming at length to the end of everything like an opening, I was compelled to rely upon an attempt to follow by sight the sledge-marks. In this I failed, for it was so dark that sometimes even when upon my hands and knees I could scarcely discover the impressions of the runners. Fearful that I should lead the party into an impassable labyrinth, I called Myouk to me. Godfrey took his whip. The superiority of the long practised sense of the savage over mine was at once seen; for the lines which I could not trace, except when stooping, he followed, for the most part, in an erect attitude. Occasionally he was compelled to grope about upon his hands and knees; and twice he led us off upon a false trail, once obliging us to retrace our steps for about a quarter of a mile. Except that there was no moon, that we were much fatigued at starting, and that the distance was twice as great, this journey through the mass of impacted ice was much like the passage already described from Northumberland to Herbert Island.

The dilapidated hut at Anoatok was at length reached; and the party, twelve in number, crowded in through its broken doorway. It was partially filled with drift, and offered only a sorry shelter. We blocked up the entrance with snow from the inside to keep out the wind, and we endeavored to light our lamps; but in some unaccountable manner both our tinder and that of the Esquimaux had become damaged; and after many fruitless trials we gave up the attempt. Without fire, and without skins in which to wrap ourselves, we could not long remain in this place. We were freezing, and must renew our activity, or speedily succumb to the cold.

Our failure to obtain rest at the hut was a serious disappointment to all of us; and it really seemed impossible that we could, without it, finish the march, — forty-one miles yet! As I thought of this, I confess that I did not see how the party were to bear up through the hours of exposure which the journey must require.

Down over the ice-foot dashed the sledges; across a little bay; up the ice-foot on the further side; across Esquimau point; over the ice-foot again to the level field of Bedevilled Reach! All still safe, — the most rugged part of our journey is over!

Whipple now alarmed us by saying that he did not suffer; — he was becoming stupefied by the cold, and others of us were rapidly approaching the same condition. As we passed God-send Island he fell from the sledge, and being at the rear his absence was not noticed, even by his driver, until he was a hundred yards behind. The sledge returned for him, and the teams again rushed on. The track was smooth, though devious, and we rapidly neared the northern shore of the bay.

We were soon upon the land-ice under Cape Grinnell. The dogs, excited by the unceasing cracking of the merciless whips, galloped at the top of their speed. It was a race of life and death.

The hull of the dismantled brig at length burst into view; and a few minutes afterward we were at its side. So much were my senses blunted by the cold that I remember scarcely any incident of our going on board, except that Dr. Kane met us at the gangway, and, grasping me warmly by the hand, led us into the fireless, frost-coated cabin. It was in the middle of the night, and all hands except the watch were sleeping. Ohlsen was the first to catch the sound of our coming; and springing from his cot as I entered the door, he folded me in his arms; and, after kissing me with Scandinavian heartiness, he threw me into the warm bed which he had just vacated.

The fire was kindled, and coffee and food were served to us. Such necessary attentions as men in our condition required, were bestowed upon us to the best of the ability of the sickly crew. Restoratives were applied by Dr. Kane to the frozen. These things done, we were put to bed, to sleep away the weariness caused by almost continual exposure during forty hours; in which time we had travelled one hundred and fifty miles, in a temperature eighty degrees below freezing.

There remains little more to be said. The Esquimau hunters who had served us so well remained at the vessel during the following day; and having received many useful presents, and their dogs and sledges having been returned to them, they left us well pleased.

Petersen and Bonsall had, for the most part, been confined to their beds since their arrival at the brig. They had been thoroughly broken down by their journey, and they had just begun to move about when we surprised them by our sudden appearance. It was their intention to go back to Booth Bay when their strength should have been recovered, and the moon should have come to light them on the way. Their experience had much resembled ours. After leaving us at the hut they had gone directly to Northumberland Island, where, as has been already stated, they were joined by Amalatok. Their party was afterward increased by the addition of several sledges; and, except that they had passed over, instead of around Cape Alexander, their route had been the same as our own. They had reached the brig on the 7th of December. We had been detained one day longer, in consequence of our going to Netlik, so that we did not come on board until three o'clock on the morning of the 12th.

Dr. Kane gave his bunk for my use, and under his skilful care, myself and my companions were soon recovered from our fatigue; and in three days six of our number were on active duty. Stephenson was suffering from a return of his old complaint, and I was kept prostrated by the effects of my accident at Cape Alexander. Otherwise we were in excellent health. In this respect, those who had remained at the brig were less fortunate. As had been feared they were attacked with scurvy. Every one of them was more or less affected by it; and one half of the number were actually down. Our arrival was most opportune, as we were enabled to relieve the sick of many onerous duties, for which they were physically unfit.

Although deeply regretting our want of success in the main object of our undertaking, we could not but congratulate ourselves, that at least one good had been effected; for, had eighteen persons instead of ten been crowded into the narrow cabin of the Advance, which had been much contracted in order to save fuel, and had they been otherwise subjected to the same causes of disease, we could not doubt what would soon have been the condition of the entire company. One of the motives of our temporary separation was in this manner proved by actual trial. In fact, within a few weeks the returned party were, one by one, stricken down by scurvy, and at length there were left only the commander and Mr. Bonsall who could regularly attend to the performance of the ship's duties.

The winter passed slowly away. Then spring returned, with its daylight, sunshine, and increased warmth; fresh food was obtained, chiefly from the natives; and with these aids the people rallied. Gradually the gloom which had settled over us was dispelled. The carpenter hobbled out to repair the boats; and in proportion as our strength increased, preparations were carried on for the final abandonment of the vessel.

Three boats were at length mounted upon runners, for transportation over the ice to open water; and on the 17th of May the whole company turned their faces southward. Four of the number being unable to walk were sent forward in advance to the hut at Anoatok, upon the dog-sledge, which during the two weeks previous had been constantly employed in transporting cargo to the same place. There were other members of the party who were able to perform only a moderate share of duty, and these accompanied the boat-sledges in their slow march.

We were thirty-one days in reaching the open water at Cape Alexander, about eighty miles distant from the brig. The trials of this tedious journey are too well known to need repetition. Had we been in vigorous health it could have been performed without difficulty, and probably in less than one third of the time actually consumed. The Esquimaux brought fresh food to us, and notwithstanding the severe labor we grew stronger day by day. Our greatest trial was the loss of our brave carpenter, Ohlsen, who fell a victim to his zeal. He was perhaps the healthiest man in the party when we left the brig; but he injured himself internally by over-exertion, and died on the third day afterwards. His grave is marked by a pyramid of stones on the eastern side of Littleton Island.

The boats were launched on the 19th of June, and we then set sail for Upernavik. Our progress down the coast was slow, and was almost continually embarrassed by the ice, which in many places had not yet broken up. Visiting on our way our hut at Booth Bay, it was found to have been torn to pieces by the Esquimaux; the wood had been carried away, and the Ironsides had been wantonly destroyed.

Upernavik was reached on the 6th of August, after an exposure of eighty-one days. There we remained until the 6th of September, having in the mean time shared the simple though kindly hospitality of Governor Flaischer, the Missionary Kraigh, and the people of the settlement generally. We were there met by the Danish brig Marianne, which plies annually between this port and Copenhagen; and we were received with great kindness by her warm-hearted commander, Mr. Ammondson. In this brig we took passage for Denmark. Halting at Godhavn, the inspectorate of North Greenland, we were welcomed by Mr. Olrik, and were there overtaken by the ships, which under command of Captain Hartstene had been sent to our assistance by the government of the United States. Captain Hartstene had made a bold and vigorous search for us, reaching within fifty miles of the winter-quarters of the Advance; and had abandoned the ground only when he learned from the Esquimaux that we had gone southward.

From the accomplished officers of this relief expedition we received many attentions, which were much needed and were gracefully bestowed. Transferring our quarters from the Danish brig to the American vessels, we returned in these to the United States, and landed in New York October 12th, 1855, after an absence of two years four months and thirteen days.

CHAPTER XXXIV.

CONCLUDING REMARKS.

AFTER such a series of uncomfortable adventures as have now been presented to my readers, I cannot take leave of them without a word of caution and of explanation.

The reports which have been published of arctic exploration, have naturally impressed the minds of most persons with images of a character to shock the sensibilities of the humane, and to render the country about the North Pole as terrible as any of the fabled regions which have furnished themes to the pens of poets and prose romancers of preceding ages. Vast seas covered with masses of ice rushing to and fro, threatening to crush the most skilful navigator — towering bergs ready to overwhelm him — dangerous land journeys — cold, piercing to the very sources of life — savage beasts, and scarcely less savage men — isolation, disease, famine, and slow death — such are the elements of the popular conception of what is inevitably to be encountered by the explorer. Perhaps to many the chief picture suggested by the mention of arctic expeditions, is, at best, equal in repulsiveness to that described by Bulwer : —

> Huddled on deck, one half that hardy crew
>   Lie shrunk and withered in the biting sky,
> With filmy stare and lips of livid hue,
>   And sapless limbs that stiffen as they lie;
> While the dire pest-scourge of the frozen zone
> Rots through the vein and gnaws the knotted bone.*

I say that such an impression is natural, partly because the expeditions which have particularly attracted the general notice of the civilized world, have been the disastrous ones; and partly because the adventures recorded have been so different in kind from those to which our literature has accustomed us; and the scenes have contrasted in so marked a manner with those of our climate and habitual mode of life, that we are ready for the wildest fancies and the most repulsive conclusions. Although the history of every age abounds with tales of marvellous enterprise, of personal exposure, of hair-breadth escapes, and of death in a variety of forms, encountered in pursuit of wealth, of fame, or of more christian objects, yet none of these — not even the horrors of Central Africa as narrated by European travellers, appear to excite the dread which is produced by the contemplation of the polar circle.

In such circumstances I may be regarded not only as rash, in proposing for the favorable consideration of my countrymen another essay into a part of the earth so under ban by reason of its assumed inevitable perils, but also as blind to the means of success, when I send out through the press, for the criticism of the world, a volume which is almost wholly composed of chapters the most discouraging. Yet I trust it will be in the end conceded, on the one

---

* *King Arthur*, Book ix. c. xiii.

hand, that the proposed renewal of American arctic exploration is neither rashly nor hastily suggested; and on the other, that the character of the boat journey of 1854 is exceptional; and that it gives to us important means by which to discriminate the accidental causes of disaster, and to determine the real permanent elements of a rational judgment upon the prudential relations of the whole subject.

It must be remembered that the major part of the voyages into the arctic waters, and of the journeys over arctic lands, have not even as near a connection with the proposal now before the American public, as most of the efforts made during many years to penetrate the Rocky Mountains, have with the last engineer's report upon the route of the Pacific railroad. Tens of thousands of men, women, and children, with their household goods, and their herds, have travelled safely overland from the Atlantic border to the remote region where once the Oregon, " heard no sound, save his own dashings " — and to the golden shores of the Pacific, not long since uninhabited by white men. They have gone through passes which twenty-five years ago were either unknown, or had been rendered familiar to us only by often perused narratives of appalling dangers encountered by a few half-savage frontier-men. The first readers of " Astoria,"— even those of the later real romances of Fremont, — what could they depict to themselves which would be accepted now as a reasonable guide to our judgment upon the practicability of a journey between the eastern and the western limits of our national territory ? The history of our continent everywhere affords similar illustrations. What European who heard the first recital of the efforts of Balboa and of Pizarro, could have even imagined the present state of travel and trade across the Isthmus of Darien? What would Lewis and Clarke say of possibilities, could they witness the population and institutions of the Republic extending up the Missouri and its branches towards their very head-springs? The truth is, that, as in all of these instances, so in arctic exploration, the way has been gradually prepared for an ultimate success which is certain. During more than two centuries the north circumpolar region has been examined successively upon every side. England, Holland, France, Spain, Portugal, Denmark, Russia, and the United States of America, have been competing for the advantages and the glory of polar enterprise; and now, as the fruit of their expenditure of men, of money, and of zeal, we have a map and a history which enable us to speak with the positiveness of actual knowledge in relation to fresh plans of exploration. The adventures which have given reputation to Cabot, and Baffin, and Hudson, and Barentz, and Behring, and to many others whose names are less familiar in this country, were necessary antecedents to later efforts; and these, in turn, are to contribute to the more fortunate, because still later explorer.

It must also be remembered that, of the long list of arctic voyages, only a small proportion were directed towards the Pole; the others having been made in search of a northwestern, or northeastern passage to India, with the exception of such as were undertaken for the relief of Sir John Franklin's party :* and that even those navigators who endeavored to make a due north passage were aiming rather at the remote object of oriental communication, than at the nearer one of circumpolar discovery. Besides, most of the last-mentioned class of adventurers were obliged to adopt their measures with scanty information of the physical condition and changes of the northern seas; and of course without that birdseye view of the entire arctic ice-belt up to a mean latitude of 78°, which is now within the reach of every student of physical geography.

Dr. Kane, whose first voyage as surgeon of the expedition under Lieut. De Haven, in 1850, had given to him some important information upon the currents and ice-movements of Baffin Bay, carefully collated such accounts as had been published respecting the various efforts to penetrate the ice-barrier; and he thus arrived at the conclusion that the true route lay up the theretofore unexplored Smith Strait, which opens at the head of the bay. The Russian navigator and veteran arctic explorer, Baron Von Wrangel, had reached the same conclusion, which he announced to the Royal Geographical Society of London in 1847. The English expeditions up Baffin Bay had turned westward into Lancaster and Jones Sounds; only one of them, under Capt. Inglefield, having entered the mouth of Smith Strait as far as latitude 78°. 30′. To America is due the

---

* So closely have recent arctic expeditions been associated with the idea of a rescue of Sir John Franklin, or of the survivors of his company, that, for some of my readers, it may not be superfluous to say here, that my expedition has no reference whatever to the fortunes of that gallant captain and his crew. My course lies in a different direction from theirs, as the map will show.

credit of having reduced the evidence to practical results. The second Grinnell expedition, begun in 1853, added new proofs to those previously known in favor of the route by Smith Strait; and at the present time there is sufficient warrant for asserting that it is by this channel that the Pole is to be reached.

I ask now that my readers shall dismiss all thought of the long catalogue of ineffective voyages; that they shall as fully divest themselves of their prepossessions against arctic adventure as beset with perils, and as unproductive of benefit to mankind; especially that they shall guard their feelings against the influence of the recent events which have aroused the sympathies of the world in relation to Sir John Franklin; and that they shall give an impartial attention to the few, well-founded, practical considerations which are about to be presented to them.

I shall not begin at Philadelphia, nor at New York, nor at Boston, at all of which places the associations are unfavorable to a suitable estimate of the topics which ought to determine the question before us; and at all of which the mere idea of distance tends to augment the imaginary difficulties of the case; but I shall at the outset suppose that we are at Upernavik, a Danish settlement on the western coast of Greenland, where there is a healthy population, with a church, and a school, and a governor — a settlement between which and the mother-country a vessel plies annually.* Past this

---

* A reference to the "Chart of Baffin Bay," which accompanies this volume, will render the text clear to the reader. From Upernavik, at the

place, at the opening of every summer, go the WHAL-
ERS, who fish along the west shore of Baffin Bay.
We shall follow their vessels along the eastern shore
northward, until we reach the latitude at which they
usually turn westward across the head of the bay —
the route pursued by all of the English expeditions,
with perhaps a single exception. We find that occasionally some of the whale-ships cross still farther
north, namely, at latitude 77°. Well, here we are in
the good company of a hearty set of navigators,
who think it not too great a hardship to come hither
every year to catch whales. We are within sight of
the ordinary routine of nautical life; with the addition of a few peculiarities which every seaman within hail would think it a lubberly weakness to use as
occasions for pity, or as motives for shrinking, or as
means to a great reputation. Thus far, then, we are
within the limits of what is both feasible and prudent. What is the distance hence in a straight line
to the latitude of Dr. Kane's winter-quarters in
1853–54–55? Not more than from one hundred
and twenty to one hundred and eighty miles, a
large part of which distance is across what is called

southeast corner, to Rensselaer Harbor, near the top of the chart, will be found all the principal places and routes.

At the right hand of the "Chart of the Arctic Regions" is a small map showing the North Water, Smith Strait, and Kennedy Channel as far as known. On this are marked Rensselaer Harbor; and, northward from it on the western side of the Channel, under Cape Frazer, the author's proposed winter-quarters.

The intended course of the new expedition is indicated by a heavy dotted line up Baffin Bay and Kennedy Channel toward the Pole.

The northern and southern limits of the ice-belt, as reported by the explorers who have approached it on all sides, have been laid down in conformity with their accounts. Between the northern limit of this belt and the Pole there is satisfactory reason for believing that the temperature rises, as we go northward; and that the sea is never completely closed.

"The North Water," because it is mainly free from ice during most of the year.

So "beset" have been the conceptions of most of my acquaintances, by the influences of habitual association, that I am prepared for the surprise which this simple statement will produce on the part of my present readers; yet I am giving expression only to what will be readily sustained by every navigator of the head of Baffin Bay. "How then are we to account for the failure of Dr. Kane to reach the North Pole — how account for the general impression that efforts in this direction are unpromising and rash?" The only answer to such questions is to be found in the effect of narratives of ill-directed previous effort, and in the peculiar causes which thwarted the purposes of the second Grinnell expedition. These causes, which are altogether independent of previous experience, and of the skill of the commander, shall be plainly stated.

Smith Strait, which discharges its waters from the direction of the Pole, enters Baffin Bay southwesterly; but its continuation northward of Rensselaer Harbor, Kennedy Channel, has a southerly flow.* Dr. Kane, whose movements, having no precedent, were experimental, entered upon the eastern or Greenland side; he was thus exposed to the southerly drift of ice, by which he was speedily blocked in. The pressure of the current raised the ice northward of his harbor into hummocks, which rendered every attempt at exploration so fatiguing both to men and dogs, as to speedily defeat the most strenu-

---

* See the small map of these passages at the side of the "Chart of the Arctic Regions."

ous efforts to advance up the channel. The trip to the west side of the channel upon which I was ordered, and which has been mentioned in the introductory chapter, enabled me to observe the circumstances to which the company of the Advance owed their detention; and also to verify my present conviction, that on that side a good harbor exists for a vessel, from which parties can proceed successfully towards the Pole. The projection of land now known as Cape Frazer affords an ample bulwark against the southern drift of ice; and thence the travel of dog-sledges is free from the obstructions which rendered abortive the most resolute attempts of Dr. Kane and his officers and men who strove to find a way towards the object of the expedition.

It is known to the readers of Dr. Kane's narrative that he ceased the prosecution of his purpose only when the failure of suitable food and fuel had rendered his crew incapable of further effort. His departure from New York was delayed by his sickness so long, that, upon reaching the shores of Greenland, he was unable to take the time necessary for provisioning his vessel with fresh supplies of meat from the birds which frequent the neighboring islands, and with the eggs which might otherwise have been procured in large quantities. Yet, after exertions which would suffice to acquit him towards the chief promoters of his enterprise, and towards the world, he succeeded in the month of June, 1854, in ascertaining the existence of open water, beginning northward of the Smith Strait ice-belt, in latitude 80° 20′, and continuing thence in the direction of the Pole, nearly one and a half degrees, to the horizon of actual vision from the last point of observation.

Let us suppose now that we remove from the question those particulars of difficulty, which the experience of the second Grinnell expedition has proved to be easily avoidable.

First, we shall have no SCURVY. For support of this assertion I shall quote from a paper read by me before the "American Association for the Advancement of Science," at its Baltimore session in May, 1858.

"The scurvy, hitherto often a great scourge to the crews of vessels wintering in the arctic regions, can, with proper precaution, be resisted, and in this opinion I am sustained by the united testimony of the surgeons of Her Majesty's Arctic Squadron. The disease has been of very rare occurrence of late years, and wherever it has appeared, it has been owing to accidental causes, but chiefly from the long continued use of salt-meat diet, — either in consequence of the parties never having been provided with any other standard supplies of food, or of their having so long remained in the field as to have consumed their fresh stores. Indeed, I am convinced that the climate is one of unusual healthfulness. The suffering from the disease among Dr. Kane's crew was mainly owing to the above-mentioned cause. He started too early to profit fully by the discoveries which have been made in the art of preserving, fresh, meats and vegetables, and with the exception of a limited quantity of pemmican, — intended for use in the field, — he had to depend upon the ordinary navy ration, without change or variation. Casual supplies of fresh food were obtained by the hunt or in barter with the natives, and when procured, invariably enabled his men to resist the disease, or, if developed, it acted as an immediate and specific cure. The difficulty experienced in keeping alive his dogs was chiefly owing to the absence of a diet suited to their necessities. The salt of the meat acted injuriously upon them, and the insufficient quantities which they could eat did not enable them successfully to resist the cold; and a strange epilepto-tetanoidal disease was in consequence developed among them. The same was observable among his crew, and doubtless for the same reason."

I shall carry at the outset enough pemmican, preserved vegetables, fruits, and other suitable stores, to prevent the evil effects of salted food upon both men and dogs; and at the Danish islands and settlements food of bird, reindeer, and other flesh will be procured in sufficient quantity to guard the consumption of the artificially prepared meats.

A remarkable illustration of the value of these supplies is to be found in the experience of the boat journey of 1854. The party which I accompanied, and that which remained at the brig, were in the same state of health at the time of separating. The latter had the advantages of shelter in the vessel, — of freedom from the necessity for exertion disproportionate to their strength, — of fuel, and abundance of food. The former were exposed to the severest hardships, — were upon the lowest allowance of food consistent with the maintenance of life, — were without suitable shelter, and almost without fuel, — were compelled to undergo the greatest labor; and yet, wholly by reason of their having obtained fresh animal and vegetable food, though in scanty measure, they returned free from scurvy to Rensselaer Harbor, where they found their comrades prostrated by that disease. Within a few weeks after their return, every man was stricken down by the same cause.

Secondly, we shall not be embarrassed by the COLD. It has been shown by innumerable examples, that the extreme rigor of the arctic winter can be safely encountered by white men, if they be sufficiently fed, and if they live according to the customs of the climate. It is not however during the winter that attempts are generally made to push forward; but between the middle of March and the middle of July. Dr. Rae, — whose remarkable journey overland to latitude 69° is before the public, and who was the first to bring to us tidings of the relics of Sir John Franklin's party, from the neighborhood of King William's Land and Montreal Island, where Captain M'Clintock has recently found the verification of the sad story, if not its conclusion, — has personally informed me that during the months of April and May, in so high a latitude as from 66° 35′ (the position of his winter snow-hut at the head of Repulse Bay) to 69°, the whole stock of extra clothing and bedding for his entire travelling party of five persons weighed only twenty-five pounds. In Rensselaer Harbor, except in the months from December to March, almost the only external protection used by myself and companions when on out-door duty, was a pilot-cloth coat; and, even during the period of maximum depression, we frequently exposed ourselves with impunity to the most severe temperatures, when the air was calm, clothed in a very ordinary suit of thick fabric, without any furs whatever. The thermometer, during the period of our active service in the field in the performance of our explorations, was often as high as 35° and 40°, and on one occasion it reached 54° above zero. During the severer portions of the year the thermometer sometimes, (though rarely,) sank to 60° below zero; but the narrative of Dr. Kane proves conclusively that the difficulties of arctic adventure do not result from that fact; and the boat journey of which the story has just been told, bears ample testimony of the same kind.*

I speak positively, because I fear no contradiction when I say, that every navigator of the northern seas knows that the cold alone is not a serious impediment to their exploration, provided that suitable food, and even the shelter of a snow-hut, be secured.† Besides; all of my companions can testify that the wind blowing from the northward frequently brought to us a moderation of temperature; ‡ the

---

* See Dr. Kane's narrative, vol. ii. p. 78. After stating that the temperature had been as low as from 40° to 56° below zero, he adds, "but my experience of last year in the rescue-party, where we travelled eighty miles in sixty odd hours, almost without a halt, yet without a frost-bite, shows that such temperatures are no obstacle to travel, provided you have the necessary practical knowledge of the equipment and conduct of your party. I firmly believe that no natural cold as yet known can arrest travel. The whole story of the winter illustrates it."

† It is desirable to avoid inappropriate contrasts between the effect of a comfortable parlor in latitude 40°, with a glowing anthracite fire, and the lowest degree of cold among the Esquimaux. It must not be forgotten that a range from 20° to 40° below zero, occurs in portions of the United States, without preventing the ordinary avocations of the inhabitants.

‡ In confirmation of this fact, see Professor Bache's letter in the Appendix.

wild-fowl, which draw their subsistence from the ocean, flew northward to find open water near which to build their nests; and Morton and the Esquimau lad Hans, killed, northward of Rensselaer Harbor, two bears, animals which cannot subsist near an ice-bound sea. The fresh skins, brought to the ship, vouched the truth of the report of the killing. A rapid southward current brought no ice. From about latitude 80° 20′ there was an unobstructed sea toward the Pole. The water was in one locality 36° and in another 40° above zero. Even the scientific theory of the relation between the magnetic poles and the poles of extreme temperature, confirm this view of the subject. There is no authenticated experience to the contrary. It is therefore no longer merely conjectural that the cold will be found to diminish as we proceed northward from the old quarters of the Advance; and even if it were otherwise, there is nothing in any conceivable state of the facts to deter a prudent man from an enterprise of the kind in question.

Will the reader endeavor to find a reason to prove that enterprise impracticable or rash? Is it the NATURE OF THE COUNTRY? The reader is now aware that, as far as Cape Roquette, latitude 80°, (ninety-six miles northward of the latitude of the Advance's quarters,) the western coast has been surveyed by myself, my observations extending down the coast from that cape nearly to the mouth of Smith Strait; and it is a fact that all of the indications within that survey were such as to promise a safe line of travel.* Again; between the 4th of

* So impressed was the commander with the value of these indications,

June and the 4th of July, 1854, Morton, accompanied by Hans, and with a team of seven dogs, succeeded in travelling up the eastern coast to about latitude 81°, and in returning to the ship; and their journey was at an unfavorable period, and in a most inconvenient state of the ice. On the other hand, it must not be forgotten that for the main effort now proposed, due preparation is to be made. The harbor proposed for the vessel is under Cape Frazer, on the western side of the strait, in a port which has been examined by me, and from which she will be liberated upon the breaking up and southward flow of the ice, which annually recurs.

" Early in the spring, the shores of Grinnell Land will be lined with depots of provisions, as far north as latitude 82°, where a final *cache* will be established for the use of the polar boat-party; these stores to be carried forward by the dogs. One of these animals will drag upon a sledge a weight of seventy pounds thirty-two miles per day, upon an average ration of thirteen ounces of pemmican,— equal to about three pounds of dried meat; and two teams of seven each could readily carry forward ample stores for a full boat's crew of six persons. This crew should set out with their boat from the vessel in April. Within one hundred and fifty miles they would probably, as I have said, meet the open water by the middle of May or the first of June.

" The rough ice which baffled **Dr. Kane's** parties, as above observed, can be in a great measure

that he said, " Had I succeeded in pushing my party across the bay, our success would have been unequalled; it was the true plan, the best conceived, and in fact the only one by which, after the death of my dogs, I could hope to carry on the search." — *Vol. II. p.* 78.

avoided by avoiding the crossing of Smith Strait; and Kennedy Channel having a due north trend, and presenting no salient capes like the remarkable projection of Western Greenland, will, I have no doubt, be found mostly smooth. Such a track presents great facilities for travel. One man will readily walk sixteen miles per day, dragging from one hundred to one hundred and twenty pounds in weight. Dr. Rae conducted a party six hundred miles in twenty-two days, each of his men trailing after him, upon an Iroquois sledge, one hundred and ten pounds. They carried a single blanket and change of under-clothing per man, but no tent, using for periodic rest the snow-hut of the Esquimaux. These huts are readily constructed, and upon them I shall place my sole reliance while upon the ice. Indeed, the amount of labor which can be performed by a skilful use of very simple means is truly astonishing; and in spite of the cold and poverty of the ice-deserts, Kennedy, M'Clintock, Bellot, Sutherland, Pim, Mecham, Osborne, Richards,[*] and

[*] Commander M'Clintock, during his foot-journey from Dealy Island (the winter-quarters of Captain Kellet in the Resolute) to the northwest coast of Prince Patrick Island, was absent from the ship 105 days, and travelled 1408 miles, or, deducting for various detentions, about fourteen miles per day. During the early part of the journey (April 16th) the temperature was as low as 24° below zero. The weight upon the sledge, which was dragged by his men, for a portion of the time equalled one ton, or 280 pounds per man. Lieut. Mecham, from the same ship, was absent 94 days, and travelled 1163 miles. This same energetic officer subsequently performed a foot-journey of 1336 miles in 70 days, or $61\frac{1}{2}$ days of actual travel, averaging over twenty-one miles per day; thus equalling the most successful dog-sledge journey of Baron Wrangel, who, in 1823, travelled over the frozen sea from Nishne Kolymsk to Koliutschin Island and back, a distance of 2300 wersts (1537 miles), in 78 days. Wrangel was, however, subjected to many perplexing delays, and sometimes made more than sixty miles per day. The collective foot-journeys of the officers

many others of the numerous corps of their gallant co-laborers, have performed journeys which for extent would reflect honorably upon them as foot travellers in a more favored region." *

Both boats and sledges will be taken in accordance with the results of former trials. If the entire space to the Pole should be covered with fast ice, some of the most experienced explorers are of opinion that the Pole can be reached on sledges without difficulty. Captain Parry's attempt in this mode was defeated only by his having selected a route which exposed him to the full force of the great southern ice-drift.† Every undertaking of previous navigators has served to cut off sources of error and disappointment; and now that for the first time in the history of arctic exploration, a way is opened to us, not only free from the obstacles which have prevented earlier success, but offering inducements such as have been presented in connection with no other route, it is surely not the time to pronounce against the whole design as impracticable.

The distance, in a direct line from my proposed starting-point at Cape Frazer, to the North Pole, is

---

and men of Capt. Kellet's division of the British Arctic Squadron in the spring of 1853 alone, amount to 7,276 miles.

* From the paper read before the American Association, May, 1858, previously referred to.

† Dr. Rae is of opinion that such a journey is clearly feasible over ice. He has so informed me.

It is important to bear in mind that the attempt to reach the Pole is not wholly dependent upon the circumpolar waters being free from ice. However the question of an open sea may be determined, there remains ample reason for regarding my attempt as feasible. Even the single question, whether the sea is open or not, is sufficient to engage the profound interest of geographers. Prof. A. Dallas Bache calls it the "great geographical question of the day." (See his letter in the Appendix.)

only about seven hundred miles, — scarcely greater than that travelled by myself and companions, going and returning, in 1854. Dr. Kane and his entire brig's company, in the spring and summer of 1855, in two crazy boats, and beset with extraordinary perils, reached Upernavik from Rensselaer Harbor, making, with the necessary *détours*, a third more miles than lie between my starting-place and the Pole. The reader of his narrative, and of that contained in this volume, will have seen that both of these journeys were accomplished by broken-down men, in the midst of circumstances the most discouraging. Of my own, it will be remembered that more than three hundred miles, or nearly one half the polar distance, were overcome in the arctic winter night, with a temperature as low as fifty degrees below zero; and that no serious harm occurred to any member of the party. Let a comparison be made of all the peculiarities of the cases: — on the one side abundant food, clothing, shelter, relief of dogs, choice of season and state of the ice, a full force of men in healthy condition, a ship snugly harbored for a winter retreat; on the other, all of the elements of feebleness, and the worst phases of physical embarrassment; and it must be a timorous spirit which can still confound the arguments so as to make the cases parallel. So long ago as 1616, when scarcely anything was known of the northern seas, Baffin and Bylot sailed, with a little vessel of only fifty-five tons, to within seventy miles of the latitude of Rensselaer Harbor. After all that has been discovered, shall it be said that an American, in 1860, after an experimental visit to the very region of his proposed operations, cannot make his way over seven hundred miles, with the outfit and other advantages which have been described?

Is the reader staggered merely by the naked fact that DR. KANE, AFTER ATTAINING TO KENNEDY CHANNEL, FOUND HIMSELF COMPELLED TO RETURN TO THE UNITED STATES WITHOUT ACCOMPLISHING MORE NORTHERLY DISCOVERY? The narrative of that commander contains a statement of the causes of his disappointment, not one of which can be applied to a new expedition in the same direction. If he could have known, before sailing from New York, what we have learned only through his adventure; or if, when the same facts came to his knowledge, he could have been supplied with fresh food and fuel, and thus have been enabled to pass another season in the region, he would doubtless have left nothing to be accomplished by a successor between Smith Strait and the Pole.

It is my misfortune to be obliged to contend against the impression naturally produced by events which are purely exceptional: such as the boat journey towards Beechy Island, in 1854, and those towards Upernavik, in 1854 and 1855; and such as have occurred during the search for Sir John Franklin. The materials are before the reader for a better estimate; and I cannot but hope that, from this volume alone, he will have gathered such facts as may serve to convince him that the incidents which have most affected his feelings, in connection with arctic voyages, are not legitimate tests of the general character of circumpolar experience; that they are, in truth, exceptional; and that there is now no probability of their recurrence.

While the civilized world is encouraging and applauding the enterprise of men like Barth and Livingstone, in tropical Africa, whose exposure involves a greater variety of risks than await the arctic voyager, shall the latter be discouraged from an undertaking, the conditions of whose success have been made known by our countryman?*

Does the reader question the UTILITY of the proposed discoveries? Happily on this head I am spared the hazard of any reflections of my own. The subject has been maturely considered by the leading scientific associations of the United States; whose conclusions, expressed by a large number of our most eminent citizens, are to the effect that the objects contemplated are not only important to mankind, but are such as warrant a full sanction and a hearty encouragement of my expedition. Their Reports and Resolutions will be found in the Appendix.

So convincing to myself have been the actual observations made of the intended field of operations, that I should experience a feeling of mortification at the line of argument which has been followed in this concluding chapter, were I not aware of the peculiar causes which have tended to mislead the public mind in relation to the dangers of

---

* A gentleman who, during several years, prosecuted, alone, journeys from the west coast of Africa into the interior, about the Gaboon and other rivers, has, I hesitate not to say, exposed himself to more risks than can be even plausibly connected with the line of discovery up Kennedy Channel. M. Duchaillu went without a companion, and purely as a volunteer, for the collection of specimens of natural history.

northern expeditions. These causes justify the hesitation which was manifested in former years; but, now that the truth has been made known by so many reliable observers, is it too sanguine a disposition which leads me to believe that I shall see again the little flag which I planted upon the coast of Grinnell Land?

APPENDIX.

APPENDIX.

PROCEEDINGS OF SCIENTIFIC SOCIETIES

RELATIVE TO

DR. HAYES' PROPOSED ARCTIC EXPEDITION.

I.

THE AMERICAN GEOGRAPHICAL AND STATISTICAL SOCIETY.

[From the Report of the Council for 1857.]

"DR. HAYES of Philadelphia, who formed one of the heroic band, accompanying Dr. Kane in his last attempt to penetrate to the still mysterious regions round the Pole, has read to the Society a paper full of valuable details, in which he proposed to renew this attempt. Experience was shown to have done much to prepare the way for success in this noble endeavor. As Dr. Hayes expressed the intention of devoting himself to this object, and of employing time and effort in awakening the minds of our countrymen in regard to it, this endeavor may be considered to be one of those objects to which our attention will be in the future continuously directed, through the section having in charge the subject of Topography."

[From the "Journal" of the Society for January, 1858.]

"SECOND MEETING, DEC. 16, 1858. — I. I. Hayes, M. D. of Philadelphia, (late Surgeon to the Second Grinnell Arctic Expedition,) read a paper on the 'Polar Discoveries of Dr.

Kane, and a Plan for further Research.' On motion of Mr. VIELÉ, seconded by Mr. HENRY GRINNELL, it was unanimously

"RESOLVED, That the American Geographical Society cordially approve, and indorse the plan of Doctor Hayes for a continuation of the exploration and surveys of the Polar Seas, deeming it due alike to the cause of science and our national character, that the discoveries of the Grinnell expedition, reported by Dr. Kane, should not be disputed or ignored, without an effort being made to confirm the results achieved by our gallant countrymen.

"RESOLVED, That a committee of five members of this Society be appointed to coöperate with Dr. Hayes in the organization of the Expedition proposed by him; which committee shall report, from time to time, the progress of the organization, and shall give due notice of the time fixed for the departure of the Expedition.

"A vote of thanks was tendered to Dr. Hayes, and a copy of his paper requested for the archives of the Society."

THIRD MEETING, JANUARY 6, 1859. — In accordance with the resolution adopted at the last meeting of the Society, the President appointed EGBERT L. VIELÉ, Esq., HENRY GRINNELL, Esq., Hon. AUGUST BELMONT, MARSHALL LEFFERTS, Esq., HENRY E. PIERREPONT, Esq., a special committee "to coöperate with Dr. Hayes in his plan for further research into the arctic regions."

II.

THE AMERICAN ASSOCIATION FOR THE ADVANCEMENT OF SCIENCE.

BALTIMORE, MAY 3, 1858. — At half-past one o'clock, P. M., Dr. I. I. Hayes delivered in general session a paper on the practicability of reaching the North Pole. A vote of thanks having been passed upon motion of Prof. Wm. B. Rogers, seconded by Prof. A. Dallas Bache, Prof. Hitchcock moved the following resolution: —

"Resolved, That a special committee of seven be appointed by the Chair to inquire and report at this session upon the expediency of having a committee of the Association to coöperate with Dr. Hayes in reference to an Expedition to the North Polar Sea."

The resolution having been adopted, the Chair appointed the following gentlemen as members of the committee: —

Prof. Edward Hitchcock, Prof. Joseph Henry, Prof. A. Dallas Bache, Hon. Thomas Ewing, Prof. James D. Dana, and Hon. Thomas Swann.

Baltimore, May 4, 1858. — "The committee to whom was referred the subject of Dr. I. I. Hayes' proposed Expedition to the Arctic Seas report, that, —

"1. The question of the open Polar Sea, its limits and character, is the most interesting of those remaining to be completely solved in arctic geography.

"2. The statements of Dr. Hayes, surgeon to Doctor Kane's Second Grinnell Expedition, make it probable, that, with moderate means and appliances, this problem may be completely solved.

"3. The indirect results readily obtained by such an expedition in regard to the magnetism, tides, currents, meteorology, geology, and natural history of the arctic regions, and the peculiar phenomena of glaciers and icebergs, and the ethnology, are of themselves of such importance as to demand further research.

"4. Dr. Hayes is desirous of devoting himself to this line of exploration, in the difficulties, hardships, and dangers of which he has, when serving with the lamented Kane, had full experience.

"5. Therefore, this special committee recommends to the Association the passage of the following resolution: —

"RESOLVED, That a committee of fifteen members of the American Association be appointed to coöperate with Dr. Hayes in his efforts to organize another expedition for arctic research. EDWARD HITCHCOCK, *Chairman*."

The report having been unanimously adopted, the following committee was appointed by the Chair in accordance with its recommendation: —

Prof. A. D. BACHE, Prof. JOSEPH HENRY, Prof. W. B. ROGERS, Prof. EDWARD HITCHCOCK, Prof. BENJAMIN PEIRCE, Prof. J. D. DANA, Prof. JOSEPH WINLOCK, Hon. THOMAS EWING, Hon. D. M. BARRINGER, Dr. J. L. LE CONTE, Prof. J. E. HILGARD, PETER FORCE, Esq., Prof. JOSEPH LEIDY, Dr. JOHN TORREY, Prof. S. S. HALDEMAN.

On motion of Prof. BACHE, Prof. CASWELL, the President of the Association, was added to the committee on arctic exploration.

III.

THE AMERICAN PHILOSOPHICAL SOCIETY.

[From the " Proceedings " of the Society for 1858.]

"STATED MEETING, MAY 7, 1858. — A letter was read from Dr. Isaac I. Hayes, proposing to make an attempt to reach the north pole of the earth, and requesting to be informed of any measures which in the judgment of the Society it will be expedient for him to adopt, to promote the advancement of any of the sciences for whose interests it labors.

"Dr. Le Conte offered the following resolutions which were read, considered, and adopted: —

"RESOLVED, That the Society receives with much gratification the announcement made by Dr. I. I. Hayes, of his purpose to attempt a further exploration of the arctic regions, and, if practicable, to reach the north pole of the earth.

"RESOLVED, That in the opinion of this Society, such an exploration merits the zealous coöperation of the scientific men of the United States, and that, at a convenient time, the Society will communicate to Dr. Hayes such suggestions respecting the promotion of its objects as may be considered useful:

"RESOLVED, That a committee of five be appointed, to coöperate with the committee recently appointed with reference to this subject by the American Association for the Advancement of Science, and to take such measures from time to time, in behalf of this Society as shall be deemed expedient."

"STATED MEETING, OCTOBER 1, 1858. — The committee appointed on the 7th of May last, on the subject of further arctic explorations, by Dr. I. I. Hayes, made the following Report: —

"'The committee to whom was referred the subject of the arctic exploration proposed by Dr. I. I. Hayes, respectfully report, —

"'That, beside any reflections of their own upon that subject, they find in previous proceedings of the Society ample warrant for the opinion, that the verification of the alleged open sea about the North Pole, and the probable contributions to be made from that region of the earth to the collections of science, constitute sufficient reasons for an earnest interest on the part of the Society, in any reasonable attempt to complete our knowledge in these respects by further exploration. After the signal manifestations which have been given by men of science throughout the world, of their estimate of the importance of circumpolar discovery; and with the advantage of recent reports, from a high latitude, received from our lamented fellow-member, the late Dr. Kane, whose efforts were accompanied by warm solicitude on the part of the Society, your committee have believed it proper to confine themselves to a consideration of the grounds upon which Dr. Hayes rests his conviction of the practicability and seasonableness of his proposal. These have been already briefly submitted to the American Association for the Advancement of Science, and have received a very prompt acceptance by that body, the members of which referred the subject to a committee, with instructions to coöperate with Dr. Hayes. They have been also published through the Smithsonian Institution, at an invitation from which, Dr. Hayes announced them in one of the lectures of its last course. Nevertheless, your committee think proper to mention the principal of them as forming the basis of their own conclusion, that the proposal in question is sustained by sufficient evidence of its feasibility to engage the continued attention of the Society.

" 'It is well known that one result of voyages of exploration prior to that of Dr. Kane, was the establishment of an opinion that a barrier of ice surrounded the Pole; and that in order to reach open water, if such existed, a way must be found through, or over the barrier. Dr. Kane, after an intelligent consideration of the discoveries already reported, aided by the illustrations derived from his personal observation during his first visit to the arctic circle, concluded, that the most practicable course lay up Smith Strait, which he accordingly followed upon his second voyage. The difficulties encountered by him were such, that, after many gallant efforts, he was compelled to return to the United States without becoming an eye-witness to the physical condition of the region towards which his labors tended. It seemed therefore proper for your committee to inquire whether those difficulties were clearly of so constant a nature in relation to all similar attempts, as to render it prudent on the part of the Society to avoid encouragement of a project which his experience may have shown to be impracticable. It appears that the most important impediments to his complete success were

"'1st. The arresting of his vessel and her permanent confinement by the ice, in a situation which was unfavorable to the efforts of his exploring parties. This occurred in a bay to the south of Kennedy Channel, with an exposure to the main pressure of ice, which accumulated in hummocks on the north of his position; and thus the labor necessary to any exploration towards the Pole, was in disproportion to the strength of his crew, and the resources at his command. On the west side of the channel, under the cover of the projecting land visited by Dr. Hayes, (to the most prominent point of which the name Cape Frazer was given,) the ice is reported as free from the impediments above stated; and a good harbor is reported to exist for wintering a ship, with egress by the opening of the channel, or through leads in the ice during the arctic summer. The account published by Dr. Kane, shows how large a proportion of the sufferings and disappointments of his exploring parties was due to the position into which he was forced.

"'2d. The want of fresh provisions. The unavoidable delay of Dr. Kane's departure from New York beyond the period proposed by him, prevented his collecting, near the Danish settlements in Greenland, the fresh stores which abound in that neighborhood. Originally contemplating a single year's work, he was detained beyond his expectation, with scanty supplies, until his men, worn out by excessive labor, and restricted mainly to a salt diet, became the victims of fearful assaults of scurvy. His narrative shows how much of his disappointment is due to this cause. His dogs, indispensable auxiliaries, were unable to subsist upon salted meats; and thus the entire stress of the work fell upon an ill-conditioned ship's company. Dr. Hayes proposes to give two years to his exploration. The first of these he designs to employ in reaching his head-quarters at or near Cape Frazer; and in establishing thence northward, on the west side of Kennedy Channel, secure depôts of provisions, as far as the latitude assigned by Morton to the open water reported by him, or further, if necessary; and in explorations preliminary to the main attempt. The second year, or such portion of it as may be sufficient, Dr. Hayes appropriates to the ascertainment of the condition of the polar adjacencies, and to such observations as may be most important to science. Thus the expedition of Dr. Kane, which may seem to discourage further attempts in the same direction, is viewed by Dr. Hayes as really furnishing the knowledge which promises final success. Your committee concur in this view.

"'In such circumstances, your committee cannot doubt that it is proper for the American Philosophical Society to coöperate with Dr. Hayes, in such manner as may be conformable with its usages in like cases; and especially to give to him the benefit of such systematic instruction as may best further the general purposes of the Society in the discovery and diffusion of useful knowledge.

"'Your committee respectfully submit the following resolution:—

"'RESOLVED, That a committee of nine members of the Society be appointed to coöperate with Dr. Hayes in his proposed extension of arctic exploration, and to give to him, on the part of the Society, such instructions as may best promote its objects.

"'All of which is respectfully submitted.

> WM. PARKER FOULKE,
> STEPHEN COLWELL,
> R. E. ROGERS,
> WM. S. W. RUSCHENBERGER,

Committee.'

"The resolution accompanying the report was adopted, and the presiding officer authorized to appoint the committee, and announce it at a future meeting."

STATED MEETING, MAY 6, 1859. — The following named members were appointed a committee to coöperate with Dr. I. I. Hayes in further arctic exploration:—

Wm. Parker Foulke, Esq., Prof. Robert E. Rogers, Isaac Lea, Esq., Dr. John L. Leconte, Prof. E. Otis Kendall, Prof. J. P. Lesley, Rev. Albert Barnes, D. D., Hon. Edward King, Prof. J. C. Cresson.

IV.

THE ACADEMY OF NATURAL SCIENCES OF PHILADELPHIA.

[From the "Proceedings" of the Academy for 1858.]

Meeting of the Academy, May 11, 1858. — "A communication was read from Dr. Isaac I. Hayes, announcing his desire to attempt a further exploration of the arctic regions, and asking for such suggestions from the Academy as might assist in carrying out the project; whereupon the following resolutions were adopted: —

"Resolved, That the Academy has heard with great interest the communication of Dr. Isaac I. Hayes, of his purpose to attempt a further exploration of the arctic regions:

"Resolved, That the Academy will hereafter give to Dr. Hayes such recommendations respecting the objects proposed by him, as shall be deemed most likely to promote the objects of the Academy:

"Resolved, That a committee of seven be appointed to coöperate in behalf of the Academy with Dr. Hayes."

The committee was then appointed as follows: —

Prof. John F. Frazer, Dr. T. B. Wilson, Isaac Lea, Esq., Wm. Parker Foulke, Esq., Dr. J. L. Leconte, Prof. Jos. Leidy, Dr. William S. W. Ruschenberger, U. S. N.

Subsequently, on motion, Elias Durand, Esq., and Prof. Joseph Carson, were added to the committee.

Meeting of the Academy, July 6, 1858. — "On leave granted, the committee appointed to confer with Dr. Hayes in regard to his proposed Arctic Exploration, presented a Report as follows: —

"That the exploration contemplated by Dr. Hayes appears to deserve the encouragement of all individuals or societies who possess an interest in the advancement of science, and especially of those who cultivate the various branches of Natural History, for the following reasons:

"1st. The interesting problem of the existence of an open Polar Sea cannot as yet be considered as satisfactorily solved; as is made manifest by the doubts recently expressed by a distinguished geographer, in a memoir read before the Royal Geographical Society of London. Yet this problem is so intimately connected with theories of climate, not only in that region, but over a very large portion of the northern hemisphere, that its definite solution must be considered as of the utmost importance to the study of geography; and it is not impossible that its investigation may lead to valuable results of a more commercial nature. It seems probable, therefore, that this subject will attract the attention of other nations, who are engaged in an honorable rivalry with us in promoting the knowledge of the surface of the earth, and it is highly desirable that the credit of furnishing the definite solution should belong to the nation to whose energy and enterprise the interesting results already obtained are due.

"2d. The natural history of this extensive region remains, as yet, almost entirely unknown; while, from the peculiarities of its climate, and its proximity to the land of the eastern hemisphere, it seems certain that much valuable information as to the habits of animals and plants, and the connection of our Faunas and Floras, both ancient and modern, with those of Europe and Asia, may be gained by such an exploration as is here contemplated.

"3d. The excessive difficulties and hardships of such an exploration, serve to deter any but the most adventurous spirits from undertaking it; while the peculiar circumstances under which both the instruments of observation and the observers themselves are placed, render a frequent repetition of the observations necessary to produce confidence in the results. Every encouragement should, therefore, be extended to all who are willing to undertake the arduous task, and capable of properly meeting its unusual responsibilities.

"The committee therefore recommend to the Academy the adoption of the following resolutions: —

"RESOLVED, That the Academy of Natural Sciences of Philadelphia, having full confidence in the energy, prudence, and scientific capacity of Dr. Hayes, recommends the arctic expedition projected by him to the favorable consideration of all who are in a position to assist him in his enterprise, believing that its success will contribute largely to the advancement of science and to the honor of our country.

"RESOLVED, That the Academy will cheerfully assist Dr. Hayes, in carrying out his plans, by all the means in its power.

JOHN F. FRAZER,
T. B. WILSON,
ISAAC LEA,
WM. PARKER FOULKE,
J. L. LECONTE,   } *Committee.*
JOSEPH LEIDY,
WM. S. W. RUSCHENBERGER,
E. DURAND,
JOSEPH CARSON,

"The report and resolutions were adopted, and the committee continued."

V.

THE AMERICAN ACADEMY OF ARTS AND SCIENCES, OF BOSTON.

[From the " Proceedings " of the Academy for 1858.]

MONTHLY MEETING, OCTOBER 12, 1858. — " Professor Joseph Lovering, in behalf of the committee to whom was referred the communication of Dr. I. I. Hayes, dated July 19th, 1858, requesting the counsel and favorable influence of the Academy, in his proposed attempt to reach the north pole of the earth, read the following Report: —

" The announcement of an open sea within the Arctic Ocean was made in these words by Dr. Kane after the return of his man Morton from a sledge excursion in June, 1854. 'It must have been an imposing sight, as he stood at this termination of his journey, looking out upon the great waste of waters before him. 'Not a speck of ice,' to use his own words, 'could be seen. There, from a height of four hundred and eighty feet, which commanded a horizon of almost forty miles, his ears were gladdened by the novel music of dashing waters, and a surf, breaking in among the rocks at his feet, stayed his further progress.'

" The committee have quoted the eloquent language of Dr. Kane, without stopping to inquire how much of this glowing description is to be referred to the enthusiasm of an explorer, and how much is to be interpreted by a cool criticism at a distance from the scene of operations.

" The question which, it is expected, may be settled by another arctic expedition is, whether the great ice-barrier, which on some meridians, and at some seasons, encroaches even upon the 48th parallel of latitude, and which invests an area of six millions of square miles, extends northwards to the Pole; or whether, beyond the limits of extreme arctic navigation, which leaves an unexplored surface of three millions of square miles, there lies imprisoned in a zone of ice, the unfrozen waters of a polar sea. The conclusion of Dr. Kane, that the latter was the true side of the alternative, was anticipated by that of a Russian expedition, on sledges, in 1810, made upon an opposite meridian to that which Kane travelled, and of Parry in 1827 upon a third meridian.

"The impression favorable to an open and navigable polar sea, which was obtained on these occasions, based as it was upon a very circumscribed experience, and prevented by stress of circumstances from being pursued to verification, might seem to fall considerably short of a rational belief, were it not, in the opinion of Dr. Hayes and others, corroborated by various kinds of circumstantial evidence, as follows : —

"1. By the presence of bird-life, mostly marine, on what would be the icy shores of this suspected sea, and which migrate northward in spring.

"2. By the milder temperature at extreme latitude, inferred from the character of the isothermals where best determined; and which, pursued by analogy to unvisited latitudes, give the same temperature to the high latitude of 90° as to the arctic circle.

"3. By the migrations of human life; the traditions of the Esquimaux, pointing to the north as the cradle of their race. If the fact is established, that races deteriorate as they remove from the parallel of their nativity, then the tradition of the degenerate Esquimaux is confirmed by their own degeneracy.

"4. By the temperature of the arctic waters, which were observed by William Morton, and recorded by Kane, as only 36° Fahr. in June, 1854, or two degrees above the temperature of the air at the same time; the water flowing from the north and no ice being in sight. Whether this water is frozen in winter, is not, however, known.

"5. By the rise of the temperature in winter when the north wind sets in, which is also damp; as observed by Baron Von Wrangel and Sir Edward Parry. The cause of this elevated temperature in the arctic waters, Dr. Hayes thinks, may be found in the influence of the Gulf Stream flowing northward as an under-current to equalize the effects of the superficial flow southward. This direction in the flow of the deep water, is inferred from the drift of the deeply-laden icebergs northwards, while the lighter ones move southward. Moreover, what compensation for astronomical exposure may not the drainage of five millions of square miles from the northern water-sheds of Europe, Asia, and America, introduce into the temperature of the great arctic basin?

"If these mild waters, embosomed for centuries in a zone of ice, are to be reached by civilized man, Dr. Hayes thinks that the best invitation to success comes, not from a purely nautical expedition along the easterly coast of Greenland, but from more westerly meridians, to be traversed by boats and sledges.

"The committee do not feel called upon to examine, singly or collectively, the force of these various arguments in favor of an open polar sea. It is certain, however, that human curiosity will not be satisfied until the mystery on this subject is cleared up by new expeditions. To postpone these expeditions to another generation, when much of the personal experience already gained will have been forgotten, and when the services of those best qualified to conduct them can no longer be commanded, would not be a wise economy.

"With these few hints on the views and objects of Dr. Hayes, in his appeal to the Academy for scientific aid and sympathy, your committee conclude with the recommendation of the following resolutions: —

"RESOLVED, That the American Academy of Arts and Sciences appreciate highly the laudable ambition of Dr. I. I. Hayes, to continue, and, if possible, consummate, the arduous exploration for which he has already sacrificed much, and is willing to sacrifice still more; and that the Academy tender him their sympathy and influence.

"RESOLVED, That a committee of seven be appointed, from the members of the academy, to coöperate with Dr. I. I. Hayes, and to render him such scientific counsel as may make his new effort, if undertaken, secure the greatest advantages to science and humanity.

JOSEPH LOVERING,
HENRY L. EUSTIS, } *Committee.*
JOSEPH WINLOCK,

"On motion of Professor FELTON, the resolutions were adopted unanimously, and the subject was referred to a committee, consisting of —

" Prof. JOSEPH LOVERING, Prof. HENRY L. EUSTIS, Prof. JOSEPH WINLOCK, THOMAS G. CAREY, Esq., BENJAMIN A. GOULD, Esq., Prof. THEOPHILUS PARSONS, EDWARD WIGGLESWORTH, Esq."

VI.

THE BOSTON SOCIETY OF NATURAL HISTORY.

[From the " Proceedings " of the Society, for 1858.]

MEETING OF THE SOCIETY, SEPTEMBER 1, 1858. — " A letter was read from Dr. I. I. Hayes, to the President, announcing his intention of making another attempt to reach the north pole of the earth. On motion of Prof. PARSONS, the subject was referred to a committee to be nominated by the President, and reported on at the next meeting."

MEETING OF THE SOCIETY, SEPTEMBER 15, 1858. — "The President nominated, as a committee on the subject of Dr. Hayes' proposed Arctic Expedition, Prof. THEOPHILUS PARSONS, Dr. A. A. GOULD, and Dr. S. KNEELAND, Jr., and they were chosen."

MEETING OF THE SOCIETY, NOVEMBER 3, 1858. — " The

committee, to whom was referred the letter of Dr. I. I. Hayes, announcing his intention of making another attempt to reach the north pole of the earth, would report: —

"1. That we regard the proposed expedition with no ordinary interest; and receive assurance that it will be successfully prosecuted, in view of the near approaches which have already been made in that direction; the reasons by which it is shown that the obstacles hitherto encountered may be, in a great measure, evaded; the personal experiences of its conductor of the dangers and rigors to be met, and his ability to forestall them; and, especially, in his acquaintance with the residences and characters of the natives, on whom he must mainly rely for extra aid, — an acquaintance, probably, superior to that of any other person.

"2. That while the hopes of former expeditions may not have been fully realized, yet, that in view of the additions made to human knowledge, as to the Metereology, Geography, and other natural features of our globe, as well as the proofs they have given of the physical endurance, perseverance, and moral energies of our race, enough has been attained to entitle them to be considered as anything but unsuccessful; and that we anticipate similar results from this, results in no way inferior to those attaching to previous expeditions.

"3. That whatever of encouragement or countenance can be derived from this Society, we wish to tender to Dr. Hayes, assuring him that our best wishes will accompany him; and of our confidence that his return will be fraught with fruits most valuable to science.

"All which is respectfully submitted.

    AUGUSTUS A. GOULD,
    SAMUEL KNEELAND, Jr., } *Committee.*
    THEOPHILUS PARSONS,

"The report and accompanying resolutions were accepted and adopted as the sense of the Society, and the corresponding secretary was directed to communicate a copy of the same to Dr. Hayes."

VII.

THE NEW YORK LYCEUM OF NATURAL HISTORY.

Meeting of the Lyceum, December 28th, 1858.

The committee appointed to prepare resolutions in reference to the proposed Expedition of Dr. Hayes to the Arctic Sea, reported: —

"That notwithstanding the many expeditions that have explored different positions of arctic America, much yet remains to be learned, respecting the Physical Geography and Zoölogy of those regions; and Dr. Hayes having at our last meeting given an outline of his contemplated explorations, we cannot, as Naturalists, but feel a hope that in the prosecution of his project, much valuable information may be obtained to perfect the knowledge we now have of the productions and zoölogy of the extreme north.

"On this account it seems proper that some expression of interest should be manifested, and encouragement given him by all scientific societies, and we therefore recommend the adoption of the following resolutions: —

"RESOLVED, That the Lyceum of Natural History in New York cordially approves of the plan proposed by Dr. Hayes, and with the expectation that if he succeeds in reaching a higher arctic parallel than has heretofore been attained, some valuable contributions to science may reasonably be expected; and the Lyceum therefore fully unites in the recommendations of his project by other societies, and willingly adds its influence, with the hope that all interested in scientific research, and having the ability, will aid him in his self-sacrificing design."

Extracted from the Minutes.

JOHN REDFIELD, *Corresponding Secretary.*

VIII.

THE ROYAL GEOGRAPHICAL SOCIETY OF LONDON.

[From the " Proceedings " of the Society for 1858.]

Meeting of the Society, June 14th, 1858. — The President, Sir Roderick Impey Murchison, said: "I ought to mention, to the honor of our kinsmen on the other side of the Atlantic, that, not content with having done so much in search of Franklin, they now, on the proposal of Dr. Hayes, the companion of Kane, contemplate a further expedition to ascertain whether there is or is not an open sea beyond Smith Sound. As geographers we cannot too warmly thank them for the spirit they have displayed in this arctic subject."

IX.

LETTER FROM PROFESSOR A. DALLAS BACHE,
Superintendent of the United States Coast Survey.

Coast Survey Office,
Washington, December 15, 1858.

Dear Sir:—I am glad to learn from you that the New York Geographical and Statistical Society has secured the reading of a paper from you before it, on Arctic Exploration. The interest which the Society took in Dr. Kane's expeditions will naturally make the members desire to complete what was so admirably begun. The question of the open Polar Sea is the great geographical question of the day: it is a question connected with the geography of our own continent, and one which Americans have taken the lead in solving. I do sincerely hope that we may follow it to the end.

You are aware that Assistant Charles A. Schott, of the

Coast Survey, has, at my request, devoted a part of his time not occupied by his official duties in discussing the astronomical, meteorological, magnetic, and tidal observations collected by Dr. Kane, in the Second Grinnell Expedition. He has recently communicated to me a most interesting confirmation of the observations bearing upon the existence of open water near the Pole. He says in a note of December 4th, which is before me, "It appears, from notes collected from the log-books of the Advance, that the southeast (magnetic), north-northeast (true) winds had the effect of elevating the temperature of the air even in the winter months, which may be supposed to have arisen from its originating or blowing over a water area, partially open (this water would have a surface temperature of 29° Fahr.). The direction points across Washington Land and Kennedy Channel as the seat of this influencing area."

The interesting character of the results of the magnetic observations brought back by Dr. Kane, induced me to say to you, at the meeting of the American Association at Baltimore, that I would gladly contribute to a new expedition, under your direction, the pecuniary means necessary to extend the observations. To this offer of course I stand.

I feel persuaded that the experience which you gained while with Dr. Kane, and the interest which you must feel in his particular line of research and exploration, make you the person, of all others, to continue the great work with which Kane's name is forever associated, and I trust that means may not be wanting to enable American enterprise to complete what it has so well begun and continued.

With great regard, yours, truly,

A. D. BACHE.

Doctor I. I. HAYES.

X.

LETTER FROM M. DE LA ROQUETTE,
Vice-President of the Geographical Society of Paris.

To Mr. E. R. Straznicky, Secretary of the Council of the American Geographical and Statistical Society, New York.

PARIS, Friday, January 21, 1859.
19 Rue Mazarine.

SIR: — It is with the liveliest interest that I have read the numbers of the "New York Tribune" (Dec. 6), "Evening Post" (Dec. 17), and "New York Times" (Dec. 18), which you have had the kindness to transmit to me. They apprise me of the new organization of the American Geographical and Statistical Society, and at the same time of the fact, that, upon the proposition of Dr. Hayes, one of the companions of the heroic and unfortunate Dr. Kane, your Society has adopted, in concert with other scientific institutions of the United States, the project of sending out a new expedition into the arctic regions, for the purpose of ascertaining the correctness of the information furnished by the latter, particularly as to the existence of an open Polar Sea, that is to say, free from ice, which would either approach the Pole, or extend to that extremity of our globe which, up to the present day, navigators have made vain efforts to reach.

From the resolution adopted by the American Geographical and Statistical Society, I perceive that the expedition will probably leave in the spring of 1860, under the command of Dr. Hayes, its promoter, and that its expenses will be covered by means of a subscription. The attachment which I have always felt for Dr. Kane, and which he kindly shared, and the honor which your learned Society has done me by electing me as their Honorary Member, leaves me ground to hope that they will allow me to place my name among the number of subscribers with a sum of five hundred francs, which I hold for their disposition.

I have already announced to the Geographical Society of Paris the truly national project conceived by the United States. I will profit by the new information contained in the numbers of the papers which I owe to your kindness, and will draw up a detailed account, which will probably appear in the " Nouvelles Annales des Voyages." I shall always receive with gratitude the communications which you will be kind enough to make to me. . . . .

Allow me to express to you, Sir, the assurance of my most distinguished consideration.

DE LA ROQUETTE, No. 19 Rue Mazarine.

THE END.

www.ingramcontent.com/pod-product-compliance
Lightning Source LLC
Chambersburg PA
CBHW030427300426
44112CB00009B/880